CW00418537

Ho... To Wreck Your Business

so that you don't

CORNISH ACCOUNTING SOLUTIONS LTD
CHARTERED ACCOUNTANTS
BUSINESS SPECIALISTS
79 HIGHER BORE ST
BODMIN PL31 1JT
TEL: 01208 74615
FAX: 01208 73116
email: info@cornishaccounting.com
Stuart Mason

i

Dedication and Thanks

Where do I start? It has to be with my long-suffering wife, Bobbie. She has lived the highs, suffered the lows, and always been there. We take "vows," and I pushed them to the limit.

My mum and dad won't read this, I lost them just a few short years after the business. They too shared the highs and lows, and a family torn apart with stress-induced family battles. Alan, my brother. Brothers fight, that's what we're designed to do. Today, we're much more mature and only fight over the bar bill. This book is for them too.

To the Ink Shop Team, I let you down. We should have nailed this. To every one of you, thank you.

To the friends that remained, thank you too. You were there through thick and thin.

Thank you to the friends who made the book possible. Royce Clarke for proofing and suggestions, John Straw for proofing and enduring hours of being read to, and to Bill Mair of Precision Presentation for keeping me *write* with the editing and spelling (joke).

Thank you to Action**COACH** for helping me find myself, I should have listened to that coach all those years ago.

Thank you to the MANY wise people I have met, and to those whose quotes I have shared. I do hope I have not missed anyone.

Finally, thank you to my CLIENTS, past, present and future. It's been my pleasure sharing this story with you.

Life is a journey, that's all it is. In the grand scheme of it, we're here for a nano second. Live it, enjoy it: life's what you make it.

Stuart

Contents

Introduction & A Warning .... Page 1

Chapter 1- School Days .... Page 6

Apologies To The Tax Payer- It Was Kris Kristofferson's Fault

Chapter 2- Humble Beginnings .... Page 19

Chapter 3- Planning .... Page 38

Chapter 4- Helicopters, Big Macs & Nuclear Submarines .... Page 79

Chapter 5- How To Wreck Yourself .... Page 95

Chapter 6- The Glory Years .... Page 120

Chapter 7- How To Wreck Your Team .... Page 137

Chapter 8- The Name's Bond, Basildon Bond .... Page 146

Chapter 9- Fire In The Hold- The Print Wars .... Page 157

Chapter 10- How To Wreck Your Dreams .... Page 174

Chapter 11- How Appropriate! (Franchising) .... Page 189

Chapter 12- How To Wreck Your Numbers .... Page 208

Chapter 13- The End Game - A Bunch of Bankers .... Page 224

Let's Wrap This Up - So What's In It FOR YOU? .... Page 235

Throughout the book reference is made to the available resources.
These are available at **www.howtowreckyourbusiness.co.uk**

As the website grows and develops, these resources will be added to and
perhaps moved- they are all there.

If you can't find what you're looking for, email the Wreck Team at
resource@howtowreckyourbusiness.co.uk

Let's Crack On...

Introduction and a Warning

Before you start reading this book I want to explain the reasons for writing it in the first place. This is not a motivational book, there's too many of them out there already. I am not a motivational speaker - if you motivate an idiot, they just go on to do stupid shit faster. There's a difference between motivation and education.

If you're easily offended, then perhaps this book is not for you. I speak very directly, very abruptly, and that may offend some people. This is a serious game, we're playing for high stakes here, and you may have realised by now that business can be tough, and unfair. Do we make it tougher than it needs to be? Let's find out.

The purpose of this book is to share with you my story so that you can learn from the many mistakes I made that cost me my business on its 20th birthday. With the benefit of hindsight, I can now share with you that every one of those mistakes was 100% avoidable. Sadly though, these EIGHT mistakes are commonplace in businesses of all sizes today.

One of the questions I am often asked is how it was possible to lose a multi-million-pound business, which at its peak had over half a million pounds of cash in the bank, and a property portfolio in excess of £1.4 million. That is the whole point of this book. Shockingly EASY is the simple answer.

The business ceased trading and administrators appointed in April of 2013. A friend asked me recently "When was it the Ink Shop failed again?" - I replied, "In the late 90s". My friend was somewhat puzzled by that as he knew it was around then that the business was really at its peak - and it was. That's when the business failed, it just never died until 2013. Of course, what I mean is those mistakes were made early on.

Imagine you have a leaking bucket. When your bucket is FULL, yet more and more water is poured into it, you don't notice your feet are wet, business is good, you have more work than you can handle. It's not until the flow stops that holes in your bucket really become evident, and yep, you guessed it, the bucket empties PDQ.

Today, I am a business coach, so I get to work with awesome business owners, all looking to take their business to the next level. The irony is that back in 2007 when the business was at its peak, I was approached by an Action Coach, it was Action International back then. Had I listened to that coach at the time I can honestly say my business would not have failed. To an outsider looking in the mistakes I was making were so obvious. I simply could not see the wood for the trees. Does this sound like you? Could this be your business?

It's a very true saying that you don't know what you don't know. In coaching terms it's a learning level that we refer to as unconscious incompetence. That was me.

I also need to share something with you that few other authors will. Even if you do read their amazing book, and you do take action, there's still a chance that it won't work for you. Let's be very clear here; what worked for them may not work for you. This book is slightly different: where following their advice to the LETTER may or may not yield success, failing to avoid the errors that I point out WILL yield results in your business, just not the results you want.

Does that make sense? This isn't a book on how to create success, it's a book on how to avoid FAILURE - there's a HUGE difference.

We're a strange bunch us humans, more likely to avoid pain than seek pleasure. We react more to losing a £20 note than finding one. We will happily spend £100 to take the pain away, yet won't consider spending £1 to avoid the pain in the first place.

As you go through this book, you'll perhaps relate to some of the mistakes made. You'll maybe shake your head at a few, you may be shaking all over if you're making them all. I would ask you to take serious action here. If this book is you, if this book is your business, then take action and fix it, and fix it soon. Park your ego - and we're going to come to that later in the book - it was a huge problem for me. Have a look at *howtowreckyourbusiness.co.uk* and click on Be a Better You. Take a look at Right Road, Wrong Track. Which one are you on?

I was on the Wrong Track for YEARS. Nothing was ever my fault, there was an excuse for everything, and a complete denial that anything was wrong with that scenario. I paid a huge price for that, and I'll cover it in much greater detail in the book. If this is you, sort that too: at best it's holding you back, at worst you're going out of business.

The saddest part of this book is that my mum and dad won't see it. They saw the highs and lows of the business and sadly I lost both of them within weeks of each other, just a few short years after the business collapsed. How much did the years of shit that the business caused contribute to that? More than I care to admit, I shouldn't wonder.

Throughout this book there will be many references to Michael Gerber, Brad Sugars, Jim Rohn, Seth Godin, and many others. I'll refer to strategies from the likes of Donald Miller (Building a Storybrand), Alan Dibb (The 1-Page Marketing Plan) and Daniel Priestley (Oversubscribed).

This is not to claim their wise words as my own, more to educate and motivate YOU. Throughout this book I'll ask you to take notes, write stuff down, be honest with yourself and most of all - CHALLENGE yourself. Most of all though, we're gonna have a bit of fun, we're gonna offend people, and if no court cases commence - well, no one will be more surprised than me.

I find it amazing that so many business owners do the Lottery. They don't realise that by owning and running their own business they have already won the Lottery; they just haven't collected the prize yet. Why is that? Is it because you believe that you'll never achieve the wealth you desire? Do you feel compelled to buy that ticket? Is it because money isn't your main motivator in business? Seriously, are we meant to believe that crock of shit? If money isn't the motivator then why are you buying the lottery ticket? Just asking for a friend.

Every industry has movers and shakers, every industry has those who are highly successful and those who bounce from one disaster to another. Why is that? Is it luck? What is luck? Luck doesn't just happen; it is the outcome of taking calculated risks where there's more chance of success than failure. "Lucky" people are not lucky by accident, they are lucky by activity, lucky through choice.

The thing with luck is it has an equal and opposite reaction. If you're "lucky" and win that big contract, some other poor bastard is unlucky and has lost out. Was that luck, or did the victor fight for the success and the victim just not fight so well? That's my opinion on luck - you make it, you earn it, you don't just get it. You might want to go back and have a look again at the "Right Road or Wrong Track".

Here's another consideration. What the hell are you doing this for? To give you and your family a better life? Great, that gets my vote - let's now work on making sure that happens. Can I help you with that? This may be a book, however you have direct access to me via the website at *howtowreckyourbusiness.co.uk*

Finally - this book was written by me and self-edited. I left school without a single qualification, there's good reasons for that. My point is the grammar and punctuation will not be perfect. So, if you're a part-time member of the punctuation police you may be disappointed. My sole object is to allow the reader to sense my passion, share my frustration, and LEARN. If that means a typo or too (two, just kidding), then I ask for your forgiveness for that.

Let's just get stuck into the book now.

Enjoy the journey *Stuart*

If you don't know where
you want to be in 5 years,
You are already there.

Brad Sugars

Chapter One - School Days - Apologies to the Tax Payer, It Was Kris Kristofferson's Fault...

School for me was a complete waste of time. I could never figure out what practical applications such as the complex calculations of trigonometry could possibly have in commercial life.

When I was at school studying for the then "O Grades" a fad took hold that changed the direction my life would take. This took the unusual shape of a box of circuits and diodes better known as a CB radio. The film "**Convoy**" had hit the UK, and with it the explosion of Rubber Ducks and Smokey Bears everywhere - all totally illegal at this stage as "Busby" would confirm.

Unknown to me at this time, this craze was about to **wreck my schooling**, yet start an unbelievable entrepreneurial journey that continues to this day. "**Taps on the shoulder**" we call these. We all get these taps, warning us of potential opportunity, or impending doom. Maybe you think of these as nudges from your "guardian angel." Whatever you call it, we **ALL** get them.

By 1980 the CB Craze in the UK was fever pitch. Clubs were springing up in every town and city and whilst still illegal you did not need sharp eyes to detect cars with 7-foot aerials (that's 2.13 meters for young people and Europeans!) and houses with 40-foot masts (12.12 metres) - Kris Kristofferson had a lot to answer for, good buddy.

As the CB Community continued to explode UK-wide so began another phenomenon - the Eyeball. This is where CBers met each other and exchanged a printed "eyeball card" and of course talked copious amounts of utter bullshit and compared the sizes of each other's antennae. Incredible to think that we never gave this a second thought - talking to complete and utter strangers then arranging to meet them, usually at night, and generally in an empty car park somewhere - can you imagine such behaviour today? Oh my, how the world has changed! I suppose this was the 80s version of your dinner on Facebook. This was indeed the **ORIGINAL** social media, just a lot more "sociable."

Life before mobile phones, Pokemon and Facebook was much more exciting. So here I am, heading towards 4th Year at School with no clear direction in life. Academically challenged, maybe - but only through choice. The early years at high school were good for me, good grades, good subjects and I possibly led my mum and dad into a false sense of security that I was actually going to achieve the results **THEY** wanted.

See, here's the thing. This is where the education system, I believe, is flawed and still focusses on outcomes not dissimilar to those of the Industrial Revolution. Work hard, study lots, pass exams, work harder, get a job. There's a few phases of that dream conveniently missed, including get a huge student loan that takes half your working life to clear.

At school in the 80's we had "Guidance Teachers" and from what I recall they took hours of my life I just won't get back. I was a "non-conformist" and didn't fit the mould that my friends did, and that the guidance teacher insisted upon. "I want to be an architect", "I want to be a lawyer", "I want a career in banking". One even wanted to be a politician - seriously, none of us really knew what that meant. We do now: arsehole! Billy Connolly called that one right: "Anyone that wants to be a politician should immediately be banned from being one". Anyway, back to guidance classes - I boldly announced that I was going to have my own business and was openly ridiculed at that point.   Right up until that day I was pretty smart at school; the guidance teacher had successfully transformed me into an "anti-establishment" student and fuelled my determination to succeed. I do wonder to this day if that was reverse psychology although I don't think he was smart enough for that, to be honest. **The man couldn't reverse a CAR, let alone psychology**!

Is the school system feeding the entrepreneurial spirit? I don't think so. I recently did a number of talks at a few local schools on "Entrepreneurship". Only a few students "got it", and that's because their parents were self-employed. Is the entrepreneurial spirit there from day one or does it gradually grow? I genuinely don't know. My thoughts are it's there from the start.

Today we are wc still told to work hard, study hard and land a "good job" - and the biggest student loan you can possibly get?

What is a **"good job"** anyway? Seriously, I'm asking. What is a "good job"? Outwith the public sector a "good job" can ONLY be contributing to the wealth of the entrepreneurial OWNER, the person that said "fuck this" to the schooling system. The job for life is a myth that our grandparents may have enjoyed, jeez, a job for life - is that not the same as a life sentence? Time off for good behaviour surely?

I look at two heroes of mine, Lord Sugar and Sir Richard Branson. Look at the path they took. I wonder how many times they were told they would never make it. Ironically, Branson's headteacher did say he'd either be a millionaire or end up in jail.

What exactly is an entrepreneur? There are so many different interpretations of that word and I think the accumulation of wealth has distorted that. I believe that a key element of an entrepreneur is **VISION,** the ability to see things others can't. The ability to see opportunity where others can't, or won't. I also think a zoo is a great analogy. We can all be tigers: many choose to be caged and live a life being scrutinised by others, following a routine for everything from feeding to sleeping. The entrepreneur is having none of that. "Hey man, we're out in the wild having a roaring old time and seriously killing shit every day". Same tiger, different outcome.

I want to drop something else into the mix here, and this will come up a few times. I never heard this until I started my coaching practice and it's a phrase Brad Sugars uses a lot. "**You become the average of the five people you hang around with most**". If you hang around with the "glass-half-empty" and the "you'll-never-do-that" brigades get these people out your life, quick. Pick your two top business heroes - you're going to hang out with them, and Peter Jones, Richard Branson, and Alan Sugar for a few months.

Do you think that just might change your view on business and life? I would hazard a guess that's a resounding **YES.** Get rid of the morons in your life, and if that moron is you, then look out for "**Be x Do = Have**" later in the book.

Let me throw another quote at you from the late, great Jim Rohn: "Work harder on yourself than you do on your job"

Let's Get Back To School...

School days are the best days of your life. I chose not to focus on schoolwork, it was a **distraction** from far more important tasks - far more important to a 15-year-old that knew everything, of course. Even at this stage in life the entrepreneurial spark was starting to flicker. At school the paper round was the norm but not for me. I started a car washing business that brought in WAY more cash than delivering papers at 5am.

This enterprise was really to fund something a bit more fun, though. Within 6 months that booming business was banking in excess of £50 per week, which allowed the purchase of some serious radio gear. It was 1980/1981 and CB Radio had grown up. It had progressed way beyond a local social activity and progressed to long distance communications known as "DXing". Still operating in the HF 27Mhz band, some fairly inexpensive radio equipment allowed this hobby to be a global obsession. There are around 200 countries in the world, and I had managed to contact over 100 of them - more than half the countries in the world, including the then Soviet Union.

Interesting point here, all these operators also used **PRINTED** cards - you know where this is heading now, yeah?

Had I paid a bit more attention at physics I would have understood what the ionosphere was and how the 11-year sun-spot cycle affected it. Why is this important? At this time the sun-spot cycle was at its 11-year peak. Radio waves refract off the ionosphere, making it possible to "skip" them to Europe, the USA and in extreme cases, Australia. OK, so it doesn't sound so exciting reading it!

For me, everything was moving at a rapid pace now, everything apart from school work, of course. My expanding car washing business was operating at capacity and all other spare time was being used to try and talk to as many other "DXers" as I possibly could around the globe. The USA, France, Italy, Spain, Germany were becoming boring and commonplace.

CBers would dish out "eyeball cards", "DXers" would send "QSL cards" to confirm the contact. These cards would have some appropriate, or in many cases inappropriate, images on them to confirm the radio contact on a certain day at a certain time. These were good times, and it all started on the back of a **MOVIE**. Thanks, Kris.

By 1981 my parents' garage was converted into a valeting bay, the loft into a Radio Shack and to really piss off the neighbours a huge antenna was bolted to the side of the house. I think I was what would now be referred to as the "**neighbour from hell**".

This is where I must apologise to the tax payers of the late 80s: I was wasting your tax investment in education. **Sorry**, I do feel guilty about that.

In 1981 I met "Mr Noisy". Colin worked for the Council at this time and had caught on to the idea of **PRINTING** these Eyeball and QSL Cards. I was intrigued. In his bedroom in Condorrat in Cumbernauld he had trays and trays of lead type, tins and tins of ink, an Adana 5x3 printing press and orders coming out his EARS. CB Radio was the "Big Brother" of the day. If you wanted the gossip you tuned in and listened to 40 channels of complete and utter TOSH from people who hid behind "handles" such as Rubber Duck, Love Machine, Sundance, and Robin Hood. If you weren't part of this 80's movement, well, **you just let the best in life pass you by**.

Colin was giving it all up, he had left school and "**grown up**", discovered alcohol and girls and saw print as a distraction. He was looking for around £250 for his "business", including the Adana machine, all the type, inks and stock of cards - not to mention an increasing database of clients. At £250 it was a steal. I had £5, **all I needed was to source a lender for the £245**.

I approached a group of **investment bankers** and proposed my plan to acquire this business that was yet to reach its full potential and expand rapidly into the faster growing "DX" market. The need for print was **HUGE** and poorly served.

My **investment backers** agreed the project had merit and decided to fund the £245 required to secure this transaction, and without realising it at the time - a whole **multi-million-pound print business had been born**…. You were starting to wonder where this was going?

Mum and dad were of course the backers and resigned themselves to the fact that school had been a blip in my career journey, and that it was no longer a worthwhile use of their time attempting to get me to study.

By the 1982 exam period I was earning more than my dad, had a network of clients that spanned the entire UK, and between talking on the radio and printing cards I had little time to attend exams, let alone study for them. I failed them all, including physics. I never actually turned up for the physics exam as 40 orders had come that day from a Glasgow CB Store - it was a commercial business decision. The irony was my knowledge of **EXACTLY** how Radio worked had far surpassed anything taught in physics.

Leaving school at 16 with no formal qualifications makes life tough. We're hardwired and encouraged by parents to "find a job". Entrepreneurial ideas are frowned upon and unless you come from a background of businesses owners you are going to be railroaded down the employment route. I remember vividly having many conversations with my mum and dad about running my own print business. At age 17 this was **LAUGHED** at… encouragement of the day!!

To "toe the family line" I did indeed find a job. I started off on the programme of the day - the Youth Opportunities Programme - and worked in a Shell filling station. I kept the printing business going and for a while this worked well. The filling station owner was Jackie Stewart, not THE Jackie Stewart but A Jackie Stewart. Jackie didn't realise at it the time, nor in honesty did I - but my experiences there were planting the seeds for shaping my career. I quickly got to know many of the regular customers and realised that despite this being a self-service filling station if I went over and welcomed Mr Richardson and filled up his car, rewards came my way. The KPIs of the day were set around the model of the car. My **revenue** was driven by the owners of Jaguars, Mercedes, Land Rovers and Range Rovers. Not surprisingly, the owners of BMWs tipped less than the Skoda drivers, isn't that interesting?

After a few months I was making more from tips than wages and began asking what these people did for a living, in a nice pleasant way. Bingo, that's where it started to hit me. **Many had their own businesses**. I have to say a good few were lawyers and architects so the previous theory around schooling was now challenged. Then I began to do some serious market research: when super cars came in, I would make a point of talking to their owners. Almost every one I spoke to had their own business. Now we're talking. I want an **Aston Martin**.

I then went from one job to another, keeping the print very much a part-time operation. It wasn't really until age 22 that the tide of opportunity started to turn. I started working for a company in Cumbernauld called FOTEC and did a lot of print work for them whilst learning a LOT about advanced print techniques. The year was 1988(ish). Billy O'Neill at FOTEC taught me a lot and most certainly gave me the confidence to go it alone. At 22 you can imagine the "encouragement" I got from the folks. Still staying at home, I was considered the black sheep. No armed forces, no university, I could sense their disappointment. BUT, there's always a but… they **KNEW** the strides I had made at school with a business that grew from nothing. Disappointed they may have been, but deep down they knew what my calling was, and it wasn't long before they **supported it**.

The next few years I dabbled in this and that and lacked any real direction. I went from one dead-end job to another, hoping each opportunity would provide the guiding light I so **desperately needed**. The printing business was always there in the background.

Always having had a keen interest in aviation I decided to learn to fly. Who knows, that may be a great **career path**? The printing business had provided enough income to support that, and so began the route to obtaining my first pilot's licence - a PPL(A) - Private Pilot's Licence - Fixed Wing.

At the Glasgow Flying Club I was introduced to one of the instructors - George Ebner. George and I just hit it off from day one, there was something about the man that I instantly respected and without realising it at the time, he had me reined in. George was a retired BA Captain, but that's not what he was famous for - he was one of the very few, of the remaining few. When inclement weather grounded us George would keep us spellbound with war time stories of flying Spitfires and Hurricanes. There were other stories too, however, most of us switched off after Spits and Hurricanes.

The flying bug had well and truly got me now - this was what I **REALLY** wanted to do. Remember though, with no formal educational qualifications this was going to be a tough sell. Anyone who flies knows it's addictive as any drug - often described as the rocky road to financial ruin. **Every penny** was now spent on flying and building hours.

My dad found that amusing, and reminded me about a movie he took me to see. In 1975 he had taken me to see Airport 75. I still have no idea how a ten-year old got in to see that film. Airport 75 was the one where the Cessna hit the Boeing 747: carnage, crew killed, the usual. Everyone left the cinema reluctant to ever fly again, I left the movie determined to be a **PILOT**.

We're now up to the early 90s and I was the ripe old age of 27. Yes, in RAF terms this is OLD. I had applied to the RAF and never got to first base with my initial enquiry. George learned of this and was surprised - he knew that I could have that little Piper Tomahawk eating out of my hand, and with a bit of sadly-lacking discipline - the world could be my oyster.

To this day I don't know what George said to that RAF recruiter but whatever it was it WORKED. I sailed those interviews, blew away the first, second and third selection tests and then got that letter - **ACCEPTANCE** into the Royal Air Force.

George sent me a card, all it said was "**Per Ardua Ad Astra** - and less of the Ardua", signed, George. "PS stick in and get that commission". The RAF motto roughly translated means "Through struggle to the stars", so what George referred to was "less of the struggle". The PS was important - George always said that the RAF is for officers and those who are privileged enough to hold the "Queen's Commission" virtually guarantee themselves any career outside the RAF.

I never saw George again, he passed away during my time in the RAF and his friends were unable to contact me. I never got the opportunity to thank the man who changed the direction of my life. George, wherever you are, sir, per ardua ad astra... **and less of the ardua**.

At 27 and having been an "**entrepreneurial nomad**" I was deemed "high risk" by the RAF - but they too saw something. The careers office was very clear that I was a risk, a wildcard at school, a fly-by-night entrepreneur with a distinct lack of any form of respect for authority. You can perhaps see why a military organisation would be concerned?

After basic training the training team confided in me those concerns, then conceded they had been proven completely wrong. They were amazed at how well I fitted in to the RAF. Next step - RAF Shawbury, Air Traffic Control College. Again - high risk, but knowing it this time. I set out to prove a point.

When I graduated from RAF Air Traffic College Shawbury I left with some interesting paperwork. Not just the Certificate of Graduation but a Certificate of MERIT, and a letter of commendation from the CO stating my test scores had been the **highest in the history of the College**. Thanks, George.

You see, I had learned that achievement is not academic, that's just the way we're conditioned to think. I had out performed 1000s that had gone before me. Many much younger than me, many with O Grades and Highers, some with degrees and varying college certificates - yet none of them held the highest average test scores. **Isn't that interesting**?

In life we need a reason to achieve. At school that reason was not clear - I had higher priorities. In the training days of the RAF the priority was "don't let George down" and by now **I was determined to succeed**.

As anyone who has progressed through training in the RAF will know, a passing out parade is something special. A sense of achievement for sure, yet also sadness as the friends you have made are now all going in different directions, different career paths, and for some, in harm's way.

Stationed at RAF Lossiemouth my urge for adventure resurfaced. What the hell was I doing in a glass box **TALKING** to these guys? I was a **PILOT** for God's sake and needed to be out there.

The next few years were nothing short of extraordinary. I got involved with numerous activities at Lossiemouth, including deputy editor of the Station Magazine, running the station Print Club. I then decided to utilise the superb education facilities at the station and get all the qualifications I needed to progress to the sharp end of an RAF career. Higher maths, English and law were quickly gained, a special recommendation from the boss and I was ready to progress. I was being pushed by Squadron Leader Tolman, DSATCO (Deputy Senior Air Traffic Control Officer) - D-BOSS as he was better known. We already agreed that the first pint bought in the Officers Mess would be on his tab. **What could possibly go wrong**?

What could possibly go wrong indeed? I had settled in well at Lossiemouth. I had secondary duties usually reserved for those of much higher rank, I had a boss who offered support and encouragement and life was good, **really good**.

Aircrew was a must, so I spent a week flying with the Herc crews at RAF Lyneham and came back from that totally focussed on what needed to be done. I was now determined to get my commission (thanks George) and quickly set that process in order - with a LOT of help. **What could possibly go wrong?**

In the early 1990s, **Options for Change** was a Defence Review - a radical re-shaping of the Armed Forces - after all, Russia was our friend, the Soviet Union had collapsed. Recruiting was cut, trades were closed, and I was going nowhere fast. Age was against me, and at 28 the clock wasn't ticking, the clock had stopped.

That was a bitter blow, to be so close, yet so far left me very disillusioned. There's no way I was going to be happy in a glass tower, spending years thinking what could have been. Options for Change did bring one advantage. They were so desperate for redundancies that leaving was easy. After a heated debate with my Wing Commander I was back on Civvy Street in **less than 6 weeks**.

It's important to take five here. I left the RAF because I had tasted something SO GOOD that nothing else would have come close, I knew that. I am often asked by friends, colleagues, clients and family about my thoughts on their kids going into the RAF. I don't even pause to think about that answer. Yes. I was, and still am **immensely proud** to say "I **served** in the ROYAL Air Force".

I then add that they should "play the game", study hard, get the qualifications and COMMISSION - George was right there. We may live in difficult and changing times, however she's now 100 years old and I don't think anyone would argue that our Royal Air Force is the best in the world. **Lest we forget that**.

I left the RAF in March 1993 and within weeks, The Ink Shop was born...and now the story really starts. One hell of a story.

The Formula For **Success**
The Formula starts with you.

Dreams

x

Goals

x

Learning

x

Planning

x

Action

=

Success

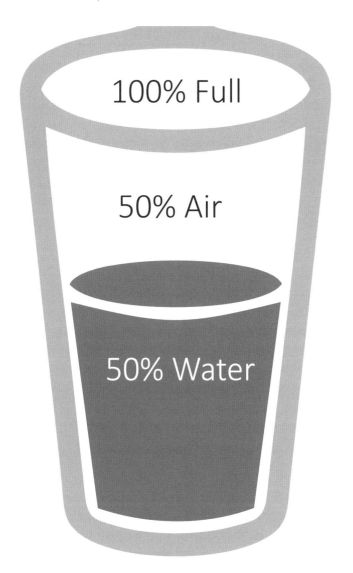

The glass is always **100% full**
50% water + 50% air = 100% FULL

Chapter Two - Humble Beginnings

The purpose of writing this book is to share the Ink Shop story. The title of the book is **How to Wreck Your Business** - clearly so that you **DON'T**. I just wanted to be clear on that from the get-go: it'll save so much time in pending litigation!! With the current levels of business failure in the UK the **last thing** anyone needs is guidance on how to "wreck a business."

Business failure in the UK is a national outrage, yet in many cases avoidable. If you are in business or considering going into business you MUST read Michael Gerber's **The E-Myth Revisited**.

If you have read that book, great - this will make sense. If you haven't read Gerber's masterpiece, close this book right now and go and download it. Let me do you the courtesy of being extremely blunt. As I have said many times, had I known during my 20 years at the Ink Shop what I know today, that business would not have failed - I mean that 100%. Had I read and implemented what is highlighted in The E-Myth, ditto. If you think simply reading something is enough to change your business then you need to go and have a look at the "Right Road, Wrong Track" (see graphic) - there's a big chunk of denial going on with you right now. **There are no free lunches**.

Without taking action, then you're simply wasting your time. In fact, be one of the 80% that won't take action and bin this book now - **save time**.
I know this annoys people; it's done for a reason. I am not intentionally trying to piss you off, well, actually I am, I'm just not doing it for any other reason than I want you to take ownership and take **ACTION**.

The statistics on business failure vary from report to report. The broad consensus of opinion is that 80% of new businesses fail in the first five years. **From the remaining 20%, 80% of them will fail in the next five years**.

Let's put some figures on that. If 100 businesses start in 2020, 80 of them will have failed by 2025. 20 will continue, of which only 4 will see 2030. 100 excited "entrepreneurs" embarked on a life-changing journey, full of excitement, full of enthusiasm, and no doubt dreams and aspirations of being the next Richard Branson. The reality: 96 families are torn apart by those businesses **FAILING**.

Only 4 out of the 100 will see ten candles on their Business Birthday Cake, and it **doesn't** have to be that way.

If you were told that of the 100 flights departing your airport, 96 will crash and burn, you can bet your arse you'd get a ferry. Then why do so many of us continue to start our own business? We know the deck is stacked against us - yet off we go, often with nothing more than a few quid and an **awesome idea**.

Why do we do that? We do that because of **DREAMS**, our desire to be better. The dream of building a better life for ourselves and our family. Here's the strange thing though: when I ask business owners about dreams and goals, they often look at me as if I'd asked for the title deeds for their house. Why is that? Every one of us that starts a business has a dream, a vision - what was yours? Has it become a bit faded? If so, why? Why is it business owners are often reluctant to talk about them? Is there now an embarrassment because the reality differs from the dream? Is there a sense of disappointment or frustration that the dream has not been achieved?

If there's one thing I hear and see a lot in business it's this: for most it's **harder** than you expect. For many it's **more expensive** than you budgeted. For the majority it's like playing the human version of Snakes and Ladders. Just as you get up the ladder, along comes a snake, and you're back down a few levels. Remember though, just like Snakes and Ladders, while there may be ups and downs, you must and can push through. Why do I mention this?

Simple. I played Snakes and Ladders for 20 years. As the business progressed the ladders became bigger and the snakes smaller. That was until the Perfect Storm started to gather pace and all of a sudden some pretty big fucking snakes appeared. The mental fitness a business owner needs, in my view, is phenomenal. Back in the day we never talked about mental fitness, I do wonder though just how close I came to total meltdown?

You will deal with more data in your head in one day than most employees could manage in a month. You'll have weeks where you'll be dealing with more shit than a dairy farmer. You'll have all that going on and you'll still need to make the right decisions and keep that British stiff upper lip. Being self-employed is the **loneliest "job" in the world**, few get it, fewer still want to get it.

Here's a tip: get an "**Entrepreneur Buddy**." Not a mentor, not a coach, not an inspirational guru, not a relative or business partner, and definitely not some guy you know that just talks pish. I am talking about a business owner that is at the same stage as you, or slightly ahead. Even better, get a small group, and meet up for a beer once a month. Not in work premises though. Unless you've been there, or are there, then you haven't a clue, and I mean that. Too many people in business only see the destination and have no idea of the journey. I got a lot of shit for driving a £186,000 Aston Martin - yet no one remembered the early days of living in a static caravan with no heating and driving a Metro Van.

This is something I think the UK is dreadful for: **Jealousy**. Everyone loves the underdog taking on the big corporate giant. Actually, that's not what they are doing, I also thought that. Now, I believe it's a wish for the successful owner to be "brought down a peg or two." I often hear people refer to Brewdog as having "lost their roots." I totally and utterly disagree with that. The guys, and the dog, had a **VISION**, they kicked ass and made it happen and have built a business of modern folklore. Have they changed, hell yeah, they **HAD** to. Are they still passionate about their business? I'll drop them a line and ask, I'm connected with them on Linked In - they can't be that fussy!!!

You'll be pleased to know there is actually a Formula for Success - seriously, there is. I'll explain it briefly here. Look around at any successful business, any successful entrepreneur and you'll find that the formula for success is in place. Following the formula will **not guarantee success**, not following it will almost certainly make success way more difficult to achieve. I laughed at this when I first heard it, then I thought about it letter by letter - not laughing now, I can tell you. I first saw this at an Action Coach event, it's powerful stuff.

Here is the Formula for Success: D x G x L x P x A = Success

Try and work out what this is. Yes, you could Google it, in which case it will mean nothing other than a string of words. **THINK** this through. What is the **FORMULA** for success? What do successful people do every day, every waking moment? What did Branson do that I didn't?

Successful people and successful businesses have all these components nailed. When a business, or business owner is NOT where they want to be it's simply because one or more elements are missing.

So here it is. **Dreams x Goals x Learning x Planning x Action = Success**. Every one of us had a *dream* when we started our business. Have those dreams become a bit faded? Why do we let challenges in the present prevent us dreaming about the future? That's the wrong way around. Dreams of the future should allow us to overcome the challenges in the present. You also need to be prepared for the people that mock your dreams. If a "friend" ever tells you your dreams are shit or unachievable - you need that arsehole out your life, like yesterday.

Then we set *goals* to start realising that dream. Yes, write them down. A goal that's not written down is simply a wish, an idea, a maybe, a might: get it written down and commit to a date that the goal will be achieved. SMART Goals, Specific, Measurable, Achievable, Realistic and Time-agreed. I get clients to work on SMART ARSE goals by adding, Accountability (to who?), Results (expected), Shared (is the goal shared?) and most importantly, Enjoyable (it should be fun growing your business). It can be damn hard work and still be enjoyable.

There's a lot of crap on social media at the moment about working long hours, "Hustle and Grind," as Gary Veynerchuk refers to it. Then others say you are a poor business owner if you're not working 4 hours a day - 4 days a week. It's time to get real, - running a business is hard work at the start. This is where the systems come in, this is where I never joined the dots. For me the hard work **CONTINUED** - that's not right. Expect hard work in the early years, expect hard work in the growing years and expect hard work in the difficult years - you will have them all. However, the business needs to breathe, it needs systems and structure. Without that you quickly go from being the business's biggest asset to its biggest liability. I did not see that - now, Christ, it's obvious. **I Wrecked My Business**. I Wrecked My Business because no one told me this stuff.

We then move onto *Learning*. Once you set goals and start to achieve them, what do you need to learn to be a better business owner? Every day should, indeed MUST, be a school day. Then we come to the old favourite, *Planning*. This was a huge part of the Ink Shop's demise. The journey for that business was simply not planned. You can only fly by the seat of your pants for so long. The plan needn't be long nor overly detailed. Many business owners today use my one page "**Vision Planner**" - you can download that at *howtowreckyourbusiness.co.uk*. This simple plan allows you to see where your business is today, in 12 months, 2 years, 3 years and 5 years. "If you don't know where you will be in five years then you are already there" - when I heard that from Brad Sugars I nearly fell off my chair.

After all this is in place the final part of the formula for success is of course, *Action*. There are plenty of businesses out there that actually think that writing it down, giving it some thought means it will magically happen. In a world of delusion that may work, for the rest of us, action is needed. What and when, why and by who. This is why we use 90-Day Plans: it makes the day-to-day and week-by-week tasks much easier to break down into "bite-size chunks." Use the 90-Day Plans from the resource section on the website. Don't try and be too ambitious with your first 90-Day plan. Commit to a few tasks every week and add more as you become confident with the process. If you add too much, you'll miss deadlines, get pissed off and stop doing it, **then become even more pissed off**.

That's the Formula for Success. As I said, using it does not guarantee success, not using it will almost certainly prevent it!!!

Humble Beginnings

This chapter is called "Humble Beginnings" - because they were. As previously mentioned, very few people care to remember the early years, the long hours, low pay, seven-day weeks of hard work. The truth is the hard work, lost holidays, and long hours never went away because the **structure** of the business simply wasn't there.

This is why the business coaching model appealed to me so much - it was a **HUGE BFO** (Blinding Flash of the Obvious) where my business had gone so badly wrong. I didn't have 20 years' experience, I had two years' experience, **I just did it 10 times**!!

Since 2016 I have given out over 50 copies of the E-Myth Revisited. Of those 50, some 45 have come back and said "that's me... that book has described me." The other five, well, they were so chaotic they never read the book to see how applicable it really was.

Fewer than 1 in every 100 business owners then go on to achieve the wealth they aspired to at the start of their entrepreneurial journey. We did, we managed it, the illusion of wealth was there, the structure was not. Business success cannot, and **MUST NOT**, be gauged by money alone.

You don't have the time to make the same mistakes. This book will point out some of the landmines, it's really up to you if you want to dodge them or jump on them.

I achieved **ALL** this, and defied the survival rate statistics. I survived the first FIVE years, I survived the second FIVE, got to TEN years, and actually saw TWENTY years, although there was no party that day. I also achieved the wealth I aspired to when I first started the business. How I then **LOST** that is a warning for all business owners.

Think

On Paper

Anyway, let's get back to **Humble Beginnings…**

I was out of the RAF, back in Civvy Street in 1993 wondering what just happened. This wasn't what I planned or expected. Or did I? I genuinely don't know. Was the entrepreneurial spark getting brighter, or did the RAF disappointment re-ignite it? I just do not know. Whatever the reason, whether fate or a sub-conscious battle plan, one hell of a journey was about to start.

I bought the contents of the RAF Lossiemouth Print Club and within a few weeks had sold my Suzuki Vitara jeep and had amassed a fortune of £5,000. On the 13th April 1993 The Ink Shop was born. My wife Bobbie and I set about getting this business up and running with absolutely NO IDEA what our true direction was.

This sounds really cool, and to a point it is. Yet at some point, dreams, ideas, and goals need to be committed to paper. **THINK on paper**. That's got to be the best quote / advice I have ever heard - Think on Paper. For you techy folks out there, let's agree that "paper" can be a smartphone or tablet, too. The key is **WRITE** it down, don't just think it - **WRITE IT**.

The next few pages are going to chart the progress of my business, the achievements, the highs and the lows. I often refer to the **EIGHT** Fundamental Reasons why this business failed - these will be covered later. As you read through the book it should become apparent what and where those errors were made… Isn't **hindsight** such a wonderful thing?

Running your own business can be incredibly lonely: even CEOs of larger corporations can agree with that. Few people "get it" - the Entrepreneur **THINKS** differently.

If they are not on your frequency, then they just won't "get it." I had many friends that one by one disappeared over the years, they never understood what it meant to run your own business. It's another sacrifice that many business owners find: **was it them, or was it me**?

Over the years I have amassed a number of gems of advice. The two that really stick with me are:

"Read a book a week for the rest of your life" and **"You become the average of the five people you hang about with most**."

Take a few minutes to think about that and then write down below the **BUSINESS** books that you have read or listened to in the last 12 months - there should be 52. Are there even 2?

(feel free to use a separate sheet if needed)

Then, write down the **five people you hang around with most**. Do they motivate, encourage and inspire you? Do they criticise, discourage and deflate you? This is really important, guys - if those around you are glass-half-empty types, then this is going to affect you. "Get rid of the morons in your life - tell them to piss off": another Brad quote, I know he's right, and I think you do, too. Here's an even more scary one though, and try this. You **EARN** the average of the five people you hang around with most.

1)
2)
3)
4)
5)

So, let's go to April 1993 and really get this book underway. The early years - this chapter is called **"Humble Beginnings"** so let's focus on that.

Having now decided to leave the RAF, I started working on the business idea a few months in advance. That really didn't take long as nothing was committed to plan and there was no cash-flow forecast. There was an IDEA, passion and enthusiasm and not a lot else. I'm an entrepreneur though, that's enough; the plan's in my head and so arrives the first warning - that rarely works. The few times that it does, it's never scalable, or sustainable.

Having worked in print prior to the RAF I knew where some of the weaknesses were in that industry. This was the era when High Street print chains dominated the market. Kall Kwiks, Prontaprints, PDCs, Alphagraphics and many others all had slick operations and impressive store fronts. Interestingly, they are now **all but gone** entirely from the High Street.

What they also had was impressive prices - this was where we saw the opportunity for the Ink Shop to "**niche**." Our first lucky break came during a visit to Glasgow, when we ended up at the famous Barras Market. In the heart of the "Glesga' Barras" was the Barras Centre - a grand plan to bring sophistication to the market - it never worked and the Centre had many empty shop units.

When we started the business, it was called the **Ink Spot**. This suited our model perfectly. The Ink Spot was going to be built on low prices - we were now in the bargain capital of the country. The Barras Enterprise Trust saw something in our idea, they liked the Ink Spot, they liked us - and I'm sure they liked the idea of renting a shop unit too. And so it was: Unit 9, The Barras Centre, Glasgow, was going to be our home, and the **Ink Spot was born**.

Upon leaving the RAF we shipped all the equipment down to Glasgow, a trip to B&Q saw the "shopfitting" done and we were ready to open on time and on budget. On time being the same day we arrived, and on budget was the cash in our pockets. Flying by the seat of one's pants doesn't even come close.

Leaving the RAF presented another problem - we were homeless. Living with parents was NOT an option so we decided we'd buy a caravan. £5000 bought us a "**functional**" home at Craigendmuir Park in Stepps and Bobbie and I, together with Dougal, our German Shepherd pup were ready to take on the world.

The caravan leaked a bit around the door, and I remember one rainy day followed by a freezing cold night being awoken by Dougal making noises of "muffled distress." I could see him lying down, so thought he was dreaming, but the noise continued. I was more than a little shocked to discover that my poor pup had gone to sleep at a wet front door which had frozen during the night and my pooch was now well and truly stuck to the carpet. It took many minutes of painstaking warm water to release poor Dougal Dog.

That's the shit you do when starting a business - **every penny is a prisoner**. Isn't it funny how in later years when £500,000 houses and Aston Martins appeared that many people chose to ignore and forget that sacrifice? Too often people see the destination and choose to ignore the journey. I also think that in the UK we are very good at bringing up the underdog, "hail the conquering hero", - only to take delight in bringing them down when they succeed. In the UK success is frowned upon by many - and that **REALLY** pisses me OFF.

The early years of trading were really interesting in a number of ways. The Barras in 1993 was by no means at its peak but still attracted 1000s of people over the weekend. This worked out really well for us as it allowed us to offer retail print at the weekends and B2B Print during the week. What really worked well was the business owners who would see us at the weekends and come back during the week.

The business was well and truly up and running and making money virtually from day one. At this stage the business was offering a variety of business products such as business cards, leaflets, brochures etc, all produced on our single-colour, second-hand press - **we were flying**.

At the end of the week we would tidy up and go from a business print centre to a retail print shop with wedding stationery being a big seller at that time.

The days were **long**, and the weeks were **longer**: the Ink Spot was open from 8am until 8pm, seven days a week. We did well catching small business owners before or after work and of course Saturday and Sundays were our retail days. **This is the shit you do in the early years**.

It was working though - this young business was establishing a reputation for offering a quality, reliable service and delivering what was needed when it was needed. Our "**disruptive**" approach to marketing was born. The Ink Shop (as it became) in later years became very aggressive in the marketplace - it is easy to see where those skills were born.

In the early years we quickly earned a reputation for disrupting the market. Our customers could sense the passion and enthusiasm and clearly bought into that. It wasn't long before our competitors were starting to sit up and take notice. This is where our business name became an issue. Another Ink Spot took exception and issued a demand that we change our name. Now, there was no Registered Trademark and no legal reason for us to do so, as there were, from memory, some 20 Ink Spots in the UK. We did however decide to change the name - even then we **KNEW** we were going to be special and as such, the subtle change was made to the "**Ink Shop**."

The business also had a "**hardness**" about it - you don't work in the East End of Glasgow and not learn how to side step a few landmines. The key was simple: see no evil, hear no evil and don't ask questions. Those who know the Barras will now be nodding their heads!!!

I remember early in The Ink Shop's life seeing a traffic warden FLY past our large front window. The poor fella had been administering a ticket on a trader's van parked illegally in what was then a pedestrian zone. The trader took exception to that and drove the van away. In fairness, the warden was having none of it and hung on well until the G forces akin to a Formula One racing car turning into a hairpin ejected him into our window. Alas, none of the 50 traders saw anything, and assumed the warden had "slipped" - it had been raining. I've never seen a human slip that fast or so high up a wall before - but slip he must have. The Barras closed ranks, as the Barras does, and we all got on with the job in hand.

For all its faults the Barras had a community feel about it - something I have not experienced before or since. 100's of businesses of all shapes and sizes, as well as varying degrees of HMRC registration, all working together for the common good. I liked that.

Business was good, very good in fact. Were we ahead of target and on plan? Difficult to say, as there was no target nor any plan but it "**felt right**." Don't underestimate gut instinct.

Space was now becoming a problem so as we entered 1995 it was time to expand. We had also managed to secure a mortgage and bought ourselves a nice flat in Glasgow's East End overlooking Glasgow Green. I remember vividly the novelty of central heating, and Dougal Dog just loved DRY, warm carpets. The simple things that you take for granted. The flat was also a five-minute drive from the shop, so great for a quick commute, and getting home after invariably long days.

It's worth pointing out that despite having such a young business it was easy to obtain a mortgage. Many referred to this as the "Liar's Mortgage", you simply put on the application what the lender wanted or needed to see. In fairness, we put down exactly what the business was doing, and that was easy to confirm with numbers. We stayed loyal to the original bank, EVERY business and personal transaction was done through "that bank" - this will become more relevant later in the book. **LOYALTY** buys you two thirds of fuck-all in banking circles, let's just get that out the way now.

Expanding the business was more exciting than our new flat - well, maybe the central heating novelty took a while to wear off. The combined print shop/retail shop wasn't working well so we convened a board meeting (stuck the kettle on) and presented our expansion plan (a doodle on a paper wrapper) and in that haphazard, Turkish-bazaar-style the decision was made to take the unit next door - trebling our floor space. That meeting took all of 3 minutes 23 seconds - but that's what Entrepreneurs do - **it FELT right**.

I jumped across the Barras Centre to speak with Willie, the Centre Manager - he was keen for us to take Unit 10. We agreed terms there and then and Willie gave me the keys to "look" around - sorry I missed that "look" bit. It was late in the day and Willie wanted away - "I'll catch you in the morning," he said, and away he went. Willie was off for a steak and bit of TV, I was off to B&Q and bought the biggest sledgehammer I could carry. Later that night Unit 9 and Unit 10 became one.

If only I had taken a photo of Willie's face that next morning. The Barras Centre had a lovely courtyard which my building work had turned into a scene resembling Kosovo - Willie was none too happy. Deep down though, very deep down, he liked the way we operated: SEE IT - DO IT - FUCK IT. 1995 and 1996 went from strength to strength - it was really at this point that the reality of possibility was dawning on me. We had secured finance and bought a brand-new press - the ITEK 3985, in its day the **MUST-HAVE** piece of kit.

It wasn't long before it had a brother and we had our first employee - then the second, then the third. Still the business plan was confined to one's head and nothing committed to paper - even at this stage it just **"felt right**."

The time then came in 1996 to take a third unit in the Barras Centre - Willie was on the ball this time, viewings were **"escorted"** and the keys retained. Terms were agreed and the lease would be altered, although a verbal agreement was enough for us to gain entry in a few days' time. A few days: in entrepreneurial terms that's the same as a few months.

After Willie went home, I noticed that at some point units 11 and 12 must have been shared as a lintel was in place and a previous opening was bricked up. Willie was away at 5pm sharp and by 6pm we had made great progress on bringing that wall DOWN. Yet again Willie arrived the following morning, yet again the courtyard resembled Kosovo and yet again Willie **LOST IT**. Getting right above the line here, I think we were the tenants from hell.

There are a few points in business where things happen - stuff that just changes the course of the business. Brad Sugars refers to these as **"taps on the shoulder"** - we've all had them - maybe a guardian angel whispering in your ear, whatever - but we've ALL had them.

Are You On The **Right Road**, Or The **Wrong Track**?

The Right R.O.A.D.

Knowing You're On The **Right Road** Means...

Responsible For Your Actions
Ownership Is Always Taken
Accountable To Yourself & Others
Decisive In Your Nature

The Wrong T.R.A.C.K.

Knowing You're On The **Wrong Track** Means...

Total Lack Of Respect
Refuse To Acknowledge Issues (Denial)
Attack & Blame Others
Change Is Always Resisted
Keep Using Excuses For Everything

Where are you?

As we were charging through 1996 into 1997 a chance conversation changed the entire direction of the Ink Shop. I was interested in a poster printer that I thought AB Dick ITEK (our press supplier) had in their product range. I called the company at their Cambuslang offices and spoke to Tom McMillan. Tom asked me to come down for a demo. On arrival, it was clear that he must have completely misunderstood me. He showed me a machine that was **NOTHING** like what I was looking for… but that was it. Without a doubt the biggest single turning point in the business. A piece of kit which was like a **golden nugget to a gold prospector**.

The real journey was about to start. And all through a misunderstanding: funny thing that. Tap on the shoulder?

This chapter has been written deliberately to show the fast-paced, carefree attitude that I had. Things looked right, felt right, seemed right - and in fairness **WERE** right. When people ask "when did your business fail?" I used to say April 2013, not now. That's just when it died; it actually failed in these early years. **That's a tough thing to say**.

Even if you have a cottage business in your garage, under the VAT levels and only a few customers, you absolutely must have the plans in place if your ambition is to grow that business. Had I been in that mindset from day one, then planning in the later years would have been second nature.

Yes, the "flying by the seat of your pants" was fun, it has a very "pirate" feel about it, but it's destined to fail. Dreams don't have to be compromised, nor should they. **If you dream big, plan big**.

The later years become a bit of a blur. We started off in Unit 9 at the Barras Centre. We then took over unit 10 and then 11 and finally 12. We were still growing and then bought our first premises, the old Clydesdale Bank Building in Glasgow's Gallowgate. Two things made me laugh there, first, the HUGE vault was still there, although it had been emptied. We did check carefully in case the odd bag had been left. The other thing that made me laugh, in a worried way, was the shotgun holes were still there after one of the **MANY** failed robbery attempts. A wee bit of Glesga' history.

It was in the Gallowgate that the business really started to fly. We had bought some serious printing gear and had gone from being an "irritation" in the market place to a real disrupter. We could do no wrong in these years, and really did wipe the floor with many of our competitors. These are the years that haunt me, not because they were bad, quite the opposite. It was in this period that we were not just unique, we were smashing the print market, really kicking ass. If the true magic had been understood at this point and a sustained plan for **SERIOUS** growth put in place, well, who knows?

If you're from Glasgow, and football is your thing, then you'll possibly be "**blue or green**." Rangers (blue) had dominated the football scene, and had amassed a number of season wins, I think it was nine in a row. 1998 saw Celtic (green) stop the "ten in a row" in its tracks. Not being football minded, I couldn't care less. What made this interesting was our location. Directly across from Baird's Bar, the most popular Celtic pub in Glasgow, it wasn't long before 1000s of supporters were celebrating - on our flat roof.

There was no point in even attempting to halt the festivities, and certainly not with a name like Mason, so we just hoped that the roof survived, which it did. It was interesting times.

We continued in the Gallowgate for a number of years, and around 1999 opened our first **CITY CENTRE** print store. This was our first "digital print centre" in Sauchiehall Street - right in the City Centre. This was a HUGE change in direction for us, and the first wrong turn, although that was not known at the time. This project's objective was to compete more directly with the High Street franchise chains and bring the brand "upmarket." This is why **PLANS** are essential, they focus direction and bring clarity - we never had that. The Ink Shop had been built on value, quality and low prices, and we were smashing it. Moving "upmarket" just put us into a saturated market where the customers were harder to get and even harder to keep. It doesn't matter a shit whether you are high or bottom end - it's **YOUR** end, stick to what you are good at.

One of our suppliers was to later hit the nail right on the head with this comment, "You were so good at being **Seiko**, why the hell did you want to be **Rolex**?" Not everything that glitters is golden.

This continued until we outgrew the Gallowgate premises and moved to Wishart Street, behind the Glasgow Royal Infirmary. We took this opportunity to sell both the Gallowgate and Sauchiehall Street shops and focus everything into one **Print Superstore**, and it was this move that really propelled us into the **super leagues**.

The year would have been around 2002/2003. It wasn't 2001, we were still in the Gallowgate then. Everyone knows where they were on **September 11th 2001**. (respect)

If I could turn the clock back I would never have moved from Wishart Street - that was the **SINGLE** biggest mistake. It was the **PERFECT** building, in the **PERFECT** location, doing the **PERFECT** work for the **PERFECT** customer base.

Every year we were at Wishart Street was a **record breaker**, the business just grew and grew. We had now moved to Heidelberg printing presses, regarded as the best in the world. The business was getting bigger and **BETTER**.

We outgrew that building and had just ordered our first Perfector press, a huge machine that printed both sides in one pass. Great machines, yet too long to fit in the building. We had hoped to extend the building into our car park, however planning consent was not approved. This was a huge blow.

Here comes **hindsight** again. We should have cancelled the press order and stayed with the equipment we had in the premises we had. Had that been done, we would have almost certainly survived the storm that was only a few years away.

We sold Wishart Street and moved to a rented industrial unit in Cumbernauld, six times the size. This would have been around 2006/2007. We didn't know it then, but this was the beginning of the end. We will cover in later chapters WHY. **Hindsight is indeed 20/20 Vision.**

The people in your everyday
life have the power to
encourage and inspire
you more than any book or
guide ever will...

Stuart Mason

Chapter Three - Planning

To successfully wreck your business it's essential that you don't let planning get in your way. Far too many lending institutions and business advisors have got this planning lark completely and utterly wrong. You do NOT need a plan. How many of the current billionaire entrepreneurs had a plan? Not many, they started off with a brilliant idea, bucket-loads of enthusiasm and not a lot of cash. That's what a TRUE entrepreneur is, right?

The plan should always be in your head, after all, things change quickly in business and having a plan means you just have to re-write the thing several times and Christ knows, you don't have time for that. Perish the thought.

The thing with planning is, it's just a total waste of time, what the hell is the point spending hours and hours planning when you could be out there cracking on with it, making shit happen and getting on with creating your entrepreneurial dream? Hell, that's what I did and it did me no harm whatsoever, so let's just agree right now - BIN the planning. Oh, hang on a minute, that didn't end so well for me. Might need to rethink that, after all, the point of the book is really How (NOT) To Wreck Your Business.

In the previous chapters it was apparent the business started with no real plan, tons of enthusiasm and truck loads of ambition, just no plan. There was a dream, there sure as hell was a dream, to build an amazing business, just no plan on how to do it.

This is one of the longer chapters, it needs to be, it's a big topic. Don't think that Planning is simply creating the Vision Planner from the website. Planning must be done in three stages. Look at the **Vision Planner** as the shortcut, do **NOT** short-cut the short cut. It just will NOT work. The three stages to creating your plan are, Preparation, Creation and Implementation.

Preparation - Plan the Plan

Be clear on what **YOU** really want. I find it frustrating when business owners limit their longer-term ambitions based on the current pain they

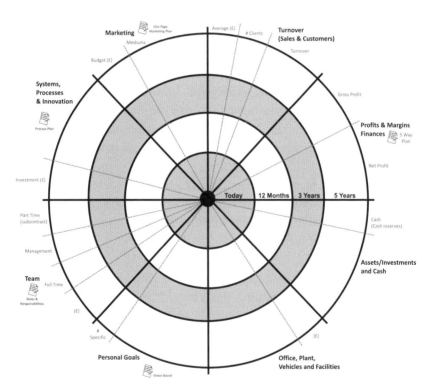

Download The 5 Year Vision Planner

howtowreckyourbusiness.co.uk

have in their business. Your longer-term vision MUST be what you REALLY want. You then create the structure and systems that eradicate that pain. This is why plans in your head rarely work; your sub-conscious is simply too aware of the current pain, and whether you realise it or not, the plan is limited based on those emotions. In my view, anyway.

Preparation also includes being clear on what a lot of your basic numbers are. Conversion rates, yes, rates (plural): there's four of them we're going to look at. If you don't know what these conversion rates are, how can you possibly start to build a plan around marketing, when you have no idea what marketing is needed to generate leads, enquiries and sales? **You can't.**

Let's be clear here, you will not build your plan on a current conversion rate that is 5% when you know it should be 60%. You will, of course, create a plan and system to improve that conversion rate, and base your longer-term plan on the conversion rate(s) you **WANT**. Can you see now why preparation is so important?

Here's a very simple statement that describes how your plan will look if you don't prepare. **Crap IN, crap OUT**. Preparation is key, agreed?

Once you have completed your Preparation, and let's be honest, a lot of this will be "best guess," you may not know a lot of these numbers. Rest easy, you WILL. Next stage is to move onto CREATION, you'll start to build your plan, in this case the 5-3-1 Vision Planner. 5-Year Vision, 3-Year Milestones, 1-Year "Must-Do's."

The rest of this chapter focuses on **CREATION**. Just remember, use a pencil.

I Love Analogies, so Here's One that Really Nails Planning in Business

Imagine you're going on holiday to some far-flung corner of the globe. You've endured the airport hell, and you're now on the jet, ready for your first G&T. You're strapped in, and ready for take-off. As expected, the Captain comes on the intercom, and as predicted the "speech"…

"Ladies and Gentlemen, welcome aboard today's "Difficult Jet" flight to…….eh, em, can't quite remember where we're going. Anyway, it's fine, we'll sort it out once we're up there. The navigation software is down at the moment, but hey, it's a big-ass sky, and there's bags of room for everyone. Sit back and relax, and once we figure out how to start the thing, we'll be off. I have never flown this aircraft type before; don't worry though, I mean, how difficult can it be? We should have enough fuel, however we may need to glide the last few miles. Anyway, enjoy the flight."

Ridiculous, YES? Clearly that would never happen? Yet for the vast majority of businesses this is exactly what **DOES happen**. Let's re-word this.

"I don't really know where this business is going, there's no clear written plan. That's okay though, I have a good idea of what I want to do, and where I want to go, and it's always worked in the past. I don't do any training, what would possibly help me? I have never needed that before. There should be enough cash to grow and sustain the business, we'll be fine, we'll get there."

The crash and burn scenario is likely in both cases.

A Kick-Ass Plan with Meaning and Purpose

The trouble is, many business owners will have read the above and agreed they do some of that - please tell me NOT all of it? Let's look at this in a bit more detail. The first challenge is around the plan itself. Lending institutions and some business advisors do need shot for the crap they get business owners to complete under the guise of a plan. Pages and pages of utter drivel that has no commercial reality at all, and sees the light of day only **THREE** times. The **first** is when it's written before being confined to the top drawer, the **second** is when you find it while looking for those triple As that are in that drawer somewhere, and the **third** is when you actually decide to throw that shit into the recycle bin. When I talk about a plan, I am talking about a kick-ass plan with meaning and purpose. A plan that is fun to create, a plan that drives and motivates you, and most of all, a plan that is less than two pages. Trust me, you're going to love this.

Head Plans Are for Headcases

Let's move back to the it's-in-my-head nonsense. Please tell me you're still not convinced about "Head Plans"? Okay, I know, that was me for many, many years. I was content that the plan in my head was perfect and the right way to run a business. Of course, I was oblivious to the fact that emotions varied that plan almost daily. Good days saw me wanting to globalise the brand and take on the world. Bad days saw me wish the whole business was back to me on my own. How can you even begin to structure a business for sustainable growth in your head? The simple answer is you can't. **Head Plans are for headcases**, and that's the simple and brutal truth. Again, in my humblest of opinions.

Whether your business is a garden shed enterprise or a growing global brand, the need for that plan is the same, although the complexity of it will change, for sure.

What Got You Here Won't Get You There

Marshall Goldsmith has a great quote, another one of my favourites, and it's so applicable for this. "What got you here won't get you there." That's it - that's the one for me. What got me to (this point) was never going to get me to the (next point). Yes, many entrepreneurs started with nothing more than a dream, £5.75 in loose change, a car worth £500, and enough enthusiasm to drive a steam train. That's how you START a business, it's not how you grow a business, and it's sure as hell not how you build a business that isn't reliant on you at every stage.

You need to decide right here, right now what kind of business you WANT. Do you want nothing more than a job, a business that can't function without you being involved in even the most basic of decisions? Are you ready and willing to work harder for less, and your reward, if you survive at all, is a business that is worth two thirds of fuck all because no one wants to buy the "job" you have created? Is that what you want, are you kidding me?

Don't get me wrong, the early years are always going to be "hustle and grind," long days followed by short nights. It must be temporary, though.

Wouldn't it make more sense to start to build a business that in the years to come can work without you? A business that works without your every waking moment reliant on its success - or failure? Do you want a business that will have a value when the time is right for you to exit the business, a return for the many, many hours of hard work over the years? **I'm just guessing here that this is more appealing**?

Then of course we come to my favourite line, and one I used many times myself. "**Things move too fast and change too often to write a plan**." It was a shame that I realised that's WHY a plan is vital a few years too late. Let me again be brutally honest - if this is your excuse, then it's actually more of a reason TO create the plan rather than the excuse **NOT** to.

The disadvantage you have about using all the bullshit excuses on why a plan shouldn't be written is **I have used them all**. If you're struggling to find a bullshit excuse for not creating a plan, email me, I have archives of 100s of them. That includes: "true entrepreneurs not having a plan", and some didn't, in fairness. They may not have had a plan when their business started; they sure as hell have them in place now. **What got THEM here would never have got THEM there**.

Think on Paper

Does that make sense so far? This needs to click, otherwise it's a waste of time. Creating a plan is simply committing a dream to paper, it's the ideal, a best guess, and MUST be fluid because it will change. Going back to aviation, you're flying from Glasgow to the southern coast of Spain, heading over north-west France en route to Spain... that's the plan. The French Air Traffic Controllers are on strike (shocker there, eh?) and advise of severe disruption in France (no shocker there) - you change direction, you adjust your journey to make sure you arrive at your destination alive and intact - delayed maybe, yet arrived. Your business is exactly the same. **You can and will have to divert to avoid a few storms**, the plan will change, the outcome may change, that's the whole point of it. Having the right plan in place will allow you to see what needs to change, why, when and how. It will ensure you reach the destination.

I recently had the honour of listening to Sir Clive Woodward talk about his Rugby World Cup glory. Now, for a Scotsman, that was tough, although let me tell you, the learning was worth it. Sir Clive talked about "T-Cup" moments, and this is exactly what the aviation analogy is all about. T-CUP stands for **Thinking Clearly Under Pressure**. In the cool light of day, and with a clear head, you plan for the moments that DO NOT go as planned. "Should this happen, we immediately do that." Does that make sense? In effect, in a genius way, you are planning and preparing for the unplanned. I wonder what percentage of business owners do that? I don't think my calculator has enough decimal points! Like everything in planning, write it down, including random thoughts, ideas and notes, **THINK** on paper.

I really hope this does make sense. **Let's get back to PLANNING**.

My business had no plan, well not a written one anyway. As crazy as that sounds, there was **NO WRITTEN PLAN**. Everything from day one was in my head. When you have a small business, having no written plan rarely works, although you might get lucky. When you have a growing MULTI-MILLION-pound business it simply CANNOT work, and if you still think otherwise, close this book, burn it - because you are delusional. I know that some of you are now saying: "Well fuck you, I do have a multi-million-pound business with no WRITTEN plan!" I wonder what you would have if you **DID** have a written plan in place? Just asking.

Can your business survive without a plan? Of course it can. Mine did for 20 years. You're just stacking the odds heavily against yourself, and making life harder than it needs to be. Is it not hard enough already in business? Would you not rather be benefiting from the clarity a plan will give, rather than re-inventing the wheel every month? That's exactly how I felt, it was horrible. Every month the "Head Plan" was being re-written. The trouble with that is, you actually become **comfortable being uncomfortable**.

If you read this chapter, then act upon it, and do little else in the book, then you'll see the benefits. You'll see **massive** benefits in fact. That's why the 3rd stage in the Plan is always **Implementation**. The best plan in the world that lives in a top drawer will be beaten every day by a poor plan that's perfectly executed. Action wins every time.

80% Will Do Nothing? Are You One of the 80%?

The vast majority that read this book, around 80%, will NOT take any action. 80% of businesses fail - isn't that interesting? Do you want to re-think that decision? Thought so. You see guys, this is it - if you expect to READ this book (or any book) and be safe, you're in trouble - you really are, go and get a job now and save us all the effort. If you change nothing, then NOTHING will change. If you commit to change... commit to action, well hang on, here comes success.

There's something else, I want you to write this down...

Go on, write this down: "**You can only improve what you accurately measure**." Seriously, write it down. (I will start it for you)

You Can Onl

Feels weird huh? Good, it's meant to. Unless you come out of your comfort zone and commit, then nothing will change. As we go through this book one thing will shout at you. "**You can only improve what you accurately measure**." How in the hell can you change anything if you don't know what you are changing, or why?

Why did I ask you to write it down? Michael Leboeuf sums it up: "*When you write down your ideas you automatically focus your full attention on them. Few, if any, of us can write one thought and think of another at the same time. Thus, a pencil and paper make excellent concentration tools.*"

You commit tasks to memory too, hence why I say, "think on paper." How many times have you been out and about, walking the dog, in the car, out with friends and you have thought of something, only to forget what it was later? No? Is it just me then? Maybe an age thing!!

You see, any planning you do "in your head" will have the same issues. You'll remember some of it, you'll probably remember MOST of it. It is almost certain though that you'll not remember some of the finer details, you know, the ideas that you had when out walking the dog. More often than not it's those smaller, intricate details that can make the biggest difference.

Today of course, it's easy to "write stuff down," it doesn't need to be paper. I have a Galaxy Note (sorry Apple lovers) and use the note pad facility all the time. I'll use the "pen" and write down notes, doodle stuff, take photos etc, it's great for all this random stuff that flies about, and easy to use too.

This is why the plan is such a powerful tool: it works. You're not simply writing down a list of targets and goals that may or may not be achieved, what the hell is the point of that? You're building a living and breathing planning document that has clearly defined **OUTCOMES** and **BENEFITS**. They are going to be realistic, otherwise the plan becomes a de-motivator, and most of all, they are going to be time-specific with temperature checks taken along the way. Too often I see business owners with an agreed, achievable goal with a specific time set. They then get to that week, are nowhere near completing the goal and simply shrug their shoulders and move the date forward. **What's the point in that**? You're kidding yourself. If you have a target set to achieve "X Goal" in "Y Weeks", then your plan will have a number of "temperature checks" to make sure you're on track to meet that deadline. Of course curve balls will get in the way, of course deadlines will move, of course other priorities will come along - that's fine. As long as it's not the NORM, as long as it's not the EASY way out.

You Can Only Improve What You Accurately Measure - and ACT ON

You will accurately measure everything in your business, you'll set up numerous KPIs (Key Performance Indicators) that will allow you to quickly and accurately see the performance of your business in seconds. We'll cover KPIs and KPI Dashboards later in the book. However, if you don't commit to PLANNING, well, chances are that will be a total waste of time, best go and watch daytime TV.

Despite my business having a turnover in excess of £2.7m there were no REAL KPIs in place. Of course, performance figures were looked at, that's the issue, they were **LOOKED** at. There was no consistency in checking those figures, and no system in place for capturing and interrogating the data. Turnover, quality, client satisfaction, etc were all watched carefully but there were no KPIs in place to track and monitor progress, they were not accurately measured. You can ONLY improve what you accurately measure.

I'll say that again, you can only improve what you accurately MEASURE, and ACT on. I just added that final bit as a timely reminder that USING the data is vital. Don't laugh, there's 1000s of businesses out there that are exceptional at collating data and analytics, then DO NOTHING with it. Not you, right? Do not allow yourself to get into "**Paralysis by Analysis**", you are just kidding yourself.

Conversion Is the Key to Everything,
It's the Business Equivalent of The Big Bang

What's your sales conversion rate? If you have answered that question with any of the following phrases, then you don't know, it's that simple: "I think," "It's about," "It's around," "Pretty good, actually," "John does that," "Jane knows that," "It's pretty high," "I don't need to know" or "The accountant does that." This is where I went so badly wrong. This is why this chapter will be BRUTAL and unforgiving, it's **THAT** important.

When I ask "what's your conversion rate?", what do you immediately think of? More than likely you are thinking of the **conversion to SALE**? That's not unreasonable. Not unreasonable until you go to my web site at howtowreckyourbusiness.co.uk and go to "Planning Tools." There you'll find my Magic Matrix (apologies for the cheesy title), and that will challenge your thought process around conversion rates. The example on the website explains this in much greater detail. You may be surprised to learn there's actually **FOUR** conversion rates you **MUST** know in your business. Before we dive into Planning, we're going to look at this in more detail. It will help if you have this printed from the website, and start

How To Wreck Your Numbers

The area within the Business	The Monthly Figure	The cost for each	Get better by 5%	and see the reduction...
Marketing Reach	12,000	the marketing spend was £5000 for the month. = 42p per engagement	12,000 This figure and the marketing budget stay the same	the marketing spend was £5000 for the month. = 42p per engagement
x				
% Conversion	10%		10.5%	
=				
Initial Enquiries	1200	£4.17 per enquiry	1260	£3.97 per enquiry
x				
% Conversion	25%		26.25%	
=				
Qualified Leads	300	£16.66 per lead	331	£15.11 per lead
x				
% Conversion	50%		52.50%	
=				
Quotes Issued	150	£33.33 per quote	174	£28.74 per quote
x				
% Conversion	40%		42%	
=				
Customer Sale	60	cost of acquisition £83.33	73	cost of acquisition £68.49
x				
No. of Sales	2	cost per sale £41.67	2.1	cost per sale £34.25
x				
Av. Sale Value	£495		£520	
=				
Monthly Turnover	£59,400	every pound of turnover required 8p investment	£79,716	every pound of turnover required 6p investment
x				
% Margin	30%		31.5%	
=				
Profit	£17,820	every pound of profit required 28p investment	£25,110	every pound of profit required 20p investment

What are YOUR Numbers?
Can you see how a small 5% improvement can make a HUGE difference?

Download the "Vital Statistics" pack from the website and complete
your own numbers. www.howtowreckyourbusiness.co.uk

How To Wreck Your Numbers

How to Wreck Your Numbers is really easy, just don't focus on them, and the rest will take care of itself. Go on, switch on the TV, there's a really good soap on. If you choose to take a bit of time and focus on your numbers though, you'll be pleasantly surprised how a **few small changes can make a huge impact**.

This mock example is a small business's **monthly** figures. Let's look at all these figures in a bit more detail. This company invests **£5000** per month into their marketing and that generates an estimated 12,000 "reach." That is people engaging on social media, coming in-store, receiving literature, meeting their sales team, receiving a mailer etc.

You'll notice there's **FOUR conversion rates**. The conversion from overall reach to initial enquiry. From an initial enquiry to qualified lead. Then from qualified lead to a quote being issued. Last, and by no means least, the conversion from quote to sale. **Qualification** is one area that many businesses neglect. It's essential to **QUALIFY** those leads.

Once you know your figures and your marketing costs, it's easy to see what engagement, enquiries, leads and sales "cost."

You now know how many **CUSTOMERS** have been gained, so now look at five other important figures. The number of sales that customer gives you. The average sale value. The monthly turnover obtained. The margin made. Finally, the profit for the month.

Why is this important?

These figures first of all give you end-to-end transparency. What results your marketing is delivering, what the associated costs are, and more importantly, it allows you to track every stage of **CONVERSION** in your business.

If you want to increase SALES (and who doesn't?) Don't even consider increasing your marketing spend until your conversion rates are right. **Does that make sense?**

When these figures are right, you can instantly see what your cost of acquisition is. If you want £xx more turnover, simply increase your marketing to £xx. Simple isn't it?

Everything starts with knowing your numbers. Use the blank template from the website and start to build your own numbers. Use the figures as an "average" month. Some clients prefer to do this as an annual illustration. It's whatever suits you best.

collating and writing down your own numbers.

First up is your **Marketing REACH**: how many people are seeing your message or adverts? "How the hell can I possibly know that, I can't do that?" That's the common answer. "Bullshit," is my common reply, of course you can. You can track views of articles on LinkedIn, you can track likes, comments and shares on social media, analytics will tell you everything you need to know about visitors to your website. You know how many people your sales team have spoken to, you know how many flyers you posted, you know the average reach of the magazine advert. Get the picture? It doesn't have to be accurate to the exact number, nor can it be, it does however NEED to be known.

The reason for that is simple, **Conversion Rate NUMBER ONE** is Marketing Reach to Initial Enquiry. If your marketing reach is targeting the wrong people, or worse, targeting the right people with the wrong message, then this conversion rate is going to be really low. That's a MARKETING issue, and can be easily resolved with a bit more testing and measuring. Does that make sense? Are you doing that? Are you going to do that?

Conversion rate NUMBER TWO is taking those Initial Enquiries to Qualified Leads. This is more applicable if you are issuing quotes, having further meetings, or issuing estimates, as these are a drain on your resources if not qualified. Your qualification process will be up to you, in simple terms you are checking to make sure that the prospective customer is ready, willing, and able to buy your product now or in the future. Now, here's the thing. During the qualification process, you are qualifying them. Rest assured, they are also qualifying YOU, so make damn sure that part of your process is to excite them and address the benefits they want. They don't really give a damn you've been established since 1971. **Here's a tip**, if it has "I, me, we or us," it's a **feature**. If it has "you or your", it's a **benefit**. Focus on the benefits. What's the difference between a feature and a benefit? A feature massages your ego, a benefit puts cash in the bank.

Here's a pro tip. **NEVER ASSUME ANYTHING**. The qualification process must never, and I mean EVER, make an assumption. When I bought my first Aston Martin, the dealership was joined to their Volvo dealership. I had been working that Saturday and was in "print mode," that's to say a pair of jeans, trainers and an Ink Shop sweatshirt that may or may not have had ink marks on it. Did it really matter? Anyway, I went into the showroom and immediately caught the attention of the sales executive, who remained seated. The funniest things annoy you. "The Volvo dealership is next door." The comment was bad enough, the condescending tone was shocking. "OK, thank you, sorry to have troubled you," I said, and got no further reply from the seated sales "professional." As I neared the door I turned around and asked, with a puzzled expression and tone, "Can I ask why I have to go into the Volvo dealership? I am here to pay the deposit on the black V12 DB7 Vantage that you're sitting beside."

Never, ever assume.

The second conversion, initial enquiry to qualified lead is a great way to test your marketing as well. If the conversion to qualified lead is low, then, you've guessed it, **the message is not hitting the right people**, and pressing the right buttons. Fix it, test and measure, and it will only improve.

This is where it gets exciting, **conversion rate NUMBER THREE**. Qualified Lead to Quote or Estimate. This in fairness could be a number of "next steps", including setting up a meeting to come into your showroom to buy an Aston Martin. This conversion rate is VITAL. Think about it. Your Qualification Process now identifies that you're working with **TARGET MARKET prospective customers**. You would expect this conversion rate to be high.

Conversion rates up to this point have been marketing. From this point on, it's YOU. Qualified Lead to Quote, and Quote to Sale, should be HIGH. If they are not, you need to look very carefully at your product, service, prices, scripts. Are you selling features and not benefits?

This is really important: as you begin to plan your business for the longer term it must be around what those conversion rates **SHOULD BE**. Creating strategies for improving each of the conversion rates is very easy. The example on the website also illustrates what a small 5% improvement makes. Try it on your figures, see what happens with a **5% improvement**, then try 10%. **This has all become really clear now, hasn't it**?

The purpose of digging a bit deeper here was simple. You need to know and plan around these conversion rates. There is NO POINT in starting a Marketing Plan, or a Sales Campaign without knowing these numbers. Does that make sense? If you have low conversion numbers, then an expensive campaign is **not going to improve that percentage**. If, on the other hand, you focus on improving the CONVERSION rates, then chances are you'll get the results you want from the campaign without spending a penny extra. Now that's got to be of interest. **You will almost certainly achieve MORE and spend less**.

Cost or Investment?

You'll also notice from the example on the website that you can start to work out what the costs of enquiries and leads are. Now, that's a great KPI. Look at how the figures start to change when you aim for just a 5% improvement. We'll cover that in more depth later in the book, too.

Do you currently contribute to your main competitor's marketing budget? Do you transfer money every month directly into their account? Of course you don't. If you have a marketing campaign that raises awareness of your product or industry, and your conversion rates are not where they need to be, then that's exactly what you are doing. Now flip that, nail your conversion process, and the opposite is now the case. You will probably be getting leads from THEIR inability to convert. **Nice**.

Marketing is only a cost to the business when you have no idea what's working and what's not. Remember, 50% of all marketing is a waste of time: which 50% though? That may have been the case in the 60s when that quote was first mentioned. Not so today. You can track all your marketing expenditure, and make sure every penny is an **INVESTMENT** for the business, and not a **COST** to it.

It goes without saying that I never dug anywhere near that deep. The Ink

Shop was aggressive with marketing, and we spent a small fortune on promotion every month. What should have happened is that those numbers were known, then the marketing would have been an investment in the business and not a cost to it. Had I known and implemented this, I can tell you right now I would have spent 25% of the previous marketing and delivered 400% more. How do you make a small fortune using un-tested marketing? **You start off with a LARGE one**!!

I'll summarise planning around conversion rates as "getting more from spending less." This is why it must form part of your overall planning. You'll need to know how much time, money and resource you need to INVEST into marketing to grow your business, and to hit your targets. **First though, you MUST have those four conversion rates and costs for each stage under control**.

Everything is linked, so fully expect to be adding your conversion improvement ideas into your 90-Day Plan. Complete the Matrix in the Planning Tools section of the website, and KNOW your conversion rates.
If you don't know your conversion rates to at least one decimal point then put this book DOWN and go and find out. If you don't know what a decimal point is, then it's going to be a long day.

Okay, so you don't need to know the decimal point. The important thing, before the letters start, is to make sure your answer is "my conversion rate is 41%," and NOT "I think it's around 50%."   Since I started business coaching in 2015, I have not met a business owner yet who did not over-estimate their conversion rate, sometimes massively, when they didn't know the TRUE figure. Somewhere in the region of 5% of business owners knew their conversion rate, for others, it was often a WILD guess. If you have taken a guess, then chances are it's 10-20% (at least) lower than that. **You can only improve what you accurately measure**.

I Love it When a Plan Comes Together
Before we get back onto PLANNING, are you thinking that your conversion rate is either not important, irrelevant, or too difficult to measure? **Do you really believe that**? Businesses that supply quotes and

estimates can measure conversion rates easier, I get that, there's no argument there. However, EVERY business needs to know their conversion rate. How else can you POSSIBLY know what part of your Marketing Plan is working? You can't, it's that simple. If you're a retailer then you MUST know what is bringing those customers IN to the store. You MUST also know how many are BUYING. You want to know WHY they are buying so that you can replicate that and do MORE. If they are NOT buying, you need to know WHY NOT before the next person through the bloody door is an administrator.

Are your prices too high, is your product range crap? Is your store poorly laid out? Is it easy to BUY? Are your staff inattentive? Are your staff too pushy, or not pushy enough? Is your store too busy, too confusing? What is it? why are people coming in and NOT converting? Don't you think this is good information to know?

Going back to The Ink Shop, our conversion rate was high - **well, I think it was**!! The crazy part of conversion is knowing what's **not converting** is as equally as important as knowing what is. What system do you have in place that tracks and records why sales never converted? Oh, as good as that?

If you do, what's then done with that information? What action do you take weekly and monthly to fix the issues that are preventing conversion? Don't think for one minute just because you are good that, "**So what? We'll get another sale**!" is anywhere near acceptable. That's the arrogance I had. Remember this, every sale that you don't convert is turnover and profit for a competitor. **Your inability to convert is making your competitor stronger** - let that sink in for a moment.

This is where it all starts to come together: the **Preparation** stage of Planning will make your eventual plans considerably more accurate.

Plans Achieve NOTHING - Sad Yet True

When Planning or creating a Business Plan is mentioned, many business owners roll their eyes. I know I did. Emotionally scarred by the multi-page irrelevant document that financial institutions seem hell bent on getting business owners to complete. What happens with these "plans"? There's a great deal of enthusiasm when writing it (perhaps). Then what happens? They are confined to the top drawer, and the next time you see it is when you're hunting for the triple A batteries that you know are in that drawer somewhere. "Oh, the plan," followed by a brief moment of renewed enthusiasm followed in turn by "Shit, we never did any of that." Then, once again the drawer is closed, since you have now found the triple A batteries, confining the plan to more months of darkness and inactivity. **Plans like that achieve NOTHING**.

There is a direct relation between the success of your plan and the hours of daylight it sees. I get business owners today to put their plan on the wall. There's usually a reluctance at the start, followed by the "excuse" they don't want staff to see it. That may be the case, although I doubt it. I'll go out on a limb here and suggest there's a bit of embarrassment there, or maybe the **F.E.A.R** of the plan not working. **False Expectations Altering Reality**, that's what I think **FEAR** stands for. You allow false beliefs to alter what you are TRULY capable of, and that's just criminal. If you don't believe that, I have another version of F.E.A.R you can use, Fuck Everything And RUN.

Yes, plans do achieve nothing, if that's what you permit to happen. In business, you get what you tolerate. If you tolerate a lack of planning, a lack of preparation, a lack of implementation, then that's exactly what you're going to get. **You GET what you tolerate**. The outcome of your plan is your actions. Don't make the same mistake I did. My book title should have been "**How to REALLY Print Money**," and it so easily could have been. The recipe for success WAS there, it WAS working, and had PLANNING been there…

Lies, Damned Lies and Statistics

I personally believe that business statistics are all linked. We know that 80% of businesses fail in the first five years, yet 80% of business owners fail to take any action after training events, seminars etc - despite taking LOADS of notes. In 2018 and 2019 I held several seminars and workshops for business owners, all free, and all were usually FULLY BOOKED or at least well attended. There was always LOADS of energy in the room, frantic note

How To Wreck Your Dreams

You need to navigate through the interference - **no one is going to do it for you**. Don't downgrade the dream, **upgrade the ACTION!**

taking, yet the action points people were asked to take were rarely actioned. What is that all about? What's the point in taking notes, then not committing those notes into an action plan?

More interesting, less than 4% of UK businesses have a turnover exceeding £2m and less than 4% of businesses have a WRITTEN business plan that they follow. Isn't that interesting? You may recall that 4% of businesses survive to see their 10th Birthday. The same percentages come around again and again.

It's not a coincidence, it can't be. Planning cannot, and will not, be a guarantee of success. Run away from anyone who tells you otherwise. What planning does do is move the odds in your favour. Look again at the business survival statistics and let me tell you, you really want every bit of help you can get.

As I grew my business towards £1m it was obvious, with hindsight, that the "flying by the seat of your pants plan" would not work. At the time I convinced myself, that's what entrepreneurs do. How in the hell can you grow and develop a business when you have no CLEAR idea where that business is going? It can be done, it's just very difficult and almost certain to go pear-shaped.

Here's something else to be mindful of, it's what separates someone who is self-employed from an entrepreneur. When self-employed you tend to spend TIME to save money. An entrepreneur will of course spend money to save TIME. Money can be earned, money can be made, time, not so much - you have what you have and what you do with it is up to you. When you're creating your plan a huge part of that is related to the above - it's maximising your time effectively.

I am often asked "can you help me manage time?" My reply to that is simple: NO. I am not Doctor Who, I can't manage time. What I can do is help you with managing YOURSELF, so that your use of time is more effective. It's a huge part of planning in your business, planning your time. **Use the Four D's** to help you manage your time better. **Do It** - do the stuff that will drive your business forward. You should only do what only you can do. **Delegate it** - pass the task on to someone else in your team, or outsource it. What the hell are you doing the £15 an hour stuff for? **Defer it** - not everything needs done right now. It may be important, you may need to do it, but does it need done right now? **Drop It** - this is the one business owners struggle with. If you don't need that shit cluttering your desk or your day, **DROP IT**.

How Much Are YOU REALLY Worth?

Another thing that frustrates me, only because I was the world's worst for it, is business owners doing shit they should not be doing. Washing the van, working in the factory, out in the delivery van etc etc. Try this exercise. This is a handy tool for Planning your tasks.

You are a business owner, the top dog, the head honcho. You work hard and have a heap of responsibility. **What should your salary be**? Not what it is, what it **SHOULD** be? Let's say it's £100,000. That is NOT a big salary for an entrepreneur. Heck, Jeff Bezos probably gets that for a half day now.

That works out at roughly £2,000 a week. On a 40-hour week that's £50 an hour. YOU are a £50 an hour ASSET to your business. You are a mover, you are a shaker, you are the creator of **WEALTH** and the **DRIVER** of the business, not the driver of the van. You are worth more than £50 an hour, in my opinion. I know you do a load of wee cash jobs too, we'll keep them between us, OK?

My point? **Would you pay someone £50 an hour** to wash the car, stack the shelves, be out in the van… I suspect not. Then what are you doing it for? Why are you paying yourself £50 an hour for that? It's because YOU are sacrificing **TIME for MONEY**. Your mindset needs to shift - sacrifice **MONEY for TIME**, pay someone £15 an hour, and let you focus your TIME to do the high level £50 an hour stuff.

Does that make sense? Obvious isn't it? You knew all this, though? I never got that. I'm embarrassed to admit it. Even driving around in an Aston Martin whilst opening print centre number 6, I never got the mindset of

Your Hourly Rate **Challenge**

What salary should you be earning? Not what you are, what you SHOULD

£ [ ] [ ] [ ] , [ ] [ ] [ ]

Pro Tip - note the use of the number of boxes !!

Now work out the following from that

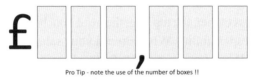

example; £100,000 pa = £8333 per month = £1923 per week = **£48 per hour (roughly)**

Now, here's the question. Would you
PAY someone **YOUR** hourly rate to do some
of the tasks you do? Would you pay
someone £48 per hour to wash the van,
do the invoices, empty the bins,
drive the vans?

No? Then WHY are you doing many of these tasks yourself?

Outsource or delegate these tasks, and leave yourself free to do the
higher hourly rate work that is going to drive your business forward.

sacrificing MONEY for TIME. I would still end up doing stupid shit that was a drain on my time, and prevented me focussing on what I should have been doing, the BIG PICTURE stuff. I would (wrongly) think that being "multi-talented" was entrepreneurial, it's NOT. Nothing wrong with being multi-talented, as long as those talents are all business-growth focussed.

Learn Before You Earn

I wanted to add this into the Planning Chapter because another plan you should have is YOURS!! Your own plan for learning and self-improvement. What can you learn today, that you didn't know yesterday? What's going to make you better tomorrow? One thing is sure, Brad Sugar's quote, "You'll never out-earn your learn" is 100% right, or put another way, **"the only time earn comes before learn is in the dictionary**." Today, I have a simple plan. A list of books and courses I want to read and attend: simple, easy and focussed.

I have a personal plan that improves my coaching, marketing, business development, self-improvement, time management and amateur radio skills. It doesn't always have to be business improvement!

Going off topic a bit here. You read that the whole business was started through a radio hobby? Some FORTY years after all that, I finally went for my amateur radio licence. You can teach an old dog new tricks. Very interestingly I passed that exam with 100%, back to **DRIVEN** achievement again.

Now, I just want to add something here before the letters start. I know plenty of highly successful entrepreneurs who DO go out in the van, who DO wash the vans, because they WANT to, because they ENJOY it. That's absolutely fine, if you are making those decisions through **CHOICE** and not **NECECCESITY**, then that's absolutely fine - to a point!!!

I Google Your Business in FIVE Years. What Do You Want Me to Read?

I want to introduce you to the "Vision Planner," a superb, one-page plan. When I talk about PLANS, I talk about ones that are simple, accurate, and will work. Take that multi-page pile of crap and light a fire with it - not in the office though, please. Why do these plans rarely work? In fact, why do plans in general rarely work? The answer is simple - execution. Right at the start of this chapter **Implementation** was listed as the **third part of the planning process**. You could have the best plan in the world, and you will, yet without **ACTION** it's nothing more than wasted ink. The simpler something is, the more likely it is to get done. You'll see that with the entire Planning System that accompanies this book. A ONE-page "Vision Planner", a ONE-page "Marketing Planner," a ONE-page 90-Day Planner. It's not that we couldn't be bothered investing more time to create these, it's just that we know **ONE-PAGE Plans work**.

Think carefully about this. We're going to fast forward five years, to the end of your five-year planner. I am going to **Google your business**. What do you **want** me to read?

There's one other thing I need to mention. As obvious as this sounds, if your product or service is shit - then the best plan in the world won't be much help initially. The reason I say initially is because your plan will contain the roadmap to excellence and will improve that. Keep in mind that an **EXCELLENT** business with a poorly executed plan is simply letting opportunities sail away, usually towards your main competitor.

To summarise, a great plan is only a great plan when it's followed by execution, commitment, accountability and measurement. Remember the formula for success? D x G x L x P x A = Success. The P is **PLANNING** and the A is **ACTION**. This is what this chapter is all about. If you're still reading this, great, have a coffee, sit back - now we're really getting started.

If you don't know where your business will be in five years, I'm guessing you're already there. I also hear a lot "I've got 10 years' experience doing this." Actually, no. You have one year's experience, you have just done it ten times. How's that working out for you? This was ME, so relax, I'm having a go at me, not you. I was making the same, stupid, dumb-ass mistakes time after time, year after year. We quote Einstein here, the definition of insanity, **"doing the same thing time and time again and expecting a different**

result." Business owners do it all the time.

We're going to look at various plans here, and not dive too deep into them. The "Planning Tools" on the website have all the Planners and Guides on how to get the best out of them. We'll just cover the basics, so you know what to look for, and **what to get started with first**.

The Vision Planner - Always Start HERE

Your plan is going to start off by using the 5-3-1 Vision Planner. As the name suggests, this looks out to where you want the business to be in 5 years. This is YOUR vision. This is the Google bit. We'll then look at what your 3-year milestones are. **Where the business needs to be in 3 years** to make sure you're on track for your 5-year plan. Be aware that growth is unlikely to be linear: years 1 and 2 may be slow starters followed by accelerated growth. **It's your business, just be aware of that**.

Then comes the really exciting bit - the 12 month "**MUST Do's**", what you need to do in the coming year to start this journey. Does that make sense so far? Now, here's the rules. The 3- and 5-year plan CAN change. It's best guess, and needs to be fluid and flexible. Your "**12-Month MUST DO's**" **are exactly that, the non-negotiable tasks that MUST be done.**

There's great debate about Five-Year Plans, some agree, some disagree. There's no right or wrong. In my opinion you must have a 5-year VISION. How can you even begin to plan for today when you haven't considered tomorrow? I was actually being polite and diplomatic there. Not having a 5-year VISION is just plain stupid. You may want a 10-, 15- or 20-year VISION, that's fine - hey, dream BIG.

The Vision Planner is really simple. There's **EIGHT** key areas of the business to focus on. **Turnover, Profit, Marketing, Team, Facilities, Investments, Systems, and Personal Goals**. The outer ring of the planner is year five. As you add these figures, each section challenges the others. You may want £x turnover and £x profit, yet when you add your figures for the team, systems and marketing, and the fact you may have to move to bigger premises, it may challenge those initial profit figures.

Once you're happy with the five-year numbers, you have the **VISION**. Then start creating your three-year **MILESTONES**. Where you need to be in three years to hit those five-year numbers. Remember though, growth is unlikely to be linear, so make sure you look at the "**Growth Chart**" in this book and plan accordingly.

Once you have the three-year milestones in place, you want to start really thinking about the next 12 months. The "**Must Do's**" to get this journey started. What MUST you do in the next 12 months to hit those three-year milestones? Some clients change this to 2 years, that's fine, it's your plan.

You'll see that the Vision Planner has a book icon on some of the sections, that simply means that a more detailed plan or supporting document is needed. Marketing is a good example. Headline figures and activity are fine for this, however, you'll need a LOT more detail. Lucky for you we have a **Marketing Planner** on one page too.

And that really is the 5-3-1 Vision Planner - here's a Pro Tip: use a pencil. There is a Vimeo link on the website that explains the 5-3-1 Vision Planner in more detail.

90 Day Planner/Quarterly Planning

Now, we talked about **action**, and **implementing** the Vision Planner, this is how you do it. The key to delivering results is breaking the plan down further into 90-Day Plans - Quarterly Planning. Agreeing a number of tasks and projects that are going to be done in a particular quarter. The key here is not to add too much. The "Planning Tools" on the website also has your 90-Day Planner ready to complete.

These are your **12-Month Must Do's broken down into FOUR Quarterly Plans**. Most business owners do these one quarter at a time. Just be sure to add your next 90-Day Plan onto your 90-Day Plan!

On the 90-Day Planner we ask you to consider a few more things. **Your #1 Business Goal** for the coming quarter. There's also space for **THREE personal goals** for that quarter too, don't forget them. For your first plan, be

How To Wreck Your Numbers

The **Growth**Curve

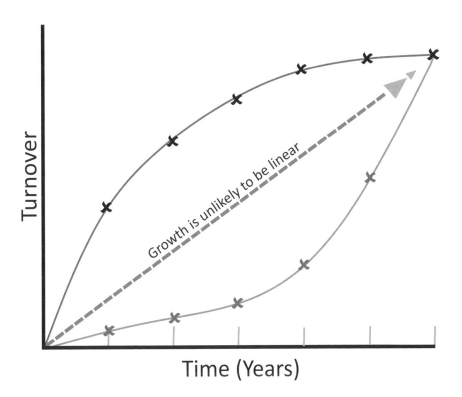

Know your "Growth Curve", it's unlikely to be linear.
It may take 1-3 years for systems and planning to take
effect before rapid growth in years 3-5.
There may be RAPID Growth in years 1-3
which may plateau in years 4 and 5.
It's **YOUR** business, it's **YOUR** plan.
What's your Growth Curve?

easy on yourself. The temptation is to put too much on it - easy, tiger. Better to complete tasks and bring others forward, than see your plan slipping before the first month is complete.

We're often asked, "what do I put on the 90-Day Planner?" That really is up to you. This is personal preference, focus on the **DRIVERS**, what's going to make a change to you and your business. It's better to have FOUR items on your Planner and have a 100% completion, than have FORTY and achieve nothing. Two thirds of fuck all equals??

You may choose to use our proven **Jigsaw System**, that's great. Jigsaw works by creating a strong focus on tasks that YOU want to achieve, and delivering them in a timescale that works. Jigsaw alone may fill your 90-Day Plan. I have taken the decision to **REMOVE** the Jigsaw System from the website. Not because I don't want to share it, I do. **I will ONLY share it with the business owners who want to take action**. I know that's a small percentage. If you're not going to take action, then you're not going to dilute Jigsaw.

Jigsaw focusses on **12 AREAS** of your business, ie sales, Marketing, Customer Service, etc. Within each of the **12 areas** there's **12 systems**, processes or actions. Simply put, it's 12 x 12 - **144 systems and processes**. Look at "Jigsaw" as the business equivalent of "Pick n' Mix" for Business. Where Jigsaw really scores is that it's **adaptable to suit virtually every business**. It's not a "one size fits all". If you want to see how "**Jigsaw**" will help you and your business, message us through the website.

Use **SMART** for your 90-Day Planning. **S**pecific, **M**easurable, **A**chievable, **R**ealistic and **T**ime Specific. I suggest you should use **SMART ARSE**. Add **Accountable, Responsible, Simple & Enjoyable**. If you are enjoying doing it, it's more likely to get done and achieve the objectives required. **Have FUN**.

Your 90-Day Plan MUST be visible. Yes, I know some of you put the 5-3-1 Planner in the drawer, not so with this plan - **it must be visible**. When you see your 90-Day Plan every day your sub-conscious self is getting to work on it, even if you can't be arsed.

Take A Leaf Out of Our Marketing Plan

The Marketing Plan. Again, it's just one page. This plan challenges you to think very carefully about your marketing. You will then use this with the "Magic Matrix" to test your numbers. If you have multiple strands to your business, different divisions or departments, then you will use a separate plan for each. One size cannot fit all.

The Marketing Plan will start with FOCUS. **What is YOUR target market**? Where do they hang around in the biggest numbers? One client recently really got this. They targeted high net-worth business owners. They knew that a high percentage of their target market had kids at some local private schools, so they sponsored the Rugby and Football Teams. The leads quickly followed. **Where do your potential clients hang out in their biggest numbers**? That may be an online group, a club, a sports venue - just give that some thought.

Is Networking part of your marketing strategy? **Network with CARE**. Some events attract people who would go to the opening of an envelope. These are unlikely to be your target market, unless you sell envelopes of course. My point, sometimes with **FREE** networking events, **you're paying too much**!!

I am a big Chamber of Commerce fan, that's just me though. I would look there first.

The Marketing Plan then challenges you to think "**What is our WOW**?" For me, this is the most important element of your marketing. Being clear from the outset how you get your prospective clients to say "**Wow!**", as it's usually followed by something else, like, "I need to contact these guys right now." If you don't differentiate, then it's more than likely going to be down to price.

How well do you "**WOW**" your prospective client.? **How do you take all their pain away**? How do you make their life **SO MUCH** better? The focus

How To Wreck Your Marketing

Ignore the Single Leaf Marketing Plan and you'll soon wreck your marketing

Our Target Market

Where do our customers hang out in their biggest numbers?

Geography, Groups, Interests, Associations, Groups, Leisure, Social Media, Networks...

How do we nurture these leads and convert them?

Inform

what strategies will we use to inform, and provide REAL value?

Excite

how do we keep our prospective clients excited?

Differentiate

how do we differentiate ourselves & stand out?

WHAT'S OUR WOW!

How Do We REALLY Impress?

What makes US really stand out?

3 Marketing Mediums

online marketing mediums we'll use

pick 6 - test and measure and use the Top FOUR

offline marketing mediums we'll use **3**

HOW WE BUILD AN ARMY OF RAVING FANS

and get loads of referrals by...

To capture data we will

our biggest goal with data capture is then to:

To Improve our Customer EXPERIENCE we are going to ....

remember, customer EXPERIENCE includes everything your customer sees, hears and reads - even before you know they exist

We are awesome OUR BIGGEST BENEFIT IS

what do we have that REALLY excites our customers and our competitors can't touch?

Our Amazing "6 Touch" Follow Up Process

The Magic **6**

Initial Meeting

Quote Issued (email)

WOW!
Wow Pack Sent

Call ONE

email

Call TWO

This is just one popular example.
Consider your "WOW Pack" - what's going to impress your prospective customer, what are you doing that the rest simply miss?
Consider making touch point SIX a call, we know the majority of business is won here, yet very few of your competitors will be making this call...

Download a free copy of the PDF or order a full colour A2 poster
at www.howtowreckyourbusiness.co.uk

here is on the **BENEFIT** you provide. Let me tell you right now. If you're writing down your benefits and there's an "I, we, or us" then it's not a benefit, it's a **feature**. A **BENEFIT** can only start with **YOU or YOUR**.

Two amazing authors that you need to follow are Andy Bounds (UK) and Allan Dib (Oz). Both authors, and both GENIUSES in the field of sales and marketing. Allan Dib's book "The 1-Page Marketing Plan" is THE best book I have read. End of.

Your Marketing Plan will challenge you to build **Raving Fans**, seek referrals, and continually seek to improve your entire customer **EXPERIENCE**. Don't bang on about your "Customer Service", that kicks in after the SALE. If your **Customer EXPERIENCE** isn't better than exceptional, then there's potentially THOUSANDS that never get to see your "Customer Service," does that make sense?

Referrals, we're shit at it. I met an American Business Coach a few years back and he said "Jeez, you Brits are so good at marketing and sales, then don't ask for referrals." **What's your referral strategy**? Good as that?

Pick three online and three offline marketing strategies. From those, test and measure and retain the best four from the six. You may want more, or less. Start off with 4:6 and see how you get on.

How do you nurture leads and WIN that sale? How do you **differentiate, excite and inform**? Too many people bang on about USPs. Forget USPs. Very few businesses can be unique, and even if you managed it, it would be copied before you could capitalise on it. If you are UNIQUE, great. For the rest of us, focus on **DIFFERENTIATE**, what makes you different, better? What makes you stand out. Why would the customer buy from you, not me, and certainly not them? Get the idea?

Looking back at my business, **we were light years ahead of our competition**. Yet, the marketing focussed on features. We do this, we do that, we have these amazing machines. Had the marketing changed to being BENEFIT driven then the marketing efforts would have exploded.

Follow Up or Fold Up

If you issue quotes, estimates or have a follow-up process, then consider your "**Magic SIX**" - what is your "Six Touch" follow-up process? You see, we know that the vast majority of sales are won after the 6th touch, that's a **MINIMUM** now. Yet, bizarrely, most sales guys (guys being a gender-neutral term, before the letters start) **give up after the SECOND**. That's a LOT of business being left for the customer to decide.

If there's **NO FOLLOW UP**, and the customer is left to choose between you and them down the road (who also did not follow up) what's that decision more than likely going to be based on? **PRICE**.

We issued loads of quotes, quotes by the BUCKET load. Yet, they were not followed up. We didn't have time. **What complete bullshit**. Think about this, this was ME. Why do 100 quotes and have ZERO time to do anything other than quotes? What about doing 50 quotes to highly targeted market prospects, and **following them all up**. What do you think would have delivered better results? I'm asking for a friend.

No, we (me) were focused on getting the message out to **EVERYONE**. Every business is a potential print customer. The trouble is, when you try to speak to **EVERYONE**, you end up speaking to NO ONE. Targeted Marketing isn't just the best way, **it's the ONLY way**.

That's why being **DIFFERENT** is so powerful. If you are the same as me, and I am the same as them, then what does the customer use to make the decision? PRICE, there's nothing else. Statistics tell us that over 40% of customers will pay more to get the quality and service **THEY WANT**. It's not always about price, unless you make it so.

So that's the Marketing Plan.

It's on the website at howtowreckyourbusiness.co.uk in the Planning Tools. Download the Planning Pack and it's all there for you, free of charge. **Remember though, without Implementation, why waste your time**?

That took a while, and that was keeping it brief. I know the One-Page Plans make it all sound very easy. It's not. They do require some careful thought. The more time you prepare, the more accurate these plans will be. The One-Page Plans make it easy to **SEE**, easy to **TRACK**, and above all, easy to **DO**. Enjoy creating them, enjoy even more the success they will bring for your business.

I never did these to any degree of accuracy in my business, yet today I see clients FLY that embrace them. Just remember, there's a DIRECT connection to the success of a plan, and the hours of daylight it sees. **Our plans are claustrophobic, they hate being locked up in a drawer**.

That's the Main THREE PLANS. Here's A Few Other Planning Tips You Should Think About Too.
TO DO LISTS. As the name suggests this is your daily **TO DO** list. It can be a written list, it can be digital. My preference is written, your subconscious is way ahead of you here. **WRITE it down**. Think on paper.

Also make sure your To Do List is done the night before. I doubted this logic until I tried it. OMG! When you write your list the night before, your subconscious gets working on the list, you get up in the morning and the magic just happens. Be sure to make sure the "Frogs" are at the top. Read the book: the "frogs" will make perfect sense.

Read *Eat That Frog* by Brian Tracy - he covers this in amazing detail.

A "**NOT**" **DO LIST**. This is genius, and a new concept that I started a few years ago. In addition to my TO DO LIST - I'll often create a **NOT DO** list. Just shit that I am NOT going to allow myself to be distracted by. I'll use a NOT DO list when I have planning days or client projects. These work amazingly well. Try it for a few months, write to me, tell me how it worked for you. Remember the "Four D's" earlier in the chapter? This is a great example of "Defer." I'll do it, just not now, just not today.

Next up is the Default Diary. Before I jump into that I want to share a comment from a current client, "I'll spend more time writing plans and diaries than **doing the stuff**." Is that something you have thought about? It's total and utter crap if you have. The time saved and focus provided with these planning tools outweighs 100:1 the time taken to do them, 1000:1 in fact. It's just a bullshit excuse not to do the stuff you **KNOW** you need to do.

What is a Default Diary? Before I answer that be aware that **nature HATES a vacuum**. Nature hates space and wants to fill it. Don't believe me? **Do you have a garage**? Is there a car in it? If not, why not? For most, because it's FULL.

Do you have a LOFT? Follow the same questions, although I hope there's not a car there. Is there a drawer in your house that holds everything? Where all items from the AAA batteries to the caravan keys end up? It has everything. "Honey do you have a plaster?" - in the drawer. "Honey do you have an elastic band?".... get the idea? **Nature HATES a vacuum**. Do you have an empty garage, an empty cupboard, an empty loft - some will, most won't. **I bet NO ONE has an empty drawer though? Why are you smiling**?

Here's the thing - your **DIARY** is exactly the same. In fact, your **DAY** is exactly the same. If you leave spaces, nature will fill the damn spaces. That 40-minute job will take 90 minutes if you let it, and you won't even realise it, because nature is sneaky that way. You'll be content you "did the job," **not realising you could have done it twice**.

That's why we should use Default Diaries, and here's how simple it is. Pick tasks that you know you want to do, weekly or monthly. Writing Marketing Campaigns, Creating Systems, Staff Training, it doesn't matter - it's your tasks. Now create these as **default tasks in your diary**. Every Friday from 1pm to 5pm I work on Marketing. It's in the diary, and it's set in stone. No, of course it's not. If a prospective client wants to see me then I make a judgement call. Is marketing more important? Can I see them outwith that time, or is this a higher priority? **Be sensible,** default tasks are there as **guidance**. Rules are created for the obedience of fools and the guidance of wise men (PC alert, wise people.)

Success doesn't simply appear... "It's earned." There's no allowance for turning up

Stuart Mason

Now, there is another way to create a Default Diary, and I have used BOTH. As you set out your diary for the week you have **default TASKS** which then get slotted into available space. There's no right or wrong here - it's what works. Many business owners find their diary varies massively week to week - so this option suits them better. Try them both. I can assure you **Default Diaries** are one of the things that you ask yourself - "**why did I not do this years ago**?"

Financial Planning - Wrapping Up

Cash Flow and Budget. Now I know the eyes are rolling, I can sense it. It costs money to grow a business. You absolutely MUST have an up-to-date Cash Flow and Budget. We're back on the jet again - without the Cash Flow how do you know if you have enough fuel (money) to get there? Banks HATE when a business owner asks for funds the day they need them. Going to the bank after you forecast a lean period in 6 months' time shows you are in **total control of your finances**. Budgets are important too.

It amazes me that so many business owners I meet do not know their turnover, or the profit. "**The accountant does that**." Yes they do. However, by the time the year ends, and the accounts are back to you 18 months may have passed. Quarterly accounts allow you to f**ocus on the KEY FINANCIALS**. If your profit is not where you want it to be, use the next quarter to remedy that.

Before we move on, let's agree on an action point for **Cash Flow and Budgets**. It's essential to speak with your accountant first, they may be able to help, and may prefer that you present your Cash Flow and Budget in a specific way. Modern financial packages such as Xero, Quickbooks, etc make this much easier today, so **there's no excuse**.

Excuse me if I point out the obvious here, it usually avoids making an assumption and we all know how that ends? A Cash Flow is exactly that - the **flow of cash**. There, that didn't take too long did it? Let's grab a coffee. Alas, if it were only that simple. Your Cash Flow forecast will have your Sales and all your outgoings. Dead easy so far eh?

It's worth pointing out that in the 20 years of the Ink Shop, and during those 20 years we had a turnover of cash in excess of **£25m** or so, not **ONCE** did I do a Cash Flow. It's kind of scary when you write that down. Best I don't do that again. Just take it from me that it's really important, and convincing yourself that "I have cash in the bank" gives you some form of **Cash Flow Diplomatic Immunity** is just complete and utter crap. It's headtrash. **If you are growing your business then an accurate Cash Flow is essential**. OK, glad we cleared that up - Friends?

OK, so sales along the TOP (including VAT) - remember this is **CASH FLOW** so it's the total money IN, including VAT. If you invoice in January, and don't get paid until March, then January's sales income is in March.

Next up is the cost of those sales, all your raw materials etc. Again, this figure needs to be inclusive of VAT and shown in the month where you **PAY** them. This is really important, guys.

One thing that really fucked me up in the "dark days" when cash was tight was the fact that I DID NOT HAVE THIS IN PLACE. Along came a month where sales were quiet. The bulk of our sales were pre-paid with the order, so a quiet month was an instant, and sometimes catastrophic, kick in the nuts. What really killed us was a busy few months followed by a quiet period - we now had to PAY for busy months in a quiet period.

This is why from now, until the sun goes out, that I will constantly harass and annoy clients to have an **ACCURATE CASH FLOW** and **BUDGET** in place. It's a Critical Non-Essential (CNE). It's not legally essential you do it: there's no law or financial legislation. It is, however, a **CRITICAL** part of running your business well.

Back to the Cash Flow. We have all VAT-inclusive Sales and Purchases in now, so now we'll add our staffing costs and include all pension contributions, PAYE - anything that is PAID is on the Cash Flow.

There's plenty of Cash Flow templates out there, many are included in accounts packages too, so they will all differ, it doesn't matter, they are all going to come to the same figure. **Money IN** less **Money OUT** = what's left, if any.

The key with the cash flow is that the calculations are being done for you. I'm not saying you can't count; I'm just saying that there can be a lot of figures, and it's easy to get decimal points in the wrong place. I don't want you heading out to book a holiday in the Caymans only to discover that the decimal point was wrong.

Your **OUTGOINGS**: every penny spent is on the Cash Flow, it's that simple. I have heard people say "only put the big stuff on." They should be sent on an African safari wearing a suit made of raw meat. **Everything goes on**. The paper clips, the elastic bands - it ALL GOES ON. They will of course go under "Office Stationery" otherwise you will have a 532-page Excel document.

Remember - every figure INCLUDES VAT, and must be shown on the month that it is PAID, not the month you reccive it, or should pay it: **when you actually DO PAY IT**.

You will also need to show the VAT going OUT. In our case we were owed money by HMRC as the vast majority of our sales were zero rated.

Does that clarify what's needed for the Cash Flow? Your accountant will be the person to help out, or ideally do it for you. **Sacrifice MONEY for TIME**?

The Budget

Let's move onto the Budget now. Not the Chancellor's Budget, **your Budget**. I have a number of clients who use their Cash Flow as a template for their budgets. It's up to you HOW you do it, it just needs to be done. This is your vision into the future, you don't realise it just now, what you're actually creating is a time machine, a vision of how the future is going to look.

When you have all your sales and incoming revenues on the Budget, as well as all your projected outgoings, you can quickly see how the end of the month will look. If you have too much month left for your money, then you either do something about it, revise costs, or bury your head in the sand.

Always have TWO columns on your Budget, one for **PROJECTED** and budgeted costs and one for the **ACTUAL** figures. Over the coming months you'll get really good at forecasting your budget.

If you're looking to take on additional finance or additional staff, you simply add that figure into the Budget and see how the bottom line is affected. Same with SALES, play about with the Budget and see how the bottom line is impacted.

The key here is to **KNOW**, to be able to react to any months where cash is going to be tight. Remember, banks hate lending money - sorry, that was predictive text. Banks hate businesses that are not in financial control - that are **REACTIVE** and not **PROACTIVE** with their finances.

A great book to read on all things financial in your business, which is presented in an easy-to-read format is *The Lemonade Stand*.

The *Lemonade Stand's* full title is, *The Accounting Game, Basic Accounting Fresh from the Lemonade Stand*. If you find Balance Sheets, P&Ls, and all things accounting a bit much, try this book. It covers everything in a very clear, concise and practical way. It's humorous too - seriously, a funny accounting book.

I think we have covered the basics with the Cash Flow and Budget. When my business was at its peak, we would have over **£500,000 CASH** in the bank. It's (head trash) easy to think you don't need a Cash Flow Forecast when you have that much cash in the bank, right? **Wrong**. As the business began to slide and accrue losses, the cash reserves dwindled VERY quickly. In fact, we went from £500k in the bank to £250k overdrawn in an alarmingly short period of time. A Cash Flow forecast and budget would have made that much easier to track.

This has been a **BIG chapter**, it's also had some **BIG Learnings** and now requires some **BIG action**. If I could turn the clock back, this is the one area that would have made the difference. It's why it's the longest chapter in the book.

Here's another statistic I came across at Christmas. Business Owners in the UK, on average, spent more time preparing their Christmas Holiday Plan than they did planning their business for the entire year.

What are your actions going to be? We already know that 80% are going to do nothing. If you are one of the 20%, then what are your Action Points? Write them down. Don't try and do too much. If you feel there's loads to do, great, what's your **TOP THREE**?

Email them to me, stuart@howtowreckyourbusiness.co.uk: I bet you don't. Is this why business failure and stagnation in the UK is so high? It's **MINDSET**. I liken it to a packet of cigarettes. Basically, it says, "if you smoke these you are going to die a really slow and really painful death - and look, here's your lungs rotting to prove it," yet off they go, puff, puff, puff. Is it "**it will never happen to me**"? Is that what it is?

That was me, and guess what? **IT DID** happen to me.

How To Wreck Yourself

~~The~~ *Your* Entrepreneurial Journey

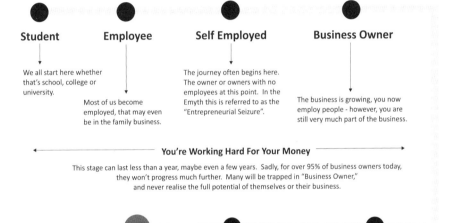

Student

We all start here whether that's school, college or university.

Employee

Most of us become employed, that may even be in the family business.

Self Employed

The journey often begins here. The owner or owners with no employees at this point. In the Emyth this is referred to as the "Entrepreneurial Seizure".

Business Owner

The business is growing, you now employ people - however, you are still very much part of the business.

← **You're Working Hard For Your Money** →

This stage can last less than a year, maybe even a few years. Sadly, for over 95% of business owners today, they won't progress much further. Many will be trapped in "Business Owner," and never realise the full potential of themselves or their business.

Influencer

You are now positioned as an Influencer. Others in and outwith your industry look at you with respect and admiration. This is how to grow a business...

Entrepreneur

The business is now capable of running without you. You can now make choices between investments, other business interests, and enjoy time off when it suits you. Levels and hours of work are now choice and not necessity. You may have sold the business, bought others...

Director

You are now removing yourself from the continual day to day operations of the business, you are now very much in control of DIRECTING the business. It's still full time, you now have BALANCE of working in -v- working ON.

← **Money Is Working Hard For You** →

As you progress towards and beyond "Director" your money is now working hard for you. You have a business that runs without you, you have investments that generate income, or you may have multiple business interests. Whatever course you have chosen, you wake up wealthier than when you went to sleep.

You now have both the time and resource to enjoy life - is that not why you went into business in the first place?

Chapter Four
Helicopters, Big Macs and Nuclear Submarines

Before I start this chapter, I need to add "allegedly" onto everything you are about to read. If I am ever called to court to testify on what's about to follow, I need to say this chapter may have been completely fabricated, or it may be absolutely factual in every detail. **Enjoy**...

When I am working with clients, I'll often quote Brad (Sugars), he's got a number of superb quotes, however, the one I often remind clients of is this: "**Business should be FUN**."

Before I dive into this chapter, business could have been a **LOT** more fun had I had the right structure to run the business. The fun incidents you will read about in this chapter however, if indeed they are true (??) were, in all honesty, few and far between. It was also in the heyday, the days when the business was making a ton of money. That money should have been invested - that's covered in "How to Wreck Yourself" - be sure to read that.

Now, "**Business Should be FUN**", that can sometimes be difficult to remember. When you are up to your arse in alligators it can be hard to remind yourself that the objective was to clean the swamp, I get that. Business should be fun, though. Write that down, ideally above your desk, "**Business Should Be FUN.**"

I had a bit of fun, I worked hard, and I played hard. In the summer of 1999, I had just completed my Helicopter Pilot's Licence, and racked up a good number of flying hours. In a moment of utter lunacy, I decided to BUY a helicopter. It's important to highlight that all this was pre 9-11, try this shit now and you'll just disappear off the radar, and no one will ask questions. If you're lucky a shoe will get washed up in some far away beach.

One fine summer's day Bobbie and I were flying out for some lunch in Arran. Arran has a lovely wee helipad, right at the harbour, which means you get to do the most amazing approach. If there's a Calmac Ferry in, you get to (legally) buzz the ferry before doing a torque turn (google it), and planting the chopper onto the pad, this is Top Gun kinda cool. After leaving the Glasgow Zone at Greenock, we dropped down low level, like sea-spray-on-the-screen low. This is what's known as flying in the "dead man's curve." If anything happened at that speed and height, you **MIGHT** have time to say, "What the f....." but that'll be about it… and even that's doubtful. Flying in the dead man's curve is stupid, irresponsible, and **incredibly amazing fun**.

On this particular day the sun was out, the shades were on, the sea was flat calm, and it was a good day - a really good day. It was days like this that made the hassles of running a print business worthwhile. As we headed towards Arran, we noticed something in the water ahead, was it a jet ski? "Let's have some fun with the jet ski," I announced.

As we approached it, the shape was wrong, there was just something wrong with that picture. After a few minutes it became clear this was **NOT** a Jet Ski - it was a periscope. I assume from one of HM nuclear submarines heading towards Faslane. Now that's something you don't see every day. We took up position behind the sub and very quickly the periscope **TURNED**. OK, time for us to bid you farewell, bon voyage, Captain. As we gained height I remember looking down in the calm waters and was blown away (not literally, although I think that was next) by the SIZE of the boat. What you see on the surface is nothing compared to the magnitude of this thing. We could see the sub blow her tanks and surface some miles ahead, and that too was an impressive sight. At least at that point we were well out her way. I tell you what, it's a brave and stupid country that wants to take on that baby.

After a pleasant lunch, we behaved ourselves and waited for clearance to enter the Glasgow Zone. When the controller came on and asked what our route OUTBOUND was, I was certain we were about to experience a shit storm of biblical proportions. He simply came back and thanked us, he hadn't noted our route on the way out, we were promptly given clearance to re-enter the zone, and toddled back to Cumbernauld where the helicopter lived.

You always behave yourself in controlled airspace, like 100% by the book behave yourself. We're lucky in Scotland, just passed Greenock and you're out the Glasgow Zone, and it's just one big play park, uncontrolled airspace. Yes, there's a few rules to obey, and a few people to talk to, bizarrely none of which is a legal requirement. I always made a point of talking to "Scottish" - a bunch of incredibly friendly controllers based at Prestwick. It was always good to have a least a broad idea of where the charred bodies were in case something went wrong.

This was a pretty memorable day, so that takes care of the Helicopter and the Nuclear Submarine, how can a Big Mac possibly fit in with this story?

You don't want a Helicopter breaking down, you just don't, it's bad all round. To prevent that (us Helicopter drivers) we kind of check things VERY carefully and adhere to a very strict maintenance schedule. Although my helicopter was for private use, I kept it on a Public Transport Certificate of Airworthiness.

That meant that the helicopter needed stringent 50- and 100-hour checks by a licensed engineer, and the closest, and best, was based in Kintore just outside Aberdeen. Yes, it was a pain, although I always took the view that safety was paramount. On this particular day I was doing some further training with Donald, my old instructor. Every year a pilot needs a competency check, and mine was looming, so now was the time to get the emergency procedures sharpened up.

The idea was we would fly up to Aberdeen and do a bit of instrument flying, that was easy, it was a crap day. We'd land at Kintore, drop off the chopper, and jump into Aberdeen for some lunch while the chopper was being serviced and checked. We'd then fly back to Cumbernauld and do some training on the way back. The bit us pilots hate is "engine failure," in a helicopter it's more dramatic than a plane. An aeroplane WANTS to fly, it's gracious, it will glide like an eagle. A helicopter, well that bastard just wants to screw you into the ground as quickly as it possibly can. Should an engine fail in a helicopter you have seconds to drop that collective lever. Fail to do that, and it's too much load on the rotors, followed by "rabbit ears,"and congratulations, you are now in command of a flying brick, knowing your 6ft 2inch height is going to be reduced substantially any second. It's not pleasant, and it's why instructors are a real pain in the arse during a competency check. A helicopter will autorotate after the engine quits, that simply means there's airflow through the rotors, it's effectively an autogyro now and you're hurtling towards the ground at around 1,800 feet per minute.

Are helicopters any more dangerous than aeroplanes? Well, the answer sadly is yes. Fixed-wing pilots can expect to crash 7.28 times for every 100,000 flying hours. Helicopters tend to fall out of the sky 9.84 times for every 100,000 flying hours. That means helicopters crash around 35% more. "Do they not have two engines?" I am often asked that. Some do, the Augusta 109, and Eurocopter Twin Squirrel are helicopters I flew with two engines, the majority don't. Robinson R22, R44, Bell 206 Jetranger and McDonnell Douglas 500E that I also flew all had single engines. In reality, for the majority of private pilots, the second engine simply takes you to the scene of the accident.

What I mean by that is simple. When you're flying a single-engine aircraft and the engine quits, you simply go into "forced landing mode," your training kicks in, you select a safe (or safest) landing spot and you begin your descent towards it. There's great debate about twin engine helicopters, the fact is some models simply cannot support the weight of the helicopter, fuel, passengers and baggage on the remaining one engine - so the end result is the same. Sir Isaac Newton is now the pilot in command, and he's taking you down, you're simply the passenger, and select the landing site for Sir Isaac. Too many private pilots have become so obsessed with the remaining engine that they fail to pilot the damn aircraft, and end up in an even worse situation.

Helicopter flying is relatively safe, it's like everything else, you only hear about the incidents and accidents and assume it's dangerous. Crossing the road is dangerous, driving up and down the A9 is way more dangerous than flying a helicopter. That said, the danger is why I gave it up. There had been an incident with a McDonnell Douglas 500, the same helicopter I was due to fly. The MD500, or the Hughes 500, was the helicopter Magnum P.I. flew, remember him? An amazing helicopter, very powerful with its Rolls Royce C20B engine, and five-bladed rotor system. In helicopter flying, a tail rotor failure with full power applied in the take-off configuration is the ultimate nightmare due to the torque being produced by the main rotors. That's exactly what happened in this instance, causing the aircraft to crash, killing all on board. Not good. That sharpens you up, and after that I decided to give up flying. It had been worthwhile; I'd learned a hell of a lot, and even taken flying to commercial level. For me, though, it was supposed to be fun, and the fun had stopped.

Anyway, flashback to before the fun stopped. You are possibly wondering where "Big Macs" fit into this chapter? During the aforementioned 50-hour check at Kintore, the day got kind of complicated. I had a print shop in Aberdeen, and called in there during the day. One conversation led to another, and another, and I ended up leaving the shop late and returning to Kintore to get back to Cumbernauld before the light faded. No time for lunch. After a hurried check we were soon airborne, and out the Aberdeen zone on our return to Cumbernauld. Hungry!!

It was a dull, cloudy day as we returned to Cumbernauld, and with the strong headwind right on the nose, it appeared the cars below us were going faster, and they actually **WERE**. We had 90 knots indicated, but with an estimated 40-knots headwind, it was slow going. Have you ever seen the movie It's A Mad, Mad, Mad, Mad World? The scene where the giant "W" is seen? We saw it, we actually SAW IT. This time it was a glorious "M," a big glorious yellow "M," beaming out its light for all hungry travellers (and pilots) for miles around, - inviting them to stop by. It was of course the **Forfar McDonalds**. If you know this branch of McDonalds, you'll know it sits right on the A90 Aberdeen to Dundee road.

It had been a full-on day, we were HUNGRY, and this massive yellow "M" shone like the North Star against the dull, grey sky on the horizon. Did you know decisions can be collectively (no helicopter pun intended) made with NO talking? We looked at each other, and within minutes had begun the descent, and flight checks required for landing at an unfamiliar site. After two circuits of the landing area, we had decided that the disused and fenced area to the east of the restaurant was a safe spot to land, and duly popped the chopper down, jumped the fence and headed off for a well-earned Big Mac.

Now, if you have ever eaten one of the aforementioned Macs then you know how quickly they cool down. We had placed our orders and were getting a barrage of questions from customers, staff and indeed the restaurant's owner. The attention was nice, and in truth, I was loving it. The Big Mac and usual accompaniments arrived, and we were just about to tuck in...

The **flashing blue lights** of the Range Rover attracted everyone's attention. I hoped their destination was not the helicopter. The next thing I remember saying, and out loud too, was "Oh, fuck!"

Donald seemed to know the restaurant owner. With the recent attention on the chopper I hadn't realised they were deep in conversation. Turns out he was something to do with one of the football clubs, maybe Aberdeen. I'm not a footy fan so he could have been a centre-forward for the Gallowgate Stank Lifters for all I knew.

I said to Donald, "I better go and speak with these guys." The cops were now at the helicopter. "Can you get into trouble for this?" asked the owner. "Yes and no" I replied. "Technically we need the permission of the landowner to land." "Ocht, you're OK then, I own that land - just tell them you asked me earlier." **That was a huge relief**.

I took a bite of my now cold Mac and walked over to the cops. "We got reports of a helicopter in trouble." I was thinking "define trouble." "No, we just dropped in here for a break and a bite to eat before heading back to Cumbernauld." "Can you do that?" one of the officers asked abruptly. "Yeah, we can pretty much land anywhere which is safe and with the landowner's permission. As you can see, the area here is fenced off and pretty well secure." The second officer then radioed back to base as one of the senior officers there used to be at the Glasgow air unit. Within a few minutes the cops knew that was indeed the case and were pretty chilled out about it. The usual 1001 questions followed about helicopters, that's always fun.

I left the police officers to their own devices as the clock was ticking, and I wanted to get back to Cumbernauld well before sunset. I had a current night rating (licence) for the helicopter but I didn't like flying after dark. There are only two things that fly at night, **bats and twats**. Bad enough trying to land a chopper during the day if the engine quits. At night the best advice is "**head for the dark bits**." Seriously!

My Big Mac was now colder than a McFlurry, I needed to lose a few pounds anyway, and in a helicopter, pounds = knots!! I noticed Donald was still engrossed in football conversation, completely oblivious to the attention we seemed to have created. As we were walking out of the restaurant, we noticed a dark blue estate car fly past and pull up beside the helicopter. Donald and I looked at each other in silence, we both looked away, then back at each other. "The Campaign Against Aviation?" Donald wondered. "Naw, can't be the CAA that quick, and even if it was, we're cool." As we walked over to the helicopter, we noticed the crowd had increased significantly and there seemed to be a lot of hilarity, another WTF moment.

Once we got closer it became evident what all the amusement was about. The estate car was a local press photographer and the police had jokingly put a parking ticket on the nose of the helicopter. In fairness, we thought that was pretty funny. We jumped the fence and on request posed for a photo with the police. The photo was hilarious as you saw me reaching my arm out in desperation to cover the helicopter's registration which was on the tail boom of the machine. Later that week, we made the papers: "**Hungry Pilots in McDonalds Fly Through**".

I did a quick safety check and then asked the police to ask everyone to step well back. We fired up the helicopter and within a few minutes had lifted out of the landing area and routed "direct Cumbernauld."

The flight back was quiet. "Don't even think about practice engine failures" I mumbled to Donald. He looked and grinned, paused for a second and then.... rolled off the damn throttle!

So that takes care of Helicopters, Big Macs and Nuclear Submarines. Why has this even been mentioned in the book? There's a number of reasons. As a business owner you're more than likely, especially in the early days, to work harder and longer than most. You probably get a lot of hassles and have days where having any hair left is a bonus. It's the cost of doing business. However, business should be fun, you **NEED** a release, and flying was mine. There are loads of other stories, like flying under the Skye Bridge, or flying to the Isle of Man and almost having to make an emergency landing on a container ship - God knows where that was going. We can talk about them over a pint.

That's not the reason I wanted to include this in the book, there's a much more **SERIOUS** reason. Later in the book we're going to cover Education, and the need for all of us in business to continually learn and develop. This is relevant here though. This was all around 1999 - 2000, the business was making some serious money here which afforded the toys that I have been talking about. Have you figured this out yet?

The simple fact was this. The business was making money and tons of it. I would re-invest in the latest kit, and we had one hell of a production facility and owned all the shops and units we used. That was smart. What wasn't smart was blowing significant sums of cash on flying for FUN. Cars are fun, bikes are fun, golf is fun, helicopters are the rocky road to financial ruin. That money should have been invested in the business. The business was cash rich, not that cash rich. A good friend of mine told me something too late in life, "don't live like a millionaire until you are one." **Do you see where I am going with this**? "Son, your ego is writing cheques your bank can't cash."

That money could have been better invested in **PEOPLE**. Creating the right structure of management that was so lacking in my business. That realisation came around too late. The irony is, had the money been invested in **PEOPLE** then the return on that investment would have been tenfold and afforded a bigger helicopter.

The business at this point had a turnover of around £2m, and would be sitting with significant cash balances. We'd been trading for about 7 years at this point. It's easy to "**THINK**" you've made it. That's why I referred to the "illusion" of wealth earlier. That's what it was, "an illusion." While the business didn't fail until 2013, some THIRTEEN years later, this period was indeed a factor as it shaped the business for years to come. This is where the business failed, **this is where I failed**.

I can't remember who said this, "You can grow a business to £1m with nothing more than blood, sweat and tears." I would agree with that, and the quote continued, "to get a business beyond £2m and £3m requires structure, systems, key staff, plans and **KNOWLEDGE**. "Bullshit, the entrepreneurial spirit is all you need," I **WRONGLY** thought.

Here's another **MUST READ** book; the relevance of this book is given away by the title. "Billionaire in Training" by Brad Sugars. Once again, I will hammer home - had I known all this, my business would have taken a VERY different road.

My issue here was twofold. First let's look at the **COMPETENCY** levels we go through in business, indeed life.

We start off as **unconsciously incompetent**; that pretty much means we don't know what we don't know. We progress to **consciously incompetent**; we now know what we don't know.

After a while we become **consciously competent**, we know what we know. Then finally, we become **unconsciously competent**: we're good, and perhaps better than we realise. NOT a know-it-all, a continual learner who knows that unconscious incompetence lurks behind all new business tasks.

Now think of your business journey. We start with good ideas, we start with big goals and big dreams. We start with more energy than Hunterston B, and very quickly we are running a business. We know the "job," we know the "trade" - we know jack shit about BUSINESS. At this stage most new business owners are "unconsciously incompetent" and happy to "learn as they go along."   You need to get out of that state very quickly, however, do you **KNOW** it?

How To Wreck Yourself

Your ~~The~~ Levels Of Competence

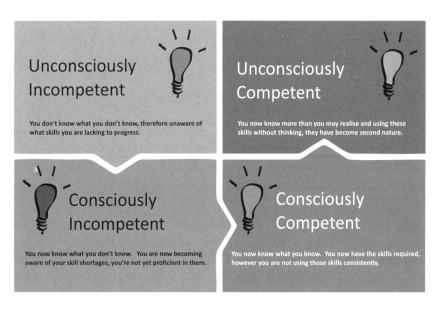

Unconsciously Incompetent

You don't know what you don't know, therefore unaware of what skills you are lacking to progress.

Unconsciously Competent

You now know more than you may realise and using these skills without thinking, they have become second nature.

Consciously Incompetent

You now know what you don't know. You are now becoming aware of your skill shortages, you're not yet proficient in them.

Consciously Competent

You now know what you know. You now have the skills required, however you are not using those skills consistently.

incompetent
/ɪnˈkɒmpɪt(ə)nt/ (adjective)
not having or showing the necessary skills to do something successfully.

Incompetent does NOT mean stupid or careless.

Think of all the stuff you need to know and **LEARN**. What is business, it's just a word, what actually is business? You need to learn sales, marketing, business development, accounts, bookkeeping, and loads, loads more. That's before you even begin to look at your trade learnings. You need to know all this stuff, even if you don't have to actually DO IT all.

It doesn't stop there, nowhere **NEAR** it. You need to learn people skills, you need to learn recruiting, training, managing, to say nothing of employment law and health and safety - that's years of learning on their own.

The competency levels move continually. Just because you're now unconsciously competent at one task doesn't mean you're not unconsciously incompetent in another one. There's nothing wrong with that, it's part of business life. The key is realising it. This is where continual learning plays such a part in business today. Take marketing and sales as two examples. Strategies and working practices that worked exceptionally well 10 years ago no longer work today. At the time you may have been unconsciously competent, just to allow a slide back to unconscious incompetence. Does that make sense?

I want to move on to what the real cost of all this **REALLY** was. It's worth pointing out that the Helicopters and Super Cars were at different times, it was one, THEN the other, not both. If that was the case the title of the book would have been *How To REALLY, REALLY Wreck Your Business*.

Business owners need to look at what their "**lifestyle**" is really costing the business, and again, I'll be the sacrificial lamb to illustrate this. Yes, business should be fun, however balance is needed. We all know, and agree, that cash flow is vital for our businesses? Have you looked at cash flow in THREE levels though? Here's my version of the "**The Three Tiers of Cash Flow**".

Tier 1 - Survive & Thrive: The business needs cash to survive. Pay the bills, wages, and the costs of running the business. This level should also be setting money aside for tax obligations. Obvious, yes?

Tier 2 - Invest & Protect: When the business is growing and profitable, you will be generating excess cash. This should be invested back into the business. This would include hiring additional staff, building a management structure, assets and investments. The list here is endless. The point however, is the next level in the cash flow cycle should be **INVESTMENT**.

Tier 3 - Distribution to the Owners: This again can take many forms. The point here, and this is where I went totally WRONG, Level 2 must be investment, and the excess cash generated from level 2 is what funds level 3. The helicopter and super car are level 3, however, I was using level 2 cash flow for it. Does that make sense? **INVEST** the money to create **MORE** money.

I was eating the apples rather than planting them. Being patient, and then receiving more apples than I could ever eat, once that "investment" had matured.

A friend said to me when proofing this book, "You should create a character like Gerber did in The Emyth." Great idea, so I set about creating a mythical character that would be gender neutral, of no definable race or religion, nor be of any specific country of origin, just so as not to offend anyone. That didn't work out so well, so reality wins. **The character is me**.

What do I mean by the "TRUE Cost" to your business? First of all, let's break that down into Cost vs Investment. You need to be very clear what is a COST and what is an INVESTMENT. I would argue till the cows came home that the Aston Martin was an investment in fun. Sadly though, being realistic, that was a COST to the business, and a big one at that.

What did the Aston **"COST"** me? It was around £2,000 a month in payments alone. Running costs were of course on top of that. The car cost £2,000 a month, that's the way most people look at it, me included. Can I (the business) afford £2,000 a month? Yes, then we'll be having it then.

Hold on, it's not as easy as that. First of all, you don't even consider having

The**3Tiers** Of**Cashflow**

Tier ONE Cash Flow - Survive and Thrive
Your business needs cash to survive, pay the bills, meet the payroll.   Once you meet ALL of the business overheads **COMFORTABLY**, what's left becomes Tier Two Cash Flow. **Tier one meets the COSTS to the business**. New leases as the business grows will of course be Tier One Cash Flow.

Survive and Thrive

Tier TWO Cash Flow - Invest and Protect
You now have surplus CASH.   Invest and Protect.   This can cover **MANY** elements, for example, training and development, investing in PEOPLE, as well as systems and processes.

Everything here should be an **INVESTMENT** in the business. Every £1 invested should return £10+ (directly or indirectly).   Where Tier One meets the costs, Tier Two MUST be for **INVESTMENTS.**
Nothing in Tier Two should be a cost to the business.

Invest & Protect

Warning: I was spending Tier Two Cash.
That became the Three "Tears" of Cash Flow

Tier THREE Cash Flow - Distribution To Owners
The surplus cash after Tier One and Tier Two now becomes Tier THREE. Think what you have created here. You are investing at Tier Two which feeds and allows **MORE** cash in Tier THREE. Only now can the owners and investors start buying Aston Martins. The cash can now be taken out for the owners WITHOUT damaging the continued growth and development of the business.
Tier Two won't allow that.

Distribution
To Owners

When completing the 5 Year Vision Planner you will see there's a section for Investments and Cash. This is your **2nd Tier Cash Flow**.   Personal Dream and Goals, that will be your **3rd Tier Cash Flow** an Aston Martin Vanquish S as a company car, the benefit in kind would pay off the debt of a third world country. No, you buy this personally, therefore you need to take extra TAXABLE income out of the business. Does that make sense so far?

Excluding the tax implications on the earnings, the car costs £2,000 a month, yes? NO. The payment is £2000, not the cost. Let's say your business is making a 10% net profit. What does the business need to bring in in order to generate the £2,000 a month you want to spend on a CAR? Easy one, that, it's £20,000. Crude way to do it? Maybe. It does show that the car is actually a £20,000 a month car - that's a bit more than even I would expect to pay.

Many will argue that's a ridiculous illustration: is it really? If you don't look at it that way, then how is the payment made? Magic? The Fairies? This should be looked at for ALL costs to the business, because let me tell you, when you start looking at it that way it sharpens your focus as to what's really important when it comes to **COSTS**. What are the **COSTS** in your business? What are the **TRUE** costs of those costs?

Now let's look at **INVESTMENT** in the business. You'll read in the book that structure in the business is really important. Having the "right people on the bus" - yes, ok, it's a cheesy quote, what about having the right people in the right seats on the bus? It's not everyone that wants to be a driver. I made this mistake, "promoting" otherwise EXCEPTIONAL people in the business into managerial roles. They didn't want to be a driver. Then what happens? Good people LEAVE. WTF? This is why having a clear recruitment strategy in your business is essential - that's the ultimate way to invest in your business.

Anyway, back to **INVESTMENT**. We already know the £2,000 cost would require £20,000 of turnover. In those glory days our net profit was over 20%. I have chosen not to illustrate that, first of all - DRAMATIC purposes, you need to see the shock and horror picture, and secondly the net profit dropped to 10%, then to 8%, then to 5%, then to zero.

The recession created a new phrase, "**negative growth**." What the actual fuck is that? Is that to pacify shareholders? You can just see the CEO reciting, "Negative Growth this year is in line with expectations at 45%" - some will be **DELIGHTED** with that until they get the annual shareholders report and realise that it's a 45% loss!!

Let's say that I viewed that £2,000 as an investment and not a cost. What about instead of buying the Aston Martin I "invested" that towards getting a Managing Director in place? Someone who could take over the day to day running of the business and let me get on with the growth and development. Now, that's an investment. How much would an MD cost back then, £60,000? £5,000 a month? How much would that investment have returned? An MD focussing on costs and structure, systems and savings, recruitment and finances, get the picture? How much more would I have contributed focussing purely on big picture growth of the business?

I don't have those figures; however, I am certain that the return on that investment would have paid for the Aston TEN times over. It's back to the Three Levels of Cash Flow. Working with 100s of business owners over the years this is very common practice. It's not a "common mistake", because it's not always a mistake. Look at the Entrepreneurial Journey illustration again and you'll see what I mean. Some business owners are happy at the self-employed and business owner stage, and that's fine. If it's through choice and not necessity, that's absolutely fine.

For the vast majority of business owners, it's **lack of clarity** that's holding them back. It's what prevents people from realising their full potential, and that of the business. This is where the plan comes in, think about this. If right from day ONE your vision and clarity is clear, then you'll know that these initial steps are temporary, and indeed required. You'll have your plan carefully thought out and you'll know the road the Entrepreneur needs to take.

This is all covered in other chapters. The purpose of this chapter was simply as a reminder that business should be FUN, with the occasional Big Mac thrown in. **May I suggest the DRIVE-through though**!!

The ability to meet
the finance payments
is **NOT** wealth. That's the
illusion of wealth.

Stuart Mason

Chapter Five - How to Wreck Yourself

There's been a number of people involved with proofreading this book and providing valuable feedback. One of the comments was, "I think you are being too hard on yourself - you did more right than wrong." Now, let me be clear, I disagree with that: had that been the case, the business would **not have failed**. Yes, the early years were the "Glory Years", they were also when the mistakes were made.

No Sympathy Required

I want to be hard on myself because I want **YOU** to feel and sense the pain. If this book sounds like a mild inconvenience, then you are less likely to act. When you taste my frustration, share my pain, and understand that this brought me to a VERY dark tipping point in my life, then I hope you will sit up and take notice, and more to the point, **take ACTION**. Especially when you understand the **majority of these errors were 100% avoidable**. No sympathy required; action would be better.

I could not control the downturn in the print trade. I could, however, control the market we served and I could have moved away from non-profitable work to more niche markets. A lower turnover with a higher profit makes sense for any business.

I certainly could not control the recession that was about to devastate the global economy. I could, however, have made sure my business was lean and mean. The business was **not lean and mean** and ready to brave the storm. It was built on a foundation of sand, and the tide was coming in.

I accept that I did a lot of good stuff, and in the early stages made more right decisions than wrong. However, the fact remains that the business failed, and failed for a variety of reasons. I was slow to react, too. For people who know me, that is unexpected: for someone that was so impatient and spontaneous in so many ways not to have reacted quicker comes as a surprise. You only have to refer to the "Right Road or the Wrong Track" to understand why this was the case. I was on the **Wrong Track, DENIAL** was the killer here, that, and blame. This wasn't MY fault; how could that be the case?

The sooner you can recognise this negative behaviour in yourself, the easier progression is going to be. I'm not sitting on my righteous high horse preaching here, this was ME. This **WAS** me, not now. No one showed me this stuff, or perhaps **DARED** show me. You have a big advantage. I'm sharing **NOW** what you **MUST** look out for. You, like me, are your business's biggest asset. **DO NOT** allow yourself to become the business's biggest **LIABILITY**.

How to Wreck YOURSELF

This chapter is going to cover **How to Wreck Yourself**. I am not going to get all "woo, woo" here or go deep into psychological mindset, self-sabotage etc - sod that. I am going to share what I now know was wrong with me at the time.

I'm also not going to mention health and fitness, the need to eat healthily, and get the right amount of sleep, etc. I'm guessing that's there's maybe a book or two written on those subjects already. Can we agree that this is a **GIVEN**? Can we agree that a healthy business **OWNER** precedes a **HEALTHY BUSINESS**? Great, then we can have a sugar-laden coffee, some chocolate digestives, and crack on.

The feedback provided pre-publication was that this chapter is too long, there's too much in it. Yes there is, it's rammed without a doubt. Rather than split and dilute the chapter, I would suggest you read it, **highlight the important areas** you connect with, then go back later and re-read it.

Be sure to **HIGHLIGHT** the areas that you can relate to: you need to fix these, soon.
I have mentioned this book before, and in this chapter, it becomes an essential read - **The Chimp Paradox** by Dr Steve Peters. I had the privilege of meeting Steve, what an amazing guy, and what an amazing book, although heavy at times.

You Can Only Grow Your Business to
YOUR Level Of (in)Competence

Let's dive right in with the **Levels of Incompetence** we encounter in ourselves. Now, before the letters start, I want to be very clear what I mean by incompetence, it's the literal meaning (incompetent, the inability to do something successfully), so I am not calling you incompetent, as in some kind of fool. Have I explained that OK? Everybody happy?

Here's a phrase that may annoy you, it's why I positioned "incompetence" right at the start. "**You will only grow your business to your level of incompetence**." I can't remember who said that. I think it was Brad Sugars, it certainly sounds like a Brad quote. Wow, just wow, sore one isn't it? When I look back at my business it's as obvious as it is TRUE. Unless you have an outside influence, of course you will only grow your business to your level of incompetence. You can easily change that quote to read, "You will grow your business to your level of **competence**." Same thing, it's just not as powerful or annoying!

When I saw this presented for the first time it really got me. It wasn't until this point I realised that I had been the business's biggest **LIABILITY.** It's so obvious. If you are the Top Dog, the Head Honcho, and making all the decisions for the business, the **QUALITY** of those decisions can ONLY be limited by one factor, YOU. More importantly, **YOUR** level of expertise and knowledge. You can only grow your business to the level of your **INCOMPETENCE** - wow, just wow!

The four levels of (in)competence are

Unconsciously Incompetent: You don't know what you don't know. Now it goes without saying that when you start anything new, this is where you'll more than likely be. The key here is **awareness** of not knowing. When I start anything new, I position myself at this level, and then make damn sure I'm not here for long.

Conscious Incompetence: You know what you don't know. You are now conscious and aware of your shortfalls. In business that could be anything:

marketing, accounts, IT, planning. The key now is you are AWARE. The question is, **what are you doing about it**?

Consciously Competent: You know what you know, you're comfortable. You're good and you know it. Now, this is a danger area. And yes, I made this mistake once I attained conscious competence. It is possible to go back to unconscious incompetence. In the ever-changing world we live in you can easily and quickly go from the expert to completely out of touch, very quickly in fact. The other consideration is you are "complacent" - in your comfort zone. Be aware at this stage there's always more to learn.

Unconsciously Competent: You know more than you realise. Most of us progress quicker than we realise and become better than we sometimes believe. This is unconscious competence - you're better than you realise. Tasks are now second nature.

Earn Never Comes Before Learn, Except in a Dictionary

This is why I always bang on about learning and development. I am now obsessed with continual learning and development in all areas of business. I make sure I read or listen to a book every week. I try and vary that too, marketing, selling, coaching (obviously), self-improvement, planning - anything. I have also created my Top 20 book list in this chapter. Books that I have read or listened to that have been real game changers. If you're serious about **YOUR** competency levels, don't pick one or two. Read/listen to them all. These are all available in print or audio book.

Without learning, you restrict your earning. You will never, **EVER** out-earn your learn. Another way to look at it: the only time EARN comes before LEARN is in the dictionary. I know, you don't have time, where's my thinking? How many miles did you travel last year? What did you listen to when driving? Why not open an Audible account and turn your car or van into a mobile university? The vast majority of the books I listen to are in the car. Over 200 books have been listened to. Now, in fairness books like the Wealth Coach, 1-Page Marketing Plan and Building a Storybrand have been listened to multiple times.

How To Wreck Yourself

~~The~~ *Your* Levels Of Competence

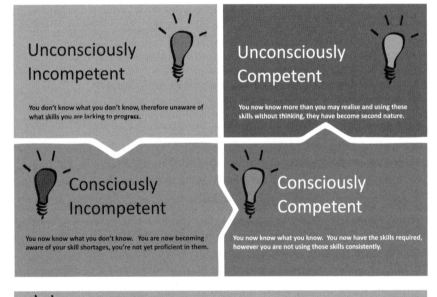

Unconsciously Incompetent

You don't know what you don't know, therefore unaware of what skills you are lacking to progress.

Unconsciously Competent

You now know more than you may realise and using these skills without thinking, they have become second nature.

Consciously Incompetent

You now know what you don't know. You are now becoming aware of your skill shortages, you're not yet proficient in them.

Consciously Competent

You now know what you know. You now have the skills required, however you are not using those skills consistently.

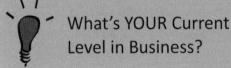

What's YOUR Current Level in Business?

incompetent
/ɪnˈkɒmpɪt(ə)nt/ (adjective)
not having or showing the necessary skills to do something successfully.

Incompetent does NOT mean stupid or careless.

You Get What You Tolerate

Next phrase I really want you to get tattooed on your arm is this: **You Get What You Tolerate**. There's nothing more guaranteed to Wreck Yourself than that. **You Get What You Tolerate**. When you accept behaviours in your business or personal life, well that's it "deemed as accepted," good luck changing that later. This could be behaviours from your team, your clients, your family - even **YOU**.

I see business owners today putting up with all kinds of shit. **Why is that**? I usually get some ridiculous answer like "better the devil we know," or "they can be very good," or "what if they went to a competitor?" Get the picture? I'm guessing it's because you have become comfortable **BEING uncomfortable**. The thought of change is **preventing change**. Are you here? Have you been there?

Think of your business as a rowing boat with **TEN** people on it. The three at the front are your STARS, and they are rowing like crazy, driving your business forward. Now, picture FIVE people in the middle of the boat, they are rowing, turning up, doing the regulation minimum. These five are driving the boat forward, just nowhere near as good as they **could or should**.

Then we get to the two at the back of the boat. These two Charlies are throwing the **ANCHOR** in and deliberately trying to disrupt the others on the boat, and not just slow the boat down, they are trying to sink it. These people need to exit your business rapidly. **DO NOT** be comfortable being uncomfortable.

Here's another thing. Good people rarely bring bad people up, it's usually the other way around. Having that negativity in your workplace is like having a **VIRUS amongst your team**. Find a cure, quickly.

The technical terms for the good guys are "**Very Engaged**," the middle five are "**Disengaged**" and the two clowns at the back are "**Very Disengaged**." Who do you work on? The two at the back? No, they're a lost cause. The three at the front? NO. They are already stars, just make sure they KNOW it. The ones you work on are the five in the middle. Good leadership brings the cream to the top. Now imagine your boat again, this time you have SIX "Highly Engaged," FOUR "Disengaged" and ZERO "Highly Disengaged." Now, you have a business that is flying, that people WANT to work for.

You Attract the People YOU Deserve

The above can be extended further into another great quote, "**You Get the People You Deserve**." If you have a business that is disorganised, chaotic, poorly disciplined, that's the kind of people you are going to attract. Conversely, an organised, structured, tidy and disciplined working environment is going to attract that type of person. In Chapter 7 (How to Wreck Your Team) I am going to dive a lot deeper into this. It's important to mention here though, a sure way to "wreck yourself" is by not having the right people behind and beside you, or even worse, **HAVING** the right people and not giving them the **opportunity to grow and shine**.

Now that you have removed the "Highly Disengaged" dead wood, and focused on the "Highly Engaged" people, do you think your business is going to attract more of the "Highly Engaged" people to join your team? Of course it is.

Are You an Entrepreneur?

Before we get really deep into the chapter, I want to cover the "Entrepreneurial Journey" again. Download this worksheet from the resource section on the website. It's in the "Be A Better You" Section.

The reason why this chapter is important is simple. If you don't understand the entrepreneurial journey, then you will become a slave to it. When you're at the Student to Business Owner phase you are **working hard for money**. As you move along in your journey then **money starts to work hard for you**. I am guessing here that the vast majority of people reading this have their own business? I'll further hazard a guess that there's aspirations for a lifestyle that may or may not be wealth driven? Finally, the ideal lifestyle sought is superior to that achievable by being employed. Yes? Then the journey is important.

Book Check. An all-time classic. When you're starting your own business, it should be a legal requirement that you read this book: *The E-Myth Revisited*, by Michael Gerber.

The Student: we all start here, whether that's school, college or university. Many argue this is where some of the issues start as the current educational system is "Industrial Age" in thinking, and not up to date with Entrepreneurship. That's a whole debate for another book. "Study hard, get a good job!!"

The Employee: most of us become employed, probably because it's what we're conditioned to do. It may even be in the family business. It's rare for people to go from student to self-employed, although it does happen, just not enough. It's important to realise **WHAT** you are doing here, almost certainly you are contributing to the wealth of someone much further up the "ladder."

Self Employed: Gerber refers to this as the "Entrepreneurial Seizure," here you go from working **FOR** the idiot boss, to **BEING** the idiot boss. Now, here's the thing, you are **NOT** an Entrepreneur yet, IMHO. That's a title that needs to be earned. The journey often begins here, the owner or owners with no employees at this point. That's not always the case of course. "Self Employed" is as much a state of mind as a legal business entity.

Business Owner: the business is growing, and you now employ people, however you are still very much part of the business. You're still working more **IN**, than **ON** the business.

The above stages are the progression for most business start-ups. During these phases you are working hard for your money. As the business grows, as you grow, the money starts to work hard for you. Well done though, on getting to this point.

How To Wreck Yourself

~~The~~ *Your* Entrepreneurial Journey

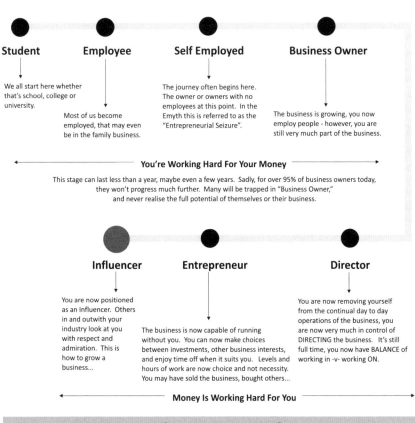

Student

We all start here whether that's school, college or university.

Employee

Most of us become employed, that may even be in the family business.

Self Employed

The journey often begins here. The owner or owners with no employees at this point. In the Emyth this is referred to as the "Entrepreneurial Seizure".

Business Owner

The business is growing, you now employ people - however, you are still very much part of the business.

You're Working Hard For Your Money

This stage can last less than a year, maybe even a few years. Sadly, for over 95% of business owners today, they won't progress much further. Many will be trapped in "Business Owner," and never realise the full potential of themselves or their business.

Influencer

You are now positioned as an Influencer. Others in and outwith your industry look at you with respect and admiration. This is how to grow a business...

Entrepreneur

The business is now capable of running without you. You can now make choices between investments, other business interests, and enjoy time off when it suits you. Levels and hours of work are now choice and not necessity. You may have sold the business, bought others...

Director

You are now removing yourself from the continual day to day operations of the business, you are now very much in control of DIRECTING the business. It's still full time, you now have BALANCE of working in -v- working ON.

Money Is Working Hard For You

Where are you?

As you progress towards and beyond "Director" your money is now working hard for you. You have a business that runs without you, you have investments that generate income, or you may have multiple business interests. Whatever course you have chosen, you wake up wealthier than when you went to sleep.

You now have both the time and resource to enjoy life - is that not why you went into business in the first place?

The Director: (not in the legal sense.) You are now removing yourself from the continual day-to-day operations of the business, you are now very much in control, and DIRECTING the business. It's still full time, however, you now have the **BALANCE** of working **IN** vs working **ON** where it needs to be. Decisions on working in certain elements of the business are now made through choice and not necessity. To sense-check this level, you can now take days off at random, go on holidays and not have the phone glued to your ear. You also come back to calm and not chaos. Is this enough though?

Entrepreneur: Congratulations, you made it. Let's take a moment this day in memory of the 100 people that started the same day as you. 1 or 2 others have made it this far. The sad fact is you can probably **hold your class reunion in a phone box**. The business is now capable of running without you. You can now make choices between investments, other business interests, and enjoy time off when it suits you. Levels and hours of work are now completely through choice and not necessity. This is what I call an **Entrepreneur**. That's just me, though.

An Influencer: You are now positioned as an influencer. Others in and outwith your industry look at you with respect and admiration. Don't think this is Dragon's Den stuff. Personally, I despise that show. "Great idea, it'll be worth billions, so I'll give you the £1000 you need for a 75% stake" or, they ridicule raw talent for good TV ratings - **sorry, not for me**. An "Influencer" could be a LinkedIn Influencer, or simply a well-respected business owner in the local community. Look at your local Chamber of Commerce, there will almost certainly be "Influencers" there.

That's my theory of the "Entrepreneurial Journey." It's a journey that could take a few years or many. Sadly, it's a journey that the vast majority of business owners will never complete. Not necessarily through failure, although many will fail, the majority will simply **not progress past the level of their competence**. Does that make sense?

Back to the book - where do think I got to on that journey? I got to DIRECTOR. There were investments, however I never got the business capable of running without me. I could choose to do certain things through

100 Businesses Start **TODAY**

The **20th** reunion can be held in a TELEPHONE BOX

choice and not necessity. I also still worked too hard for my money. The real kicker is the **PEOPLE could do the job** but I was reluctant to "let go" and give them the opportunity. This is really **How to Wreck Yourself**.

Features, Benefits, Egos and Growth Mindsets

I wanted to add this into this chapter, it's more to do with marketing though. The reason that it's added here is to make sure your ego isn't driving marketing decisions.

I found some old literature about the Ink Shop recently, and a few things really grabbed me. First thing was just how bad it was. We this, we that, we have this machine, we have that machine (picture of machine) etc. It worked, hell it worked - not sure HOW, if I am honest. I call that "Ego-Driven Marketing." **All about me, never about YOU**.

It still amazes me today that so many businesses have this persistence about their logo, their machines, about them. You'll have seen the advert where the logo is one third of the page. The only people interested in your logo are you and your parents, not even your partner, hell they are the same as your CLIENTS, they want to see **BENEFITS**. We have been established since 1974 - so what? Is that a benefit or feature? It's a feature, argue all you want. As soon as you say "I, we, me" it's a feature, end of. We'll cover AIDA in a later book, and have a download on the website that covers this in more detail. Pay attention, it will save your life. Many business owners now refer to this as First AIDa. **AIDA** is **A**ttention, **I**nterest, **D**esire and **A**ction. The recipe for **success**, to be blunt.

What I did read in the Ink Shop literature, and this really surprised me, was how mindset THEN and mindset NOW are poles apart. The phrase in the brochure was, "**you're more likely to find me in the print room than the board room**." Now, at that time I thought that showed passion and commitment, and maybe the customers did like it, they probably did. What did it say about my mindset, my entrepreneurial mindset? That I'm more happy working **IN** the business than **ON** it. That I'm happy being a "Business Owner" and not progressing? This is exactly what I mean by growing a business to the level of your incompetence. I wasn't really tuned in to the next levels nor had anyone educating me. Even if I did, would I have listened? Now that brings us to DISC.

Eagles, Owls, Parrots and Doves

This chapter is **How to Wreck Yourself**. A sure way to wreck yourself, your team, your customers and your business is not to have a grasp on DISC profiles. Now, DISC is a book on its own, so there's no way we're ramming that into this chapter. There's a download workbook on the website for DISC which has kindly been provided by Dr Tony Alessandra, and allows you to **REALLY** dig deep into DISC Profiles. When I started to understand DISC, it was the starting point of **changing me**. As you can imagine, **I strongly suggest you spend some time there**.

DISC is a **behavioural style**. We all behave in a certain way, react to situations differently, want to receive and send information in a particular manner. We also react to personal situations differently. There's no good or bad, right or wrong with DISC, we are what we are. However, **knowing** what your **strengths** and potential **shortcomings** are is gold dust in business and personal development. When you understand why someone behaves and reacts the way they do - it's their DISC profile.

I saw an illustration recently that illustrated "birds" with DISC Profiles. There a lot of truth in that. Let's look very briefly at DISC. DISC stands for the four areas of behaviour. **Dominant** (The Eagle), **Influencer** (The Parrot), **Steady** (The Dove) and **Compliant** (The Owl). When you're overly dominant in one area, it's referred to as "**High**." For example, my DISC profile is HIGH D. That can be very good for getting shit done, however it can be a problem when I show the empathy of an Amazonian Mosquito towards people. Now that I fully appreciate DISC, and that challenge, **I work around that**.

I'll cover the basics of **DISC** here to provide an understanding. Why mention this? Simple, when you know how you behave and why, it's easier to avoid areas that annoy you, even better when those around you know too.

More importantly though, if you have an understanding of DISC with your team, suppliers and customers - well, you're taking your communication to a whole new level.

Dominant Style, "D," The Eagle

Dominant Styles do not like detail, they like short, sharp, straight to the point facts. Bullet points and very much "Why use 25 words when 2 would do?" A "High D" tends to be **decisive, competitive, daring, direct, innovative, persistent, adventurous, problem solver, and results orientated**. Can you see how this could be an advantage to a business owner?

Conversely, "C" Styles CRAVE detail. Don't send 2 paragraphs when 20 pages are available. Now imagine you're communicating with a "High C," can you see where the clash is?

Influencer Style, "I," The Parrot

When communicating with an Influencer individual, share your experiences, allow the "I"-style person time to ask questions and talk themselves, focus on the positives, avoid overloading them with details, and don't interrupt them. High "I's" are people people, so be prepared for a chat. A High "I" tends to be **charming, confident, convincing, enthusiastic, inspiring, optimistic, persuasive, social and trusting**.

Steady Style, "S," The Dove

When communicating with a Steady individual, be personal and amiable, express your interest in them and what you expect from them, take time to provide clarification, be polite, and avoid being confrontational, overly aggressive or rude. Steady Styles do not like change, and like "I's," are people people.

A High "S" tends to be, **understanding, friendly, good listener, patient, relaxed, sincere, stable, steady and a team player**.

Compliant Style, "C," The Owl

When communicating with a Compliant Style individual, focus on facts and details; minimize "pep talk" or emotional language; be patient, persistent and diplomatic. Remember that, like "D's," "C's" are task- and NOT people-focussed.

A High "C" tends to be, **accurate, precise, analytical, compliant, courteous, diplomatic, detailed, fact finding and objective**.

Have a bit of fun with DISC and download the DISC booklet from the website. You'll soon be able to identify yourself, then others. This is a great exercise to do in a team environment.

Are You on The Right Road OR the Wrong Track?

Another sure way to Wreck Yourself, and this also relates to behaviour, is to operate "on the wrong Track." The illustration of the "Right Road, Wrong Track" challenges how you behave. Being on the "**Right R.O.A.D**" means you taking **R**esponsibility and **O**wnership for your actions, you are **A**ccountable to yourself and others and **D**ecisive in your nature.

Now, should you drift "**off T.R.A.C.K**," and we all do from time to time, then you can develop a **T**otal lack of respect, **R**efuse to acknowledge or deny anything is wrong with this picture, you may be quick to **A**ttack and blame others, **C**hange can be resisted, defaulting to "always done it that way" and finally, **K**eep using excuses for everything.

See, here's the thing. When you stay on the Right Road it's almost impossible for arguments and disputes to occur. If responsibility, accountability and ownership is being taken, then heated debates or disagreements are killed stone dead.

Conversely, if both parties are on the Wrong Track, well, wars have started that way. There's blame, excuses, no respect and a refusal or denial from parties that anything is wrong with them. Does that make sense?

Are You On The **Right Road**, Or The **Wrong Track**?

The Right R.O.A.D.

Knowing You're On The **Right Road** Means...

Responsible For Your Actions
Ownership Is Always Taken
Accountable To Yourself & Others
Decisive In Your Nature

The Wrong T.R.A.C.K.

Knowing You're On The **Wrong Track** Means...

Total Lack Of Respect
Refuse To Acknowledge Issues (Denial)
Attack & Blame Others
Change Is Always Resisted
Keep Using Excuses For Everything

I was on the WRONG TRACK for **YEARS**

Where are you?

The reason I created the "**Right Road and Wrong Track**" was simply as a business owner I spent far too much time on the **Wrong Track**. Yes, you guessed it, High "D," and in denial that there was anything wrong with that picture. I was too quick to blame others, wouldn't respect or sometimes even allow an opinion, and kept an excuse for everything. It's the trade, it's the economy, it's you, it's them, it's the world - **never me though, hell no**!

Can you see how destructive it can be on the Wrong Track? Can you see how powerful and progressive keeping on the **Right Road** is? When you challenge yourself on this, it becomes second nature. When you and your team nail it you will definitely be on the **RIGHT ROAD** to build your business.

I mentioned previously about the amazing *E-Myth Revisited* by Michael Gerber, and the need for every business owner to read this. Another sure way to **Wreck Yourself**, and ultimately your business is to not understand the reference Gerber makes to the "Technician, Manager and Entrepreneur." To be clear, this is the same person, just the different roles they play in the running and growing of their business. Let me explain, this is important.

Technician, Manager and Entrepreneur

The **TECHNICIAN** is you "doing the job," so if you're a joiner, you're building stuff, a hairdresser is cutting hair and a mechanic is working on a car. You're working IN the business, and you're working in the PRESENT - doing what needs to be done to "get by." Most small business owners will spend 75%+ of their time here. Working IN the business, working in the PRESENT.

The **MANAGER** then has a job to do, you need to (hopefully) be doing the books, managing invoices, preparing quotes, follow ups, all the things a manager needs to do. This has all happened, so the manager is working in the PAST, still working IN the business though. Most small business owners spend around 20% of their time here.

Then we come to the **ENTREPRENEUR**. You're now working ON the business, planning, creating, strategising - the stuff that is the most rewarding and FUN to do. But hey, how does that work? Most business owners devote around 5% (at best) of their time to working ON their business, and planning for the **FUTURE**. How's that even possible?

The answer is simple. The vast majority of small business owners can't get past the "Technician" phase and end up having a JOB. Gerber's theory is this is why so many businesses fail. The Technician is **GREAT** at the job, yet knows little about business. The Entrepreneur learns and invests time in **themselves** to be better.

Can you see how this is all linked to Competency Levels, Right Road / Wrong Track? **It's powerful stuff if you take action**.

The key is of course **BALANCE**. As a small business owner, you WILL be the Technician, The Manager and definitely the Entrepreneur, it's getting the balance right.

A friend described this in a phrase that I think sums up business owners today, "**you need to come out of the engine room up to the wheelhouse**." BOOM, that's it! Thanks Royce.

My own view, as a small business owner, growing a young business, you can't avoid being all three, you **can't avoid hard work**, and you **can't avoid long hours**. I think if anyone tells you different then they are on the Wrong Track. In my opinion. What is **NOT** acceptable is for that to continue, this is why your **PLAN** is so important. You're not just planning for the growth of the business, you're planning for the growth of yourself too. **Graduating** from self-employed "worker," working IN the business to a **savvy entrepreneur** working ON the business. Send me an invite, I want to come to your **graduation**.

Who's Your Business Buddy? Get a Business Buddy

You'll no doubt have your "bestie"? Someone you can call to laugh, talk, moan, cry, and maybe share a bit of gossip, too. It's unlikely they will understand what it's like being **IN BUSINESS**, unless they are a business owner themselves. Get a Business Buddy. Ideally a business friend who is maybe up a few more rungs of the ladder than you. Go out for a drink, a meal, whatever, have a bit of fun with a like-minded business owner. **They have been where you are, it's almost certain**.

Learning Styles

It's worth finishing off the chapter with **LEARNING** styles, VAK: Visual, Auditory and Kinaesthetic. Whilst DISC is gold dust to know, it covers **behaviour**. VAK is a **learning style**. Now, over the years there's been a few additions to VAK, however, for this illustration we'll stick to the main THREE.

Visual people learn best through SEEING. What does that mean? They tend to think in pictures, prefer to see notes and illustrations, write things down. When you're communicating with a Visual person you would use phrases like, "**How does that look**?"

Auditory people learn better from listening, often read aloud, listen to others. When you're communicating with an auditory person you would use phrases like, "**How does that sound**?"

Kinaesthetic people learn through doing, moving and touching, they prefer to work as a group, would rather see a demonstration, and definitely a hands-on approach. When you're communicating with a kinaesthetic person you would use phrases like, "**How does that feel**?"

Another great book that nails this is "*The Law of Connection*" by Michael Losier.

Why is this important? Knowing how people learn is crucial. One sales manager admitted some time ago that he was very Auditory and "told" his sales teams what do. Everything was verbal because that was his natural style. However, a few in the sales team never "got it" and their performance was a reflection of that. VAK was explored, and as expected the non-performers were both VISUAL people. It didn't take long to SHOW these team members, introduce graphic presentations etc and soon the entire team was performing to **record-breaking levels**.

How does that sound to you? How does that look now? Does that feel better knowing that?

Be x Do = Have

This is an amazing formula, and when you understand it, **VERY** powerful. What is Be x Do = Have? In business we tend to be conditioned to **DO** more to HAVE more. To **HAVE** more, we simply DO more. Yes, that works, however, there's a better alternative. If we take time to **BE** better at what we do, we can multiply our effectiveness. Let's put numbers on this to explain it better.

Be (1) x Do (1) = Have, well it can only be 1.
Be (1) x Do (10) = Have (10): see, this works. Do more, then have more.
Now try this.
Be (5) x Do (5) = Have (25). BE better, do less, have more.

It's A Wrecking Wrap

Let's wrap this chapter up now. **How to Wreck Yourself** was a difficult chapter, it's the one that really requires **YOU** to change. Change can start with the basics, start reading a book, listening to audio books, **LEARN**. Why is it when we left the education system most of us **STOPPED LEARNING**, yet "Business" is harder than any degree qualification, and certainly more serious? **Why is that**?

Think of the cumulative effects of learning, getting more, and getting better every day. Do you remember ever seeing the illustration of starting with a **PENNY** and doubling that every day over one **MONTH**?

Day 1 you have 1p, Day 2 you have 2p, Day 3 you have 4p, Day 4 you have 8p, Day 5 you have 16p, Day 6 you have 32p and by the end of the first week *formula to deliver success*

$$Be \times Do = Have$$

We know to have more we do more. Do more, have more. Simple

Let's put some numbers on this
Be (1) x Do (1) = Have, well it can only be 1.
Be (1) x Do (10) = Have (10): see, this works.
Do more, then **have** more.

Now consider this.

Be (5) x Do (5) = Have (25).
BE better, do less, have more.

What can YOU do to BE better?

you have 64p. How much do you have at the end of the month, day 31? It's over **TEN MILLION**. Now think about your learning having the same compound impact. The more you learn, the better you become. Think of it this way, the more you **LEARN** the **MORE** you **EARN**.

The Top 20 Books

As mentioned, here's my Top 20 Books. These are books that have been "Show Stoppers." My first introduction to the 1-Page Marketing Plan was via audio book while driving down the A9. This is normally a 3-hour trip to Glasgow. I would listen to the book and hear something so amazing I would pull into a lay-by and take notes. That trip took five hours, hey, what a learning though.

Here's a thing about audio books, I am also VISUAL, by the way. Listen to the book a few times. Invariably when you are driving you get distracted from the book due to the task of driving taking priority - **PLEASE TELL ME THIS IS SO**. Other road users, animals, weather, traffic cops, loads of distractions, so you'll miss stuff first time around. If you don't, I genuinely worry what trail of devastation you have left behind you.

I have only added books that have had a huge impact in my business life and those business owners I have shared them with. I used to run a "Book and Beer Club." Every month we would select a BOOK and a BEER. This was held in a local Brewery Tap Room. It always became Book and Coffees, and the beer was kept for the weekend. Despite this being popular, and everyone that came along LOVING IT, it was hard work. It was becoming **HARD WORK** to get business owners to commit to attending, let alone **READING**. I mention this because the vast majority will do nothing with this list. 80%, I shouldn't wonder. **We're back to failure statistics all linking again**.

Here we go, **MY TOP 20**. This is correct at January 2020. The great thing about continual learning, you always find another "Top 20."

Building a Storybrand by Donald Miller. Absolute game changer in the way you present your brand and story.

The 1-Page Marketing Plan by Allan Dib. Getting clarity in your marketing - amazing book and even more amazing concept.

The E-Myth Revisited by Michael Gerber. This book just nails what being a small business owner is like. Essential reading for anyone in business.

Eat That Frog! by Brian Tracy. 21 great ways to get more done in less time. The key to managing your time.

Turn the Ship Around! by David Marquet. This book tells the amazing story of how decision making was changed in the US Navy.

The Chimp Paradox by Steve Peters. Why we react and behave the way we do. It's not you, it's your Chimp.

Oversubscribed by Daniel Priestley. This will change the way you market your business forever.

The rest, in no particular order, are all gems in their own right. After amassing a knowledge bank like this you'll be unstoppable. Well, you will be, providing you **take action** and don't expect shit to magically happen because you read the book.

Read a book a week for the rest of your life. Here's 20 weeks' worth. Is it realistic to read (listen) to a book a week for the rest of your life? **Enter your excuse here** ……………………….................................

Before you enter your excuse, here's a question. How many hours a week do you spend in the car again? What do you listen to? Would an audio book packed FULL of learnings not be better? Audio books vary from 2 to 6 hours. **How many hours a week do you spend in the car again**? Just sayin'… So, in no particular order;
The Pumpkin Plan by Mike Michalowicz
The Wealth Coach by Brad Sugars

Black Box Thinking by Matthew Syed
Top Dog by Andy Bounds & Richard Ruttle
The Snowball Effect by Andy Bounds
The Jelly Effect by Andy Bounds
Atomic Habits by James Clear
Jab, Jab, Jab, Right Hook by Gary Vaynerchuk
This is Marketing by Seth Godin
Laws of Connection by Michael Losier
Persuade by Philip Hesketh
How To Win Friends and Influence People by Dale Carnegie
The 7 Habits of Highly Effective People by Stephen R. Covey

I haven't added books like Losing my Virginity by Richard Branson or Legacy by James Kerr. These were amazing books that told more of a story: Branson's start from student magazine to Virgin Atlantic and beyond, and Kerr's amazing book of the All Blacks' Success. **Leadership at its finest**.

Enjoy the learnings. Take the ACTION. Work on your "BE".

World Class Customer Service is **NEVER** experienced if your Customer EXPERIENCE is poor.

Stuart Mason

Chapter Six - The Glory Years

You may not be surprised to learn how difficult it is, actually writing this book. This chapter is going to be hard. I am reviewing the notes for this chapter, and it's going to be **tough**.

I try not to look back, I focus on what's next, what are the positives in life, and I learned way too late to be grateful for what I have. This however hurts, there's lot of "what if" moments here. Armed with where these mistakes were made, and how avoidable they are hurts, badly. It's January 2020, we're heading towards the 7th year anniversary of our last day, and this is still very raw. I make no apologies for that.

Please, take action from what you read here. If it can prevent just one business going down this route, then it's mission accomplished. My sincere wish is it helps considerably more than one.

Reasons To be Cheerful

When were the "**Glory Years**," and what do I base glory on? The Glory Years were when the business was at its peak financially. When it was making seriously good money. We had Glasgow, Edinburgh, Aberdeen, Dunfermline and had just opened a new "Digital Store" in the heart of Glasgow's Commercial/Financial district in Sauchiehall Street. There would be around £500,000 cash in the bank, and whilst the helicopter was gone, it had been replaced by a shiny new Aston Martin Vanquish. The print hub was still located in our Wishart Street premises in Glasgow, this doubled as our Glasgow store. The Glory Years were therefore between 1999 and 2007, with 2002 to 2005 being the most profitable.

It's no coincidence that these were the most enjoyable years too, yet strangely you never seem to appreciate that at the time. Funny, that. There were many reasons to be cheerful, that's for sure.

It's interesting to note that in 2005 the business was at its most profitable, yet over a million away from the highest turnover period. As the business grew,

How To Wreck Your Numbers

The Dangers
Of Discounting

Just A **10%** Discount With A **25%** Margin

Danger Stickers
£1 Each

Danger Stickers sold at £1 Each

Pre Sale Revenues
5000 Stickers @£1 = £5000
Cost (75p) £3750 Gross Profit (25p) £1250

5000 units sold to make £1250 profit

10% OFF
Danger Stickers
£1 Each 90p

Danger Stickers sold at 90p Each

To Achieve the **SAME** Profit
8333 Stickers @90p = £7500
Cost (75p) £6250 Gross Profit (15p) £1250

8333 units sold to make £1250 profit

With Just A 10% Discount
This Means...

More capital tied up
More resources required to fulfill orders
Increased distribution costs
Cash flow implications
In reality the same profit is of course LESS profit
67% More SALES to make the SAME
This was just a 10% discount.

Know YOUR Numbers

£1m was bolted on without a single penny extra profit. There are lots of reasons for that, the biggest for sure was becoming more involved in trade work, which was higher volume, yet wafer-thin margins. If you look at the Discounting example you can quickly see just how discounting, even at 10 and 20%, just wipes out margin.

During the Glory Years I have to be honest, an arrogance set in, complacency. Now, Viper did say to Maverick (Top Gun) when referring to arrogance, "I like that in a pilot." I don't think anyone likes that in a business owner. This is why Chapter 5 detailed the process of "**How to Wreck YOURSELF**," so that you don't.

In the **Glory Years** we were **FLYING**, the helicopter was away, yet the business was flying higher than ever. We had one main and serious competitor, a national franchised group with whom we'd developed an interesting "love/hate" relationship, other than that - no one else was even close.

The arrogance and complacency would become a bigger issue as the years ticked by, and without a doubt would be a factor in the final outcome. Something bigger was happening during the "**Glory Years**" too, a serious issue, masked by the success. Think of the business as a 20-litre leaky bucket, we were pouring in 45 litres and never really noticed what was pouring out the bottom - nor cared. If we don't do work for A, B will be along in 10 mins. In a few years that would change to pouring 25 litres in and see 5 litres come out. The bucket is still full, life is still good, although stagnation had set in. It was also unclear **WHERE** the holes were. Sure, my feet were wet, but I didn't know why. Then of course, the final years, only 19 litres are being poured in, and the bucket, slowly at first, **starts to empty**…

We did some really funny stuff in the "**Glory Years**." Reckless? Maybe. Fun? Yes. This was the "Entrepreneurial" me, the flying by the seat of the pants renegade who made instant, on the spot decisions. The "**Just Do It**" attitude worked, we never stood still for a moment. The marketing was unique, creative and at times close to the edge, **VERY** close to the edge. This was the business though, close to the edge. At this point had things been throttled back, just a few RPM, and the bigger picture looked at, then this book would never have been written. In business sometimes you need to slow down to speed up. Two steps back to take four steps forward is still two steps ahead of where you were.

Spend, Spend, Spend

IPEX was, in its day, the biggest print exhibition in the UK. It would take over ALL the halls of the NEC in Birmingham: now, that's a lot of floor space. It was the showcase for print in the UK. The print industry's Glory Years were also **OUR** Glory Years. I had this "**indestructible**" feel about the business and took off down to Birmingham to look at some new print finishing kit. This would have been around £5000, again, no plan for it, no budget set. It just "felt" right. On arrival at the NEC our main equipment supplier was there, AB Dick ITEK as they were then. We were, without doubt, one of their biggest customers, and a big fish in a small pond. I liked that. It's also worth pointing out that the guys there **REALLY** looked after us. They were amazing, it was just "different" then, business was different then.

I should mention that it was around this time that The Ink Shop won the British Association for Print and Communications (BAPC) "**Business of The Year**." It was just what my ego (and chimp) really needed. This would have been 2005, the Vanquish had been traded in for the new Vanquish S, at a mere £186,000 an absolute bargain. Driving back from the awards Ceremony, trophy in hand, in your shiny Aston Martin Vanquish S, you do kinda think you have made it. I **HAD** made it though, I just **LOST** it, in more ways than one. When you look at the odds of business survival, I had defied all of the Grim Reaper's predictions, yet **he still got me in the end**.

On AB Dick ITEK's stand they had just launched a new press, a huge step up for them, and a huge step up for us. "Would you like a demo?" Ray Hillhouse asked. I have no idea what happened next, there was some kind of Jedi mind trick performed, and as I neared the end of the walk ways on this monster press I was shaking Ray's hand, and we'd become the **world's first** purchaser of this new equipment. From memory, this wasn't massive sums, it was £200,000 - nothing compared to the £1m we'd spend in later years on a press. Strange to think the car and press were similar amounts. One **COST** money, one **MADE** money. One broke down a lot, **and the press didn't**!!

That was me though, a magpie who collected shiny new objects. It sounds reckless, although I had a knack of playing scenarios in my head. Remember what I did **BEFORE** the Ink Shop? Air Traffic Control. I could, and still can, build living, moving, three dimensional images in my head with multiple moving targets. I could do the same with my business - okay to a point. Whilst looking at this press, I was planning new markets, our biggest customer was out-growing us, this was the ticket to growth. **SOLD! NEXT!**

What I was doing here, and **OBLIVIOUS** to it, was creating both the business plan and marketing plan as I was viewing the press. Here's the thing, 80% of purchasing decisions are based on **EMOTIONS**, backed up by 20% **LOGIC**. The show, the atmosphere, the bright shiny lights, the champagne, the crowds, get the picture? **EMOTIO**N bought that press. **LOGIC** paid for it. In fairness, this turned out to be one of the best investments. This doesn't mean the behaviour is right, it actually meant that BECAUSE I WAS right, I had convinced myself **THIS IS HOW YOU RUN A BUSINESS**. Does that make sense?

I've previously mentioned this quote, **"You get what you tolerate**." You get what you tolerate in others, this also applies to YOURSELF. I had now endorsed this behaviour, and my CHIMP was loving it.

I was down at the NEC as a guest of AB DICK ITEK, they were wining and dining me, and I was really being looked after. What a night, as stated, this wasn't just the Ink Shop's Glory Years, it was the print INDUSTRY'S Glory Years. Print, like any industry, has its characters, and there were a good few there that night. Wined and dined turned out to be wined, and wined, and wined. Ray Donnachie was their sales manager, and a good friend. I remember Ray heading for the bar, and leaving his Nokia phone, the weapon of choice in the day. I genuinely can't remember who did this, the phone was promptly changed to Arabic. Now Ray always was a resourceful guy, and knew that IPEX attracted international visitors. It wasn't long before he found a Saudi printer and soon had his phone returned to English. Always the cool character was Ray, a bit like 007.

Unknown to me at this point, a few other print owners had taken his room card and emptied the room. Not just the cases, I mean **EMPTIED** the room. Legend had it that the bed, chairs, cabinets, even the CARPET. The room was stripped bare. Blissfully unaware of this I was woken up at around 4am by the hotel management, none too pleased about it all. If you can't take a joke, don't allow 200 print business owners into your hotel, that would be my advice. Strange thing, the following morning, breakfast was quieter than expected.

Back to the show. Satisfied that this new press would meet the demands of our biggest client, and springboard us forward, I spent day two investigating other bits and pieces and made a few purchases, but mainly enquiries. Our biggest customer was an interesting business. A five-a-side Football business that was expanding massively. Now a nationwide PLC they had stayed with us from day one. Their MD, and founder, found us down at the "Barras," and what started off with a small order became a 6-digit print spend. They were with us right up to the end. An absolutely fantastic "A" customer.

Driving home from Birmingham, I was content that a "**SOLD TO INK SHOP GLASGOW**" sign was proudly stuck to my machine, the trade press was all over it, and I LOVED that. It was just what my ego needed, another boost. My 15 minutes of fame, in fact I had a lot of 15 minutes in fairness. This press had been a "**Worldwide First**" for the business. This wasn't our first "first," either: we had many. First in the World, first in Europe, and loads of UK firsts. We were, in the Glory Days, absolutely SMASHING IT. **How could this possibly go wrong**?

Banks, Finance and THIEVES

As I sat in that new car park north of Manchester, better known as the M6, I realised that I had to pay for the press before the end of the show the following day. I called the bank, explained the story, got the usual sigh, followed by an instant approval. The sigh only came from the bank hoping that one day I would have the courtesy of "asking" for finance rather than "telling" them. We also told them what rates we were paying. Oh, how those days have changed. In those days, the banks were great. Banks usually are when everything is fine and dandy.

Finance in place, I then spent the rest of the journey planning how we'd feed this new press. It had a lot of nice features, I'll not bore you with the technical shit. By the time I arrived back in Glasgow I had the Marketing Plan completed, somewhere in my prefrontal cortex, it's maybe still there, amongst all the other plans from the day.

This story takes a funny turn. It wasn't funny at the time, right enough. The finance was in place, The IPEX Show was finished, and our new press was being delivered direct from the exhibition floor. Exciting times. The required electrical work was completed, the floor painted, and we eagerly awaited the arrival of the trucks. That's another element I just LOVED. Over the years we bought a heap of big, expensive machines. Seeing the trucks arrive, laden with heavy machines was a really proud moment. As the business grew, **the trucks got bigger**, and more of them. In later years our first B2 Heidelberg came on three artics.

Anyway, sorry, the funny story. The press was being picked up by the carrier on the Tuesday after the show. Delivery with us was planned for the following day. We still had a bit of work to do, we'd be ready for delivery on Wednesday though, maybe!

I then received a call from the organisers at IPEX asking me to give them the courtesy of advising of the changed schedule. I had no idea what they were talking about. "We need to book in trucks and uplift times, there's 100s of trucks and you just can't show up, and… and…" And so he rambled on for what seemed like hours. "Hold on, I know nothing of this." I took his number, and now fuming, I called the press suppliers, who equally new nothing of this schedule change. They called the carrier, who equally knew nothing - this was now smelling like a rather large rat. Then it dawned, the press was being "jacked." A frantic call to the organisers and police were involved. We were lucky, when the security guy at the NEC went off to make calls etc the guys realised they were going to get rumbled and bailed.

Like I say, we laugh at that **NOW**. Shortly afterwards we were "joking" about insurance liability. We had paid for the press, was it ours, was it theirs? Suffice to say, we made sure that all future orders were detailed to cover that. Apparently, press thefts are not uncommon, **more the banks now though**!!

Menus and the VAT Man

In the Glory Years we had dominated one particular market, MENUS. We printed **MILLIONS** of them for takeaways and this would account for well over half of our turnover. This market was hard work, yet lucrative. If you live in Scotland, and enjoy takeaway food, it's almost certain you have used one of our menus.

I remember being at one corporate golf day and the owner of "Glasgow's premier print business" came over. That was THEIR self-proclaimed title, not mine! He mocked the "menu printers," for a minute or two until I quizzed him about a few recent jobs they had printed. Funny thing, I worked out that on a margin per sheet we were **12% HIGHER**. I said to him, the paper doesn't care if it's a menu or programme for a football club, the bank manager does. That stopped that shit, I went on to lose that damn game too, the golf that is.

Our dominance of the menu market continued, and indeed grew. You may be thinking "why not continue in this market, it's clearly a niche?" Of course it was, however, as the print industry declined and suffered from significant "over capacity," even more printers moved into this market, expecting a "quick win." The reality was that prices were simply driven down and down. There was always some **IDIOT** willing to do it cheaper. **That idiot was usually us** as we battled to retain market dominance.

Later in the book you'll read a chapter that was **NEVER** intended to be published. Recalling the story of "Fire in The Hold" was painful. This illustrated a more sinister side for the menus. That's for later, this is The **GLORY** years.

I remember doing some paperwork at the front desk, it had been a long day, they usually were LONG days. **Four very serious looking suits** walked in and flashed an ID card. Now, that card could have been for the Mickey Mouse Ice Cream Club as I paid little attention to it.

Every menu we printed had "Printed by the Ink Shop (Glasgow) - 0141 552 3337," it cost us nothing, yet brought us in thousands of pounds of business, and also brought in the occasional suited dudes!!!

Suit one, a humourless man in his 50's, produced a menu, printed by us. "Did you print this?" he barked in a rough Glaswegian manner. This guy had "don't fuck with me" written all over him. I looked at the menu, saw the "printed by" and really couldn't argue. "Yes, that's one of ours." We also had a reference number which allowed us to track the graphics files. Serious dude demanded to see the invoice and within 10 minutes we had produced it. Then, something strange happened, just at that point, the guy **SMILED**.

"Well," he said wryly, "I never expected that. We are here as part of an investigation," he pointed to his colleague on the left. "These guys," pointing to the even more serious dudes on the right, "well, they were here to prosecute YOU had you not produced the invoice." By now they had chilled a bit, and the kettle was on. It turned out these were HMRC inspectors doing some kind of investigation of one of our menu customers.

This may surprise you: I was remarkedly honest. Not that I would detail tax evasion in a book anyway!!! 99% of the menu business was **CASH**. Many weeks I would be leaving the East End of Glasgow with over £20,000 of cash in my pocket, at night, alone - bonkers. Imagine that got out to some of the "local residents?" When takeaway clients came in, they would negotiate a "cash price," which was the book price anyway. They usually managed a discount - look out for "**How to Wreck Your Margin**." They would then pay cash: credit was NEVER given, everything we printed was always payment with order. As soon as the client was out the door, I would create an invoice in Sage and put through the cash payment. At the "day of the suit dude," that saved our arse. Honesty is the best policy. Did we ever do "cash jobs"? Let me tell you in this written publication available in the public domain, **NO**.

HMRC must work on a *Chewing the Fat* principle: "Good Guy, Good Guy, w…" From that day on, we had zero issues with HMRC, 10 years without anything other than the odd call asking about a particular re-payment. I don't know, I'm guessing that HMRC then, and now, know who the rogues are?

The Glory Team

In the Glory Years we had a great team. The guys were amazing (guys referring to male, female, and I prefer not to say "members" of the team, OK? Just before the letters start.) Most of our team were the ORIGINAL people employed for that role, and all bar ONE stayed with us, right up until that fateful day.

Receivers were appointed with unbelievable speed. The end came very, very quickly. They assembled our entire staff, with Bobbie and me there, and explained that we had tried hard over the last year to trade out of the difficulties, and the business had now **ceased trading**. They were advised they were redundant, to gather their personal belongings and leave. What happened next was heart breaking, and something I'll take to the grave. I wasn't as hard as I thought I was. They all came over to us, various hand-shakes, and hugs. There was also plenty of tears let me tell you, from everyone. **Then they all went back to work**…

The receivers went out and said "Excuse me, you don't understand, you are now all redundant, you need to leave." "No, YOU don't understand," one of them shouted, "that's not how we work here, there's jobs to finish." Every one of them worked that entire week to complete the jobs the clients had paid for. That is the measure of a team. I knew we had a good bunch, and I tell you what, I never knew **HOW GOOD** until that day. That's why I wanted to add this into the **"Glory Years**," it was their efforts that contributed to those Glory Years, **they didn't deserve this end**.

I will add a chapter in the book about those dark days leading up to the appointment of the receivers. I was advised not to, fuck it, it's important to share. Yes, I made mistakes, yes, I was slow to react, yes, I was in denial, yes, I was fucked over royally by the bank - **so let's go for it**. Later.

The Glory Years, if only the business had more control, more systems, more structure. Yes, money was being made. Don't even begin to ask me where. I know that sounds really reckless, however that's where a lot of businesses are. They don't focus on the KEY areas of the business.

I know for a FACT that the demise of the business started in these glory years. That's why when asked **WHEN** the business failed, I now answer "2005." That's when it **FAILED**, it just wouldn't die from its wounds until 2013.

If I broke down the business into individual units (geographic locations), and different sectors of the business, I would have been able to see **INSTANTLY** what the most profitable areas were. More importantly though, I would have seen with greater clarity the current, and future problem areas. Remember, **you get what you tolerate**, and **you can only improve what you accurately measure**. I was tolerating far too much, and measuring nothing accurately.

The Not-So-Glory Years

It's not an excuse, it does help keep me sane though. In the years leading up to, and after, the Ink Shop's failure there were **MANY** high-profile failures. The industry was in turmoil. This can't be an excuse though, for there were MANY bucking that trend. I should have been investing in the Glory Years and planning and preparing for the **"NOT-So-Glory Years."**

We did a lot of TRADE work, that is providing print work for other printers. Now, let me tell you, this is a market where they eat their young. This is a crazy, price-driven marketplace. We used this market to fill capacity, and very quickly it became a dominant market, and with it a reliance on trade work that we could not easily turn off. As we came out of the glory years and grew more and more, the knee jerk reaction was "Feed the press."

This is where knowing your numbers is **ESSENTIAL**. The reality of trade work was **NO PROFIT**. In real terms, no profit was being made. Meanwhile, back at the bat cave, we were so heavily focussed on DEALING with this market that our attention was taken off the **CORE** business.

This was really the beginning of the end, and the topic for another chapter. The year is 2007/2008 and we're about to move again, buy a bigger press, expand the trade market and FRANCHISE the business to achieve meteoric growth. Would you like to see my plan for all of this? We were about to start a serious expansion phase. **The right idea, at the worst possible time**. Is that a question or a statement?

Something else was happening at this time. Fannie Mae and Freddie Mac were in the news. "Who the hell are they?" I remember saying. "With names like that they deserve to fail!" Little did we know the organisations with the stupid sounding names were signalling the start of a global meltdown that was going to make the 20s depression look like a cash flow glitch. Then Northern Rock collapsed, and all of a sudden panic was starting to set in.

The Perfect Storm Is Now Coming

It's worth spending a bit of time here, it was during this period that the wheels really started to come off. This book is covering the main areas of where I know I went wrong. This was a PRINT business, and was an industry in decline, rapid decline. In 2004 to 2008 the internet was still maturing, huge yeah, yet still maturing. Facebook didn't exist in our Glory Years, although by 2004 it was starting life as "The Facebook." Twenty-year-olds today, were at primary school then. It seems so long ago.

We were trapped in an industry in decline, and as we approached the tail end of the Glory Years in 2007 we were heading for the biggest global economic meltdown that we are ever likely to experience in our lifetime, I sincerely hope. The business wasn't ready for the storm.

One thing that recessions are renowned for is **killing the weak**. The mistakes made along the way in isolation would not have been fatal. It was the perfect storm of 1) Declining Market, 2) Internet Growth, 3) Recession, 4) Expansion with new press and franchise, 5) Poor Planning and Vision, 6) Lacking structure and systems. **Does that make sense**?

The reason I want to mention this (again) is because when you are BUSY you don't do this shit. You eat when you're hungry and don't think about food when you're not. It's the same with many business owners, I have seen this too many times. Businesses that are doing well, busy, making money, yet structurally unsound, as I was. My business was built on a **foundation of sand**. That's fine when the sun is shining and it's all buckets and spades and smiley faces. Watch out when the storm comes, though.

The one thing I want to hammer home for businesses is to use your Glory Days as the foundation for even more Glorious Days. Set time aside, work on the systems, work on the structure, work on the team, work on **YOURSELF** so that when the storm DOES come, you're ready.

The last chapter in the book will cover the "Final Chapter," let's just wrap up the golden years with the memories of a fun business, good suppliers, superb and loyal customers and a team that would (and did) walk on hot coals for me. **Thank you for the Glory Days, guys, you know who you are**.

Wealth - There's More to It Than Meets the Eye

Since the wealth was created in the "Glory Years" it seems appropriate to add this here.

Wealth is a funny thing, some see it as an essential driver in everything they do (that WAS me), others see as route to achieve what they REALLY want (that is me now), and others see it as the route to everything evil in our society. What is wealth? How do you measure wealth? Is it "stuff"? This is what I refer to as the "**illusion of wealth**."

Wealth is NOT simply being able to afford the mortgage, the lease payments on the Aston Martin, the ability to buy a Breitling on the credit card, that's not wealth. That's what I refer to as **stupid DEBT**. Now, I wasn't as reckless as all that. Over the years we had built up a sizable portfolio of property. We owned every shop we had, we owned the Glasgow production hub, we had a luxury holiday home and we were mortgage-free in our own home. In the day this amounted to around a property value of circa £1.4m with some £250,000 of borrowings. There was some nice equity in that, and indeed the ability to provide "passive income" should those shops be let out to third parties.

As a result of some poor advice received, and some poor decisions from me, the commercial property portfolio was all in the name of the business. This would later **HAUNT** us.

Everyone has their different view on what WEALTH is. Assets, passive income, security? What about personal wealth? I don't mean financial: reputational standing in the community, how important is that?

The simple fact is this: in business we're **ALL seeking wealth**. Before you start to email me about how you want to save the planet (please do), consider this, you need to **CREATE** the wealth to realise that dream. I'll use Bill and Melinda Gates as an example for that. Bill spent the first half of his life making as much money as possible, and the second half giving away significant amounts of money to many worldwide causes. Would they have been able to fulfil their philanthropy dream without the wealth Microsoft created? Would so many thousands have benefitted had it not been for that wealth? Obviously not.

Here's the thing, though. The rate of business failure in the UK is just ridiculous, we're covering a LOT of the reasons why. You'll recall from previous chapters that 80% of businesses fail in the first 5 years, then of the

20% that survive, 80% fail in the next five. When it comes to wealth - well, those figures just get worse. Only 1 in 200 will go on to create the wealth they aspired to when they started the business. Now, that depends on what your aspirations were. If you "aspired" to be wealthier than Jeff Bezos, then you might well be in for a 1-in-200 shocker, that doesn't mean you don't have a comfortable lifestyle. What percentage of business owners do you think make it to that level of wealth? I don't know, I'm asking for a friend.

Let's get back to wealth. The other really strange thing is people rarely consider themselves wealthy, there's always another rung up the ladder. How much is enough? You see this ambition in every element of corporate business today. In fact, let me ruffle a few feathers, it's NOT always ambition or aspiration, it's often greed. At the time of writing this book, the tax payable by a number of UK-based global brands has been released. The joiner in Govan probably paid more tax. I believe this is where the growing resentment of wealth comes from.

I have to be honest though. Too often people make "assumptions," they see the trappings of wealth, and have **NO CLUE** of the journey needed to create it. That person driving a Ferrari now, more likely than not was working 20-hour days when **you were partying**.

When I had my Aston it was rarely used. Yes, I was always busy. There was another reason though. Very often it would have Big Macs and bottles thrown at it, the usual hand signals, just the "usual" that sadly has become the norm in the UK. Again, **people saw the destination - not the journey**. They never saw, nor cared about living in a leaky caravan, driving a metro van or working 14 hours a day, 7 days a week. Work out the hours, with the back pay due on all that, **anyone could afford an Aston Martin**.

Recently, I was listening to a local radio station. There had been a story in the press of a guy that wrote off his brand-new Ferrari hours after collecting it. The presenters were talking about it, and I too nearly crashed when I heard one of the comments. "**Good**," was the broadcast comment. **They have no idea of his journey**, they just made yet another destination assumption. Is that where we are with society?

The G8 Protestors

The G8 Summit at Gleneagles, now there's a collection of wealth, this is a great story. I had been working late (as usual) and we were getting away for the weekend at our holiday home in Lossiemouth. Bobbie had given up and left earlier. I was heading off later in the Aston.

I left the Glasgow Sauchiehall Street store in a bit of a hurry. Let me tell you, a V12 hurry differs from anything else you have experienced. I settled down by the time I got past Cumbernauld, and was behaving myself. I noticed a traffic car behind me and made sure I was bang on the limit. When it became apparent I was heading north, the blues and twos came on. WTF, are you serious?

I pulled over on the hard shoulder and went over to the grass, the cops were approaching. "**REALLY GUYS**," I commented arrogantly, "what exactly is the problem?" I said, even more arrogantly.

"If you can just calm down, sir" - that made me worse. "Can I ask where you're going?" "A9 north to Lossiemouth," I belted back. "OK sir, we thought that may be the route. Sir, whilst we genuinely do appreciate your **BEAUTIFUL** car, the G8 protestors are running amok at Gleneagles. I am not sure if they will have the same appreciation of your car… if you get my drift."

"Ah… yes, I sure do appreciate that." I took the next slip road off and went home to try again the following day. Lesson learned, most of the time, the cops are actually on your side. The days that they are not - you've probably given them cause.

When it comes to wealth, boy, has my view on that changed now. One of the best books I have ever read on wealth is the "*Wealth Coach*" by Brad Sugars, not because it's an insight into wealth creation that no one has ever covered before, more because it tells the story through a family experience. Spoiler alert, the dog dies, be prepared for that.

Today, super cars and bikes do not interest me. Maybe it's because it's a case of been it, seen it, done it. Today I still appreciate Ducatis. Would I spend £46,000 on a bike now? No. Would I buy another Aston Martin, no. Well, maybe. Now, there's a lot to be said for having these things while you can enjoy them. I'm not a believer in living like a pauper until you retire, then perhaps reach an age where you can't do some of the things you want to do. I can't see me doing track days at Jerez in Spain aged 65. Then again!

That of course depends when, and how you retire. If you build up wealth with a passive income and retire early, well that's a different story. You see, no one taught me this stuff. This is why it's so important to step back from your business and **LEARN**. Read, get a business coach, **hang out with smart people**. I did none of that. **You don't know what you don't know**.

Wealth will come up time and time again in this book. *Read the Wealth Coach*, and more importantly, get your kids to read it too.

The "Glory Years" weren't long enough, a few more years would have been nice. The reality was the "Glory Years" were **PLENTY** of time to identify and **RECTIFY** the issues. **DO NOT** make that mistake. Make hay while the sun shines.

Chapter Seven - How to Wreck Your Team

If you really want to wreck your business, then this is the chapter you have been waiting for. Your most valuable commodity is your team. I know that sounds cheesy and "team" has been used to death, just park that for a moment. The **people you surround yourself with** are going to shape you, your business and your future.

I get frustrated when I hear business owners bark that there's "no decent people out there." Oh yes there is, **an abundance of them**. The sad reality is they won't come near you with a bargepole unless your business is better than awesome. Fact. Good people will work for good businesses, exceptional people will work for exceptional businesses.

Money is always important, yet research shows time and time again that when choosing an employer, it's not the driving factor. Think of Google back in its embryonic days. People chose to work there because they saw the vision, they wanted to be part of something special. It's no different in your business. If your passion, enthusiasm, and commitment are obvious, if your **WHY** is contagious, then **"you'll get the people you deserve**." If it's **NOT**, you'll get the people **YOU** deserve.

I want to challenge conventional thinking, and get business owners to focus on their **TEAM** no different than they would a TOP client. The steps businesses take to attract and keep clients should mirror the **team's development**. Is that unreasonable? You can only grow your business to the level of your incompetence. We can now add "team" to that. You simply cannot grow your business without a strong, competent, decision-making team, with **strong leadership**. Therefore, logic would dictate that you'll only grow **YOUR business** to the level of your **TEAM'S** incompetence. Put this another way, nothing will outperform a highly motivated and knowledgeable team. Do you think Elon Musk has a few highly motivated, continuously learning and inspired members on his team?

In case you ignored the previous chapter, I am using the literal meaning of the word incompetence, (inability to do something successfully) and not the adopted meaning that these are useless people, we need to be crystal clear on that, otherwise the mail I will get will just be ridiculous.

Too many business owners roll their eyes at the very mention of **Vision, Mission and Culture**. Roll your eyes if you want. While you're doing that, your competitor who grasped this is busy interviewing the right people. Just sayin'. Seriously though, how can your team join you on the journey when they have no idea what the destination is, or **WHY**?

I want to move onto an area where I know I was very **WEAK**. Training, Development and Supportive of Risk Taking. Let's look at Training and Development. It was always the bare minimum, as fast as we could, as cheap as we could. Now, "in-house" training etc is fine, it does however need structure, it needs documented and the rules of the game need to be clear. How can your team possibly know what to deliver if it's never been explained? I often hear business owners say "he's too damn slow." Was he ever told how fast he needs to be? Were the expectations ever made clear? **Communication is the RESPONSE** you get.

Today, well that's completely different, team development is a huge part of what I do. Communication, training, development, and personal development too. I also believe that if an employee wants to do any form of continual learning the business pays or supports that. The business benefits more than you will ever know with smart, motivated employees.

Annual appraisals annoy me a bit, too: often they are given lip service and done because business owners **THINK** they need to be done. It's a perfect opportunity to gain feedback on the business and the role, by the person doing it every day. It's a great opportunity to see what that person's aspirations are too. Too often though, it's overlooked or ignored.

What's that great quote? "**What if we train people and they leave? What if we don't and they STAY**?" Train and develop your team so they CAN leave, then create a business environment that makes sure they won't.

There are plenty of really good appraisal templates for this now. If you use an employment law advisor, they should have one. Remember though, these are templates. Your business is different from mine, and my business is different from hers.

The single biggest, and most obvious piece of advice I can offer is this, "**Look after your team**." The way you train, encourage, support and engage with your team will be in direct proportion to how your business matures, grows, improves, and how smoothly your transition from self-employed to entrepreneur will be. Whilst my business was chaotic at times with a lack of systems, I really looked after my team. The evidence of that was when the receivers tried to send them home. If anything, I held them back, not the other way around. **Are you holding your team back**?

We're Back to Nuclear Submarines Again

Support Risk Taking. Back to the book store. OMG, the book that nails this in a superb read is "Turn the Ship Around!" by David Marquet. David was the Captain of the USS Santa Fe, an American nuclear submarine. Funny old thing, I remember chasing something similar (allegedly!) He goes into amazing detail of how he "Turned the **NAVY** Around." How he challenged the way permission was asked, and granted. It's what David refers to as "**intent-based leadership**." I'm just guessing here, if a Commander can empower a team in a **nuclear submarine** to make strategic decisions, where such decision making is not just supported, it's **ENCOURAGED**, then I'm going to hazard a guess that the "Commander" of ANY business can do the same, just without the nukes.

This book is obviously on my Top 20. This isn't "**20 books to read before you die**," this is "20 books you need to get off your arse **NOW** and read." I'll let you choose the priority.

Back in the Glory Years this was **NOT** me. I would continually complain and bemoan staff for not taking the "initiative" to do things. "Do I have to do everything myself?" Well, that was a well-used phrase. I would be openly critical when someone did something that wasn't performed to the **EXACT** standards that I would. Often good is good enough; if the team could do it 80% as well as me, that would be a result. In reality, and this was never proved, I would hazard a guess that in many occasions, they would do it BETTER. I was doing the **POLAR OPPOSITE** of what David shares in that amazing book. I wasn't turning the ship around, I was sinking it.

Let's stay here a moment, this is gold dust. First of all, how much of the above rings true with you? Be honest now. Then, how much of this rings true with your managers and supervisors? Didn't see that one coming, did you? As obvious as this sounds, if your middle tier management aren't following the same process, then **YOUR** ship isn't getting turned around.

If You Want the Job Done Right ...

"**Do I have to do everything myself**?" - What does this mean? Are the team unconsciously incompetent, or is my training and communication programme in question? Without a doubt, it's the latter. A huge issue I see with business owners of all sizes, (the business that is, not the owner) is the lack of time devoted to training. Oh, and before the letters start, throwing people in a room with PowerPoint slides for 4 days is not training, it's **DELUSION**. We (the royal we) spend huge amounts of time learning new skills such as driving, flying, amateur radio, skiing, climbing, diving - yet I can guarantee the vast majority put a fraction of that time and effort into their TEAM. Think of the time, money and resource I spent heading towards a commercial helicopter licence . HALF that time and effort would have built a team to rival Apple. **Let that sink in**.

I read an interesting article just before Christmas, that the average business owner spent more time **PLANNING** Christmas festivities than they did on their business.

In business, the reason we feel we HAVE to do everything ourselves is simple, we choose it, we allow it to happen. **You get what you tolerate**.

I have used this quote many times, "*I had a team that would have walked on hot coals for me, I just never ASKED them to*". Put another way, many of the team **WERE** ready, willing and **ABLE** to raise their game and take on responsibility, I simply never provided that opportunity in a structured way.

"If I have told him once, I have told him 1,000 times." I think you're getting this now. What does that phrase mean? WHAT have you told them 1,000 times? Was it clear? Almost certainly not. The vast majority of employees want to do well, they want to please. Is it them, or is it your clarity of message? **Communication is the response you get**.

Get it out of your head you're the only one that can do the job. In the vast majority of cases, your team are more than capable of doing the job as well as, or better, than YOU. I know that was so true in my business, there was just that inability to let go. That cost me dearly. This is where previous experiences can be a barrier to progression. I had employed a high-end manager, and it simply did not work out. Was that the person, or the training and support? The thing is, that experience then became a barrier, **"I tried that before and it was a nightmare**." Thinking now, it's ridiculous. If it didn't work out the last time, you explore WHY, fix it, and move on. I was "comfortable being uncomfortable." I was NOT happy with my current position, indeed I hated it, yet the thought of the "pain" involved to fix it was worse.

This is where we (us humans) are a funny breed, we'll happily pay £100 for medicine to take the pain away, yet shy from paying £5 for a potion that would have prevented the pain in the first place. **Don't make the same mistake I did**, pay the £5 for the potion, train your team, empower them, encourage them, support them, then you won't need to pay £100 to take the pain away: there won't be any.

Support Risk Taking. Encourage your team to make decisions and choices. Before the letters start, I am not suggesting you let your marketing manager run amok with £100,000. Let the team breathe. If mistakes are made, do not do what I did, do not criticise openly. What happens next time? You create an entire team shit scared to make the most basic of decisions, **it goes downhill from there**.

I am going to jump in here with another gem: never, EVER use **BUT**. "Elaine, that was great, you did well with getting that client on board, **but** if you had just won that other client it would have been great." BANG! The but has just negated and killed **EVERYTHING** that went before it. Try this, "Elaine, that was great, you did well with getting that client on board, **and** if you had just won that other client it would have been great." You have gone from criticise to critique. There's a monumental difference. **One word change, huge meaning change**.

"Don't ask for my permission, ask for my forgiveness." It's an old quote, yet as valid today as it's always been. That sounds like a Hovis advert, it's true though. What is the absolute worst that can happen if an error is made? I was working with a client recently and we introduced a system where the team critiqued each other. No one ever said what was done was right or wrong, the team de-briefs would start, "**if you could do that again, what would you change and why?**" Very quickly they built a culture where the entire team LOOKED FORWARD to critiquing THEMSELVES. That team today are making decisions that the business owner HIMSELF says he would struggle with. That's when you know you have created the right culture. That's when you **KNOW** you can leave the business in VERY safe hands and progress on **YOUR Entrepreneurial Journey**. That started with ONE very simple question and a bit of support from the owner.

I was trying to think of a **HUGELY** successful Entrepreneur who is a "Solopreneur." I couldn't think of anyone. Branson, Sugars, Jones, Musk, Bezos, Jobs, their success is all down to their **TEAM**. Who is **YOUR** second in command? Who's got your back? Who walks on hot coals for you? If the answer is "no one", why is that?

Building a winning team can't be an "ideal", something you aspire to. It **MUST** be an absolute, and at the end of this chapter you're going to START that journey. Sorry, did that sound like a demand?

When you support risk taking, and don't fly off the handle when mistakes are made, you will quickly build a confident and competent team. You will build a competent team that will **outgrow YOU**, and that folks, is the key to building a business that isn't reliant on you for every decision. You will only grow your business to your **level of competence**. Change that - you will only grow your team to your **level of incompetence**.

There are many books on "Leadership" and how to get the best from your team. It's a big subject. It can however be summarised in a very short paragraph. "***Build a team through mutual respect, work hard and play hard. Communicate well, celebrate the wins, and don't dwell on the challenges. Look back only to learn, look forward TOGETHER. Aim to be better tomorrow than you were yesterday***." That's just my thoughts though, I'm a High D, so why use 20 pages when a short paragraph will do?

Let me be blunt. **This is your choice**. I can guarantee your team retention will rocket, morale will be at an all-time high, errors will plummet, and your hair will be less grey. This won't happen overnight. The best time to start was yesterday, don't wait until tomorrow, start today.

You get what you tolerate.

Now try this. On the next two pages there are a series of 24 questions. The first **12 are for your team**, with each answer being scored out of 10.

The next 12 questions are for you. You'll notice there's some similarities with the two sets. Same again, **score YOURSELF** out of 10 for each question.

You now have two scores out of 120. Compare them.

If the scores are out by more than 10% then you and your team, or team member, are **NOT** aligned. **Why**? Use the answers to find the question. "**How can we get better**?"

Are YOU Building
A Winning Team?

If you are, ask **your team** to answer and score these questions

"You Get The People You Deserve"

How would YOUR team answer these?

- Has what's expected from me, and my **RESPONSIBILITIES** been clearly explained?
  1- Never 2-4 - Briefly 5-7 - Fairly Well 8-9 - Reasonably Well 10- Very Clearly
  score /10

- Do I have the right tools and **RESOURCES** to do my job right?
  1- No 2-4 - Basics Only 5-7 - Fairly Good 8-9 - Reasonable Efforts 10- Yes, Perfect
  score /10

- Have I been **TRAINED** to allow me the opportunity to do what I do **BEST** every day?
  1- Never 2-4 - Briefly 5-7 - Fairly Well 8-9 - Reasonably Well 10 - Very Well
  score /10

- Have I received any **POSITIVE** feedback in the last week?
  1- None 2-4 - Basics Discussion 5-7 - Fairly Good 8-9 - Reasonable Dialogue 10 - Yes, Perfect
  score /10

- Does my manager make me feel that I am a **VALUED** part of the team I work within?
  1- Never 2-4 - Rarely 5-7 - Fairly Well 8-9 - Reasonably Well 10 - Very Well
  score /10

- Do I feel that my progression and development is **ENCOURAGED**?
  1- Never 2-4 - Rarely 5-7 - Fairly Well 8-9 - Reasonably Well 10 - Very Well
  score /10

- In the workplace do I feel that my opinions **COUNT**? Are they even asked for?
  1- No 2-4 - Rarely 5-7 - Sometimes 8-9 - Fairly Well 10 - Always
  score /10

- Have the **VISION** and **MISSION** of the business been shared with me?
  1- Never 2-4 - Briefly 5-7 - Fairly Well 8-9 - Reasonably Well 10 - Very Well
  score /10

- Do my team members work towards delivering **EXCELLENCE** in the business?
  1- Never 2-4 - Rarely 5-7 - Fairly Well 8-9 - Reasonably Well 10 - Very Well
  score /10

- Would I **RECOMMEND** a friend to work for this business?
  1- No 2-4 - Unlikely 5-7 - Not Sure 8-9 - Probably 10 - Yes
  score /10

- In the last six months has anyone asked me personally about **MY PROGRESS**?
  1- No 2-4 - Basics Discussion 5-7 - Some Interest 8-9 - Reasonable Dialogue 10 - Yes, Perfect
  score /10

- What **OPPORTUNITIES** have been provided in the last year to allow me to **IMPROVE**?
  1- None 2-4 - Basics Only 5-7 - Fairly Good 8-9 - Reasonable Opportunities 10 - Yes, Perfect
  score /10

Would this be **GOOD** information for **YOU** to know? *Total /120*
As the business owner, now complete the **next page**, then compare scores

Are YOU Building
A Winning Team?
If you are, answer and score these questions, then compare them

"You Get What You Tolerate"
How would **YOU** answer these?

- Has what I expect from my team, and their **RESPONSIBILITIES** been clearly explained?
  - 1- **Never** 2-4 - **Briefly** 5-7 - **Fairly Well** 8-9 - **Reasonably Well** 10- **Very Clearly**   *score /10*
- Do I provide the right tools and **RESOURCES** for the team to do their job right?
  - 1- **No** 2-4 - **Basics Only** 5-7 - **Fairly Good** 8-9 - **Reasonable Efforts** 10- **Yes, Perfect**   *score /10*
- Have I **TRAINED** the team to allow them the opportunity to do what they do **BEST**?
  - 1- **Never** 2-4 - **Briefly** 5-7 - **Fairly Well** 8-9 - **Reasonably Well** 10 - **Very Well**   *score /10*
- Have I provided individuals with any **POSITIVE** feedback in the last week?
  - 1- **None** 2-4 - **Basics Discussion** 5-7 - **Fairly Good** 8-9 - **Reasonable Dialogue** 10 - **Yes, Perfect**   *score /10*
- Do I or my manager make people feel they are a **VALUED** part of the team?
  - 1- **Never** 2-4 - **Rarely** 5-7 - **Fairly Well** 8-9 - **Reasonably Well** 10 - **Very Well**   *score /10*
- Do I provide enough **ENCOURAGEMENT** for my teams progression and development?
  - 1- **Never** 2-4 - **Rarely** 5-7 - **Fairly Well** 8-9 - **Reasonably Well** 10 - **Very Well**   *score /10*
- In the workplace do I make the opinions of others **COUNT**? Do I even ask for them?
  - 1- **No** 2-4 - **Rarely** 5-7 - **Sometimes** 8-9 - **Fairly Well** 10 - **Always**   *score /10*
- Have the **VISION** and **MISSION** of the business been shared with the team?
  - 1- **Never** 2-4 - **Briefly** 5-7 - **Fairly Well** 8-9 - **Reasonably Well** 10 - **Very Well**   *score /10*
- Do all my team members work towards delivering **EXCELLENCE** in the business?
  - 1- **Never** 2-4 - **Rarely** 5-7 - **Fairly Well** 8-9 - **Reasonably Well** 10 - **Very Well**   *score /10*
- Would I ask my team to **RECOMMEND** a friend to work for my business?
  - 1- **No** 2-4 - **Unlikely** 5-7 - **Not Sure** 8-9 - **Probably** 10 - **Yes**   *score /10*
- In the last six months have I have ASKED individuals about **THEIR PROGRESS**?
  - 1- **No** 2-4 - **Basics Discussion** 5-7 - **Some Interest** 8-9 - **Reasonable Dialogue** 10 - **Yes, Perfect**   *score /10*
- What **OPPORTUNITIES** have I provided in the last year to allow my team to **IMPROVE**?
  - 1- **None** 2-4 - **Basics Only** 5-7 - **Fairly Good** 8-9 - **Reasonable Opportunities** 10 - **Yes, Perfect**   *score /10*

Would this be **GOOD** information for **YOU** to know?
How do the two scores compare?

Total /120

Chapter Eight - The Name's Bond - Basildon Bond

Basildon Bond, it does sound like a secret agent, doesn't it? "Basildon, be a dear and pop over to the Middle East and retrieve that stolen nuke, be a good chap." I think it was Russ Abbot who started that character? Basildon Bond was also, and still is, a premium paper. How we tired of the Sean Connery accents as the printers and print finishers used it!

In Chapter 4 we covered a lot of the fun element. I wanted to return to that because business **SHOULD**, and indeed **MUST** be fun, or at least have fun elements to it. Let's not be naïve, not every day is going to be enjoyable in business, it's all about balance. I now want to add something else into the mix of achieving the "Work, Life, and Fun Balance," and that's ORDER. We'll come to that shortly. First, back to Bond.

FLYING, as any pilot or aircraft owner will know, is often regarded as the "rocky road to financial ruin." What a hell of a journey, though. During my short, yet immensely enjoyable years of aircraft **ownership** I discovered there was an even better way to blow vast amounts of cash on flying, and that's RENTING. There's a quote, "If it floats, flies or…," no, just leave that one. Let me assure you RENTING in aviation is a great way to get rid of excess cash. In fact, it's a great way to get rid of cash, excess or otherwise.

My love affair with Moray started the day I was posted to RAF Lossiemouth in the Summer of 1990. After I left the RAF we returned every year, first of all renting a holiday home at Silver Sands Leisure Park, then buying a holiday lodge there, before finally buying a holiday home, and ultimately moving to Lossie.

Fond memories indeed of the clean, warm sandy beaches that stretched for miles, crystal blue waters that reminded us of Mediterranean holidays, and Sean Connery! Sean Connery?

The Summer of 2000 was pleasant, and we often decided to take a weekend off and "head to Lossie." That was the advantage of having the holiday lodge, we could make last minute decisions. This particular weekend was forecast to be a real hottie, so we wanted to take advantage of that. I had just recently completed a type conversion course onto the Bell 206 "JetRanger," a turbine helicopter that you see in loads of movies. You'll have already worked out, this ain't cheap?

One was available for the weekend, so it was duly booked.

The Jet Ranger sits happily at 110 knots, which is slightly over 125 mph, so flying DIRECT Cumbernauld to Lossiemouth doesn't take long. Lossie is about 120 miles as the crow flies, so that flight is around an hour, and so much more fun than 3 hours+ on the A9. Did you see what I did there? **I tried to JUSTIFY it**.

This is what we do. **80%** of EVERY purchasing decision we make is based on **emotion**, we then attempt to use the **20% LOGIC** to back up the decision. Here's some real-life examples:

"I'll take the Jetranger at £450 an hour - look how much time I save"
"I'll buy the Ferrari - it's really an investment"
"I need those shoes - I have nothing to match this dress"
"I need that golf club - it will improve my game"

Get the picture?

Yes, the JetRanger to hire (then) was around £450 an hour wet (wet means including fuel.) Now, given this puppy burns around 100 litres an HOUR, that can be a cost. It's okay though, it's Jet A1 fuel which, at today's cost, is around 30p per litre. Wow, did you see what I did there, JUSTIFIED IT **AGAIN**. What a **BARGAIN**, the fuel is only 30p a LITRE, what a positively insane idea it is to even consider DRIVING now.

Now, flying from Cumbernauld to Lossiemouth requires no permissions at all, you fire up the bird and blast off... NORTH(ish). Well, not so much. Silver Sands is located right beside RAF Lossiemouth and as such is in the MATZ - the Military Air Traffic Zone. You don't even **CONSIDER** going near that without PPR. Prior Permission Required, a quick call to Lossie ATC (the old office) and that permission was duly granted. It's also prudent to talk to "Scottish" on the way up as they will provide a Flight Information Service. Only a fool wouldn't use that.

A further call to the manager at Silver Sands was needed. Not just to get permission, also to find out where to land. At the time Silver Sands had a huge flat area at the entrance, it just happened to be near the road. Permission was duly granted and an approximate time was given for arrival. They would then ensure that no one got in the way.

Here Comes Sean

Helicopters are a lot of fun to fly and watch, however when landing, your tail can be a real danger. The main rotor is above head height, however a tail rotor is at FACE height, and turning anything from 3 to 6 times FASTER than the main rotor. Get the picture? Having someone on the ground making sure that no one gets anywhere near the helicopter is essential. The guys at Silver Sands were great, they knew how it worked, and made sure there were no loose items lying around, either.

We jumped down to the airport, fuelled her up with her favourite Jet A1, did the pre-flight, threw the dog in the back, and fired her up. To this day I never tire of hearing a jet engine start, first the compressor, then the igniters, and a bit of fuel. It's a bit like starting a gas BBQ really, just more dramatic, and WAY more expensive.

The idea was to fly up, then do a few hours flying over the weekend, and fly back Sunday night. You only pay for the hours in the air, and as long as we did around six hours the flying school were happy. It made it worthwhile for them to rent.

Allegedly, there's a few areas on the A9 where you can fly along river beds and streams and LOOK UP at the vehicles on the road. I don't know, a friend told me that. It was an awesome day, Stirling Castle, the Cairngorm Mountains, it was a quick hour, that's for sure. What a breathtaking amount of scenery we have in Scotland. It needs to be viewed from the air though. We arrived at Silver Sands bang on time, the wind was westerly so the approach was from the east, over the beach low level, over the golf course low level, over the park low level and down. It didn't **NEED** to be, it was just an excuse because it **COULD** be!

We had friends joining us for lunch, so the helicopter was shut down, locked up and left. After a rather burned BBQ chicken I returned to the Jet Ranger to pre-flight it again, we had decided that an early evening Moray Coast flight made perfect sense. When we arrived at the helicopter, I was surprised, then **WORRIED**. The crowds were HUGE. The chopper attracts a crowd, it always does - however this wasn't normal. This was air show crowds. I was now worried that something had happened.

People were EVERYWHERE and cars poured into Silver Sands - what the hell was going on?

I stayed away until I knew exactly what was happening. The park manager camc over, looking a bit miffed. "Someone started a rumour," he mumbled. "A rumour, about what?" "Sean Connery. Sean Connery flew up here to play golf, it's his helicopter."

I took my flying jacket off and in "civvie mode" went over to the chopper. I was now more concerned about people pawing the machine, you don't want people fucking about with your helicopter.

No one was too near it, in fairness. A few were looking at the flight deck which is understandable, it is pretty cool. I asked the family next to me, "What's the story?" "Sean Connery is here for golf." I paused for a moment then asked, "Are you sure?" "Yes, yes, the guy next to us saw him, it's Sean Connery." Chinese whispers was alive and well.

Well, I turned to my friend and said, "No way are we lifting out of here today, there's bodies everywhere." I put my jacket back on, and walked over to the Jetranger, opened her up and took out the rotor ties, and covers and began tucking her away, ready for bed.

Well, that was a mistake. I was now of course Sean Connery's PILOT. I didn't see that one coming. Do I dispel the myth, or play the game? I played the game, I know, that was unfair. After being asked where Sean was for the 415th time, I relented. "He's playing golf, I think he's playing with the guys from U2 this afternoon." That was a REALLY stupid, unfair, thing to do, but also incredibly clever. The crowds VANISHED, well, they never vanished, they just headed "en-masse" onto the golf course. Sorry, my bad.

"OH, LOOK, we now have space to move." A quick pre-flight, an even quicker call to Lossie Air Traffic, and we were back in the air again. This time departing to the west, so no one on the golf course saw us. It's the great thing about being beside an RAF station, jet noise is normal. I think Sean must have got the private jet home because for the remainder of the weekend no one asked about him. I certainly never saw him. I got a few awkward looks right enough. I was tempted to buy a James Bond T Shirt, I thought that might have been a "Die Another Day" moment, though.

What's the Learning Here?

These reflections and stories are all well and good, **what's the LEARNING though**? How can this benefit me? I can't fly a Jetranger. These are all valid points.

Business should be fun, in fact business needs to be fun. Being in business should provide the resources and opportunities to set and fulfil your dreams and goals. **Otherwise, what the hell are you doing it for**? I'll hammer this home 100 times in this book, **and make no apology for it**.

Let me put this story into a bit of perspective. In total, before I gave up flying, I flew the Jetranger no more than three or four times. I only flew about four hours on this particular trip, an £1,800 investment in the fun bank.

Back to the Work Life Balance, and **ORDER**. Most business owners understand the importance of a Work Life balance. Whether they manage it or not is a different story. In a previous chapter I talked about the COST of the car, the COST of the helicopter, the COST of fun, and whether or not this should have been an INVESTMENT in people, an INVESTMENT in the business. At what point do you stop investing? **Do you ever stop investing**?

Let me explain what I mean here. I was very good at investing in equipment, property and other BUSINESS assets. What I was not good at, AT ALL, was investing in **MYSELF or my TEAM**. One without the other is coffee without cream. It CAN work, it's just not very good.

I was doing **TWO** things wrong here. **ONE**, not investing in people and building a management structure that was going to allow me to grow the business to the levels possible. Let's not kid ourselves here, this was an amazing business. We were UNTOUCHABLE, yet I had grown this business to **MY LEVEL OF INCOMPETENCE**. Does this make sense now?

What happens when you do grow your business to **YOUR LEVEL OF INCOMPETENCE**? The slide backwards starts. How I wish I could bottle and sell **HINDSIGHT**.

The **SECOND** thing I was doing wrong at this stage was spending **TIER TWO CASH FLOW**. This is explained further below.

Go back to the chapter on **PLANNING**: Dreams and Goals are right up there. I never had that clarity, I never set those goals, I never quantified the DREAM. Here's the thing. How can the business grow and accommodate those ambitions if they are not clear? Does that make sense? Let's say you want to have a "particular lifestyle," that allows supercars and helicopters. That lifestyle of course comes with a price tag. Once you know that, you build it into your business. You know exactly what **EXTRA** the business **NEEDS** to achieve in order to deliver that desired lifestyle. **What's more, if you DON'T achieve it, the lifestyle doesn't happen**.

This is why the Vision Planner is so important, it ties **EVERYTHING** needed for your growing business and provides instant, visual CLARITY.

The Order of Cash Flow - The THREE Levels

We all know that cash flow is the life blood of business? **No cash, no business**. The irony of the Ink Shop story is that when the business failed in April 2013, we had returned to profit in Q1 that year. **We simply ran out of CASH**.

Think of your cash flow in this order, there's **THREE** levels to consider (in my humble opinion.)

Tier ONE Cash Flow - Survive and Thrive

Your business needs cash to survive, pay the bills, meet the payroll. Once you meet ALL of the business overheads **COMFORTABLY**, what's left becomes Tier Two Cash Flow. Tier One meets the **COSTS** to the business.

Tier TWO Cash Flow - Invest and Protect

You now have surplus **CASH**. Invest and Protect. This can cover MANY elements, for example, training and development, investing in PEOPLE, as well as systems and processes. Everything here should be an INVESTMENT in the business. Every £1 invested should return £10 (directly or indirectly.) Where Tier One meets the costs, **Tier Two MUST be for INVESTMENTS**. Nothing in Tier Two should be a cost to the business.

Tier THREE Cash Flow - Distribution to Owners

The surplus cash after Tier One and Tier Two now becomes Tier THREE. Think what you have created here. You are investing at Tier Two which feeds and allows MORE cash in Tier THREE. **Only now can the owners and investors start buying Aston Martins**. The cash can now be taken out for the owners WITHOUT damaging the continued growth and development of the business. Tier Two won't allow that.

This is just MY VIEW. This is my view on cash flow, feel free to agree or disagree, I'm just sharing my thoughts on it.

This is where I went horribly wrong. I never had this explained at the time. We had huge amounts of cash. What I was doing was **SPENDING** Tier Two cash. I had invested in property, that was fine: although there was not a rental income, there was an appreciating asset base.

What I should have done was invested in **MORE** people. Recruited more Managers and DIRECTORS who would have generated profit for the business. That may have taken a few more years to filter down as Tier Three, that's okay though. I could have bought the Aston Martin a few years LATER, and enjoyed it more, as well as having a business that was now built on a foundation of **ROCK** rather than sand.

I would have argued that Tier ONE was the "only" priority, simply because it was. You should have seen our print factory, it was, without a shadow of doubt, one of the most modern and state of the art print factories in the country. We RE-INVESTED heavily in new kit and new technologies. We kept pushing boundaries, without really fully understanding WHY. It was HOW we managed to wipe the floor with so many of our competitors.

We could print and distribute in a **DAY** what would take our "larger" competitors a **WEEK PLUS** to achieve, it was like taking candy from a baby. That's why the business was profitable, that's why the business was flying, that's why the business had so much cash reserves, that's why I fucked it up, we always have to come back to that!

Looks Can Be Deceiving

I was having fun **OUT** of the business, I wasn't having much fun **IN** the business. Very often it was hell on earth. 24/7 stress and hassle. Why was that not fixed? Did it go on for so long it became normal? Normalise anything and there's no need to change it? It's back to the reference of being comfortable being **UNCOMFORTABLE**. I see that a LOT today in businesses of all sizes.

In an earlier chapter I gave an illustration of what the **TRUE** cost of spending is. A monthly £2,000 supercar payment was really a £20,000 drain on the business every month. On a 10% net profit, it requires **£20,000 of sales revenue** to generate the PROFIT to meet that payment. The ability to meet the monthly payment is not wealth.

If I had used the money spent on cars and invested that in a PA, and the money spent on helicopters and invested that in management, **what would have happened to my business**?

I may not have had such a flamboyant lifestyle **THEN**, but it would have almost certainly been an **INVESTMENT** in the growth and development of the business. It would have guaranteed that the stress and pressure was reduced, and in the years to come bigger helicopters and faster cars could have been bought, had I chosen to do so. I think "**financial maturity**" would have taken over then. Understanding the TRUE cost would have maybe led to a more prudent lifestyle? Who knows? Business should be FUN, remember. **It's not much fun when you're talking to receivers**.

From this chapter, go back to the Five-Year Vision Planner, work on exactly where YOU and YOUR business wants to be in 5 years. Be clear on what the business NEEDS, and be even clearer on what **YOU NEED and WANT**.

From the outside my business **LOOKED** amazing, and in many areas it was. It certainly had the opportunity to be **BEYOND** amazing. Looks can be, and were, deceiving.

There's **THREE** figures I want you to consider. This is really important, as there's a huge difference between NEED and WANT. This applies to both the business and YOU. For this illustration, we'll focus on **YOU**.

What Do I Need? What do I need to pay the bills and get by?

What Do I Want? What do I want to pay the bills and enjoy life?

What Is My Dream? What do I REALLY want to earn to enjoy life, and provide financial security for myself and my family? What are the consequences of not achieving that?

Three very different figures. Here's the thing though, how can you possibly begin to grow your business, and invest wisely, AND deliver the results you REALLY want if they are not all **crystal clear from the outset**?

To summarise. **I grew the business to my level of incompetence**. I never understood then the "**Three Tiers of Cash Flow**," and the result of that was "The Many **TEARS** of Cash Flow."

The**3Tiers** Of**Cashflow**

Tier ONE Cash Flow - Survive and Thrive
Your business needs cash to survive, pay the bills, meet the payroll. Once you meet ALL of the business overheads **COMFORTABLY**, what's left becomes Tier Two Cash Flow. **Tier one meets the COSTS to the business**. New leases

Survive and Thrive   as the business grows will of course be Tier One Cash Flow.

Tier TWO Cash Flow - Invest and Protect
You now have surplus CASH. Invest and Protect. This can cover **MANY** elements, for example, training and development, investing in PEOPLE, as well as systems and processes.

Everything here should be an **INVESTMENT** in the business. Every £1 invested should return £10+ (directly or indirectly). Where Tier One meets the costs, Tier Two MUST be for **INVESTMENTS**.
Nothing in Tier Two should be a cost to the business.

Invest & Protect

Warning: I was spending Tier Two Cash.
That became the Three "Tears" of Cash Flow

Tier THREE Cash Flow - Distribution To Owners
The surplus cash after Tier One and Tier Two now becomes Tier THREE. Think what you have created here. You are investing at Tier Two which feeds and allows **MORE** cash in Tier **THREE**. Only now can the owners and investors start buying Aston Martins. The cash can now be taken out for the owners WITHOUT damaging the continued growth and development of the business. **Tier Two won't allow that**.

Distribution
To Owners

When completing the 5 Year Vision Planner you will see there's a section for Investments and Cash. This is your **2nd Tier Cash Flow**. Personal Dream and Goals, that will be your **3rd Tier Cash Flow**

Chapter Nine - Fire in the Hold, the "Print Wars"

So far in this book I have adopted a very light-hearted approach, getting a serious message over in a humorous way, with a few swear words as well for dramatic purposes.

This chapter is going to be more serious, indeed **this chapter was never planned to be part of the book**. Not because it's not relevant, it most certainly is, more because of the wounds it re-opens. Arguably, wounds that were never closed.

This book has been tough, it brings back a LOT of memories, many good, some sad, and yes, a lot of painful ones, too. There have been "what ifs" along the way, isn't hindsight a truly wonderful thing? I'm not one for looking back, other than to learn and move on. I always smile when I watch Guar Gopal's YouTube video on "**Why Worry**?" Google it, it's genius.

"Do you have a problem in life? No. Then why worry? Do you have a problem in life? Yes. Can you do something about it? No. Then why worry? Do you have a problem in life? Yes. Can you do something about it? Yes. Then why worry?" Do you get the point? Guar tells this story well.

After a great debate with Bobbie, and a few friends, it was decided to include this chapter and the unbelievable stories that are linked to it. I guarantee you that everything in this chapter is true, the exact times are subject to memory, so excuse any inaccuracies there. The reason I want to highlight this is simple, at the end of the chapter, **you would never have believed it**.

When you have your own business, you are very much part of it, twenty-four seven, you rarely completely switch off, if at all. There's usually something that keeps you awake at night. Something that stops you completely switching off. For me, that was the fear of a break-in. Our business had hundreds of tons of paper, flammable consumables, expensive computers and servers, and some VERY expensive and easily damaged print equipment. A malicious break-in would be the ultimate nightmare.

The Ultimate Nightmare DID occur, only worse, MUCH worse…

You Will Never Be Prepared for This

It was Sunday 7th December 2008, a typical December night: cold, drizzly, wet, and just the kind of night you didn't want to venture out in. I always was an early starter, so being in my bed at 10pm on a Sunday was not unusual. Around 10.40pm the phone went, the phone never rings at that time, so immediately the senses **know that something is wrong**. It couldn't have rung any more than three times before I had grabbed it, eager to hear who was calling, and **WHY**. Could this be my worst fear? Yes, it was the alarm monitoring station for our Cumbernauld factory, we had an alarm activation.

In all the years since we moved in, we never had a single false alarm. By this time my heart was pounding as I fumbled about for the keys to the Range Rover. Blast off followed a few short minutes later. We lived in Dullatur, which was a short drive to the factory in Westfield North - it was even shorter that night. The superchargers were really working for a living, as was the four-wheel drive. The drizzly rain had kept the roads wet, it was foggy, it was difficult to see, and other cars daring to do the speed limit were simply a hazard for me. You would be surprised just how many cars are on the road at that time on a Sunday night. I did wonder where people were going, and if any had an urgency greater than mine.

As I approached our industrial estate my heart nearly stopped. I looked up and saw an orange glow from the south-facing part of the building. My feelings at this point were indescribable. An urge to drive faster, yet a fear of getting there. What was waiting for me as I approached the unit? Fire?

To reach the entrance of our building you had to drive past and behind the adjoining units before turning left into the courtyard. As I drew nearer, the orange glow got brighter, this was the ultimate nightmare unfolding. I drove faster and faster, and skidded around the hard left that took me behind our unit. The security lights on the building and streetlights were orange, the glow around them was intense. The drizzle had acted like a huge magnifying glass, I took my foot momentarily off the pedal and sighed, taking comfort that the orange glow was not a fire, simply the glow from the security lights. I could also now see the wooden rear fire door was closed; we always knew this was the weak point in our building. Hidden by trees, even with the big orange security light, it was easy to remain undetected there. I breathed a huge sigh of relief when I saw that door was secure.

Aware that there was still an issue I continued, albeit a bit more relaxed. As I turned to park in front of our unit, I couldn't believe it. In a few short seconds I had gone from expecting to find a display that had fallen over, to now **witnessing a fireball** that had engulfed two of the six downstairs offices. The orange glow I had witnessed just minutes before was indeed a fire. It too was magnified by the drizzle and growing massively and quickly.

I acted on instinct. I remember phoning the fire brigade within seconds. What happens next is simply horrific, all I could do was watch and wait.

Then it dawned on me, my laptop was in the office immediately above the fire. Everything was on that laptop. I ran down to open the main roller shutter which took me into reception, two offices along from the fire. I didn't have to open the doors to realise the fire was quickly spreading, three of the six windows were now cracking and breaking with the intense heat. Despite being 30 or so feet away from the flames, **the heat was intense**. I could feel my face burning in the incredible temperature. Time to fall back.

The front of the building was now starting to catch fire, and the flames were reaching the upstairs offices, my office. I called 999 again, where the hell were these guys? Just as that call started, I could hear the sirens. I had no idea how long it took the fire brigade to arrive, it seemed like an eternity; it wasn't, it was minutes. **Total respect for these guys**. They don't get paid enough.

If you have ever seen firefighters in action you know they just get shit done, quick style. Each one of them knows EXACTLY what to do, and a well-trained, and well-disciplined unit work as one. We could learn from that in our businesses. Within a few minutes the fire brigade had the door open and were tackling the blaze. LAPTOP, laptop! I ran towards reception to reach the stairs to get my precious computer. The next thing I remember is being abruptly halted by a fire chief, none too pleased with my efforts to enter the building.

I retreated back to the safe confines of the car park and could only watch as the flames quickly diminished, and were replaced by a dark, burned and broken building. The entire front of the building, once a bright battleship grey and red, was now burned black, and dead. When the fire brigade was comfortable that the flames were out, the conversation moved to me. "What the hell was I trying to achieve?" What followed was slightly humbling to say the least. There was no fire in the reception area, it never got that far.

When you enter the reception there was a large metal staircase that led to a small landing, then another staircase leading to the door for the first-floor offices. My initial crazy intention was to get up that stair and get my laptop.

The fire crew brought me in and shone the torch on what was our lovely bright red feature wall. The bottom of the wall was still red, however as you looked up the colour went from red, to deep red, to black, to a colour that resembled what hell can only look like. I remember all too clearly the fire crew pointing to the wall mounted lights, they had completely melted. Hold on, there was no fire here…

The fire chief then ran the scenario. "You would have entered here, adrenalin pumping, and flown up those stairs reaching the mid landing. You would have quickly continued to the second set of stairs. Because you know the layout so well, you probably wouldn't have noticed it was impossible to see due to the smoke. You would have then gasped for a breath of air RIGHT HERE, adrenalin only works so far, and that's where **you would have died**, having breathed in smoke at a temperature in excess of 500 degrees." "Steady on chap, gloss it up a bit for fuck's sake," was my immediate thought.

A fire fighter went up into the offices and got my laptop, it was completely undamaged as the fire never reached the upper level. The fire chief had wrapped it up neatly, and as he handed me my treasured computer, he was to ask me a question that still haunts me today. "Was it worth DYING for, sir?" I never replied with what was the obvious answer. The crazy shit we do in business.

So that was the night of Sunday 7th December 2008. This was just the beginning. Why did I want to leave this chapter out? Because in a few days, as word got out, we would be told by a very reliable source **WHO** did this. Can you now see why this was the chapter that was never meant to be, in more ways than one?

Read on, it gets a thousand times worse...

"The sooner you check our accounts and stop treating me as a fucking suspect the better this will be for all parties."

That was me on the Monday morning having been interviewed by C.I.D. That, I didn't mind one bit. What I massively objected to was the WAY we were treated. They just can't help themselves. This was very much a case of "guilty until proven innocent." In fairness, it didn't take them long to understand exactly where I was coming from. Sadly though, our "run-ins" with the police were only just beginning.

To this day I am ASTOUNDED by the manner in which this case was handled, which saw evidence missed, lost, destroyed, and blatant lies told. Best say "allegedly" here to be safe. I would have argued "no chance, not in this country" had I not lived it and seen it with my own eyes.

There will also be HUGE learnings in this Chapter, another reason why I decided to add it in. Learnings on insurance, insurance companies, and having prudent Disaster Plans in place. Let me say from the outset that our insurance broker and insurance provider were amazing. They too suffered from "must have been him," and they too got the same response as the police.

The following is factual, this shit happened. Get a coffee, this could take a while.

The Franchise Concept Saved Our Business

When we started to franchise the business back in 2006/2007, although this itself was an unmitigated disaster, it did have one major benefit: systems. With a franchise you're not selling the business, you're selling the system. In order for The Ink Shop to "sell the system," something fundamental had to happen first, it had to be **WRITTEN**. A small, minor detail!

Despite me being "Director of Everything," consultants were engaged to manage this entire process and prepare the business to be "Franchise Ready" by the end of 2007. From memory, that gave us around 18 months to systemise the business. **A reasonable time frame, we thought.**

One of the systems that was identified early on that would be essential, and require a lot of my input, was the Disaster Recovery Plan. This made sense, if you invest in a franchise where the production and supply of YOUR goods is dependent on ONE facility, you sure as hell want to know what the backup is, you want to SEE the bullet-proof **Plan B**.

Talking of "one," did you know **ONE** is the most dangerous number in business? Being reliant on **ONE** key customer, being reliant on **ONE** key member of the team (yes, that could be you), being reliant on **ONE** product or supplier, being reliant on **ONE** marketing strategy. Does that make sense? Is your business reliant on any "**One Thing**"?

I set about creating what would become known as the "**Disaster Recovery Protocol**." I think I had just seen the "Fourth Protocol" with Michael Caine and thought, "This is Defcon 1 stuff for business, so Protocol it is." There were three protocols, I honestly thought that having four would just be a step too far!

Level 1: Disruption to supply chain lasting no more than 48 hours. At the time, the vast majority of our print work was 5 working days. Disruption lasting 48 hours would have minimal impact on the business and would require some basic actions. These would include client contact, determining which orders were urgent and prioritising these. We only had a few Level 1s due to machine or component failures, severe weather, or staff illness.

Level 2: Disruption to the supply chain lasting in excess of 48 hours. This was a detailed plan as it covered eventualities of losing the production facility for a few days, or many weeks. This included having a number of strategic partners (printers) that we could send our work to. The "trigger" points for each action were very carefully considered. This plan was actually amazing. We never used a Level 2.

Level 3: On Monday 8th December 2008 the following email was sent to all Staff, Shop Managers and New Franchisees. The title of that email was, "**Level 3 Disaster Recovery Protocol Initiated**." Level 3 was "Total Loss or Significant Disruption of Unknown Time Frame." This is when you know the system works.

The fire on Sunday night started in one of the downstairs offices, and the flames, or in some cases, just the heat alone, quickly devastated that office (Planning Room), then the Accounts Office, then the Reception. There were two corridors in our downstairs offices, the fire door helped, although it did fail. The back offices were not fire damaged, although the smoke damage was horrific.

The upstairs offices were also smoke damaged and contained all our digital equipment. Our digital press, servers, and graphics studio were all upstairs. The fire was so intense that it climbed the outside wall and broke the windows, allowing smoke to enter the upstairs offices. The floor was concrete, so despite my office being directly above the seat of the fire, it escaped with fairly minor smoke damage.

The fire brigade had extinguished the fire in zip time, these guys don't get paid enough, they really don't. The downside of that is water. Have you ever seen the movie "Raise the Titanic?" The scene when she breaks above the waves and the water is flooding out from all compartments? **That's what our offices looked like**.

There was no power, no water. The press room was, by and large unaffected. A series of further fire doors had contained the blaze. Had the fire spread to the press hall it would have been a different story. Chemicals, inks, and at the time, over 100 pallets of paper.

So that was the picture on the Sunday evening. On Monday morning, armed with the Disaster Recovery Protocol, we all set about following the "checklist." Within 6 hours we had a portable office outside, portable toilets, a full display set up inside the office, laptops and PCs to access the CRM systems, and electricians working away inside the building. We had already made sure the main numbers were transferred to portable phones, the dog's bed was sorted, and a generator the size of a BUS was on hand to power the press should the electrician discover there were hidden issues with the mains. There wasn't, so the generator was only used for a day or so.

Thanks to the Disaster Recovery Protocol being in place, the business was back up and running on Tuesday at 3pm. We were making our own plates, printing our jobs, and doing all the finishing IN HOUSE, we were running at full capacity. The graphics studio was moved into the boardroom which had been unaffected. I was so proud of our entire team. When the shit hit the fan, every one of them became a superhero.

Writing a Disaster Recovery Plan in the cool light of day saved that business from untold hardship. I remember listening to a presentation recently by Sir Clive Woodward when he talked about "T-Cup," **Thinking Clearly Under Pressure**. Being clear on every area in sport where things can, and do, go wrong, and having a "T-CUP" plan for that. Utter genius. **What "T-Cup" plans should you have in your business**?

After I told this amazing story about Sir Clive, one of my friends said, "Was he not The Equalizer guy? What's he doing speaking at business events?" I paused, amazed at the utter lunacy of my friend. "That was Edward Woodward." Oh, how we laughed that day!!!

CSI Crime Scene, There Ends ANY Similarity to Professionalism

The entire downstairs offices were now a Crime Scene, and taped off like you see in "CSI Miami." That's where the similarity with anything amazing in the detection of crime ends, let me tell you.

At this point I had no idea what caused the fire and arson wasn't even considered. I was focussed on getting the business back up and running, and both the cops and fire department could see that. Very late on the Monday evening I realised one of the PCs in the account's office held vital information which was locally saved. I slipped under the CSI Miami lines and went into the office, armed with a torch. The first thing I remember was being totally distraught by the utter devastation. It was dark, it was burned beyond recognition, ceilings were gone, white walls were black, doors and light fittings had melted, it was a **WAR** scene. I made it to the office, shone my torch and grabbed the PC and other bits and pieces that I saw.

As I returned to the demilitarised zone there was a young police officer standing there. They were stationed outside. "Were you in the cordoned area?" **"YES.**" "You're not allowed in there, it's a crime scene." "Look, I had to get these vital PCs, OK?" The "You're not allowed in there" continued for what seemed like hours, he just constantly repeated himself. Eventually I snapped and said "Has your fucking cord got jammed? You're like the talking Bugs Bunny I had." I then looked up and saw the incredibly young officer for the first time. What I said next was poor, I know that, I shouldn't have, but it was a stressful situation and he was BUGGING me. "Does your mum know you're still out playing cop? If your dad sees you have his uniform, he'll go mental." He turned and walked away.

I was now done, it was something like 3am on the Tuesday morning, and I had been running on adrenalin since the phone went on Sunday night. Maybe my judgement was blurred, or maybe my incompetence filter was blocked, I don't know. **I never have been able to suffer fools gladly**.

I remember working away in the press hall about an hour or so later and heard the back door opening. A very tall, mature police officer with scrambled egg on his hat stood there, he looked none too pleased. I don't know what happened, he looked serious and ready for battle and I was ready too, I WAS READY. By the time we walked towards each other that had all changed, maybe he sensed I was just burst, and maybe I realised I had been a complete dick. Anyway, we shook hands and he reminded me why it was VITAL to preserve that scene, not to mention the dangers. I got it, I agreed, he was right. "Oh," he said, "I would appreciate some respect for my junior officers." He was right. I immediately went out, apologised, and we ended up having a right good chat about the young people who serve, the police, the army, the RAF, it was a welcome break.

Tuesday morning saw a mixture of people on site, police forensics, C.I.D, fire investigators, insurance, they were all milling around. Remember at this point I had NO IDEA what had caused the fire. What I did remember was the heat generated by chargers for radios we used. These were often too hot to touch, then it dawned on me, they had been left on, and that's where the fire started.

For a few days I was convinced this was the case. As we approached the end of the week that was ALL to change.

The people who had been in the building in the immediate days after the fire were fire investigators, police forensics and a forensic analyst from the insurance company. **That's a LOT of well qualified people**, yes? You may think that.

It was a few days after the fire, and late in the day, the CID officer in charge wanted to speak with me, NOW. "OK, come down." He appeared with the insurance forensic guy, which I thought was bizarre. He produced an evidence bag containing a plastic bottle and asked if we used any solvent in any such a container. It was a drinks bottle, so the answer there was NO. I gathered my print team and asked if anyone had decantcd solvent into the bottle. No, 100% not.

The contents of the bottle were leaking into the bag, it was **OBVIOUS** this was petrol. "Is that petrol?" I asked. "That's not been confirmed yet." I asked again, **VERY abruptly**. The same answer came back, equally abruptly. **I LOST IT**, this was taking a **VERY** serious and sinister turn. "Look, for fuck's sake, if it looks like a shite, smells like a shite, then it's a high probability it's a shite!" I had had enough of these two, I continued without taking a breath, "In your professional, *expert* opinion, do you think that is a petroleum-derived solution?" "**YES**" came the curt reply.

I can't remember when the call came, I think it was later that same week. The caller had WAY TOO MUCH information, and then the bombshell: he told me **WHO was responsible**.

I don't remember what happened next, several hours just disappeared before I was back on my feet.

It's important here to describe the front of the building. Looking left to right, the main entrance to the building via reception, the first small office with one window, the bigger planning office with three windows (where the fire started) and then the accounts office with one window, and finally the big roller shutter door to access the factory. It was a big unit, around 30,000 sq.ft.

I asked where the bottle was found and the cops agreed to show me. As we walked through, I was once again crippled by the devastation. It was dark, and although boarded up, the full picture was now evident.

We went into the first small office, and the officer pointed to the windowsill, "The bottle was found there," as he points towards the window. I started to look around and saw a large rock sitting on the worktop. "What's that?" "Oh, that fell from the roof." "No, it didn't, the roof first of all is 100% intact, nothing has broken off, besides this is not concrete, this is stone," I replied, furious that something so obvious was missed.

The picture was now building, and I presented this theory. The rock was thrown through the window. It smashed the window, went through the closed vertical blinds, and landed on the worktop. A "petrol bomb" was then thrown in, however, the plastic bottle did not make it through the blinds, fell and extinguished. We're not really sure what "their" idea was, would they throw in a burning rag after the petrol poured? Who knows? It was clearly the work of a complete moron. They had used a plastic bottle for a Molotov cocktail, it's like bringing a butter knife to a gun fight.

The police then finished, "They went to the room next door, smashed the window and poured in a large amount of accelerant and lit the fire." That was horrific to hear. I knew it, I expected it, yet to hear it was devastating. It was this ferocious fire that had triggered the alarm.

This is now where it gets worse. I had been warned about insurance companies being awkward with claims and was advised to take photos of every angle of every room. I had done that after all the forensic teams had gone. I checked these photos, and BINGO - there it was. The bottle of petrol on the windowsill **missed by every one of them**, it was the insurance guy that found it.

My argument was that he should never have removed that evidence. The people that started this fire were not the brightest, a PLASTIC petrol bomb FFS? They would perhaps not expect that bottle to survive and may have been careless when handling it. Alas, it was not to be, the bottle had been removed and placed in an evidence bag that was NOT suited for the purpose. The bottle then rolled about in his boot for a few days and had **LEAKED**. Any evidence was now well and truly **GONE**.

"Was there any CCTV?" I can't remember when I asked that. "NO, our officers went around all the units and asked." That was the reply I got.

This horror story then continued up to Christmas Eve. We had installed CCTV ourselves, now paranoid they would come back and finish the job. These were dark days, and dark times, and both Bobbie and I spent every waking hour either in the building or watching it at home on CCTV.

What was interesting was just how much wildlife there was. The CCTV would regularly pick up a variety of hedgehogs going about their nocturnal business, badgers, loads of foxes, they are really nosey, and a variety of deer that seemed to wander around the industrial estate as if they owned it. Maybe they did, the rent after all was really 'dear'!!!

The exact dates become a bit blurred for the next bit. This was on or around Christmas Eve. I was driving out of our unit and drove past the unit that faces the back of ours, it's the only road in and out of our part of the industrial estate. I noticed four golf ball cameras on the side of the building. An immediate U-turn followed, and I went in to enquire. The security manager comes out and explains he was waiting for the visit. "**I assumed they would have asked,**" he said. "They did, I replied." "**Let me tell you, no one has asked me about this**." Within a few minutes we play back the CCTV from Sunday night. Twenty minutes before the alarm activated a vehicle drives up the road and turns left, that takes you RIGHT to our unit. This was clearly a Mitsubishi Shogun-style vehicle and although the images were black and white, you could easily see the two-tone paintwork that was common on these vehicles. A few minutes AFTER the alarm activation time, this vehicle is once again seen driving out, this time, so fast it skips a few of the CCTV frames and is seen again heavily braking at the junction. There was not enough detail to see any registration.

I was fuming, this evidence was several weeks old. It was burned onto a CD (it was the way it was done then), and I proceeded very quickly, and very angrily towards the local Police Station.

I just couldn't contain myself, I was "incandescent with rage," that was how THEY later described me. I demanded to speak to the officer in charge, and demanded to know why I had been lied to about local businesses being asked about CCTV. Somewhere in the conversation it was mentioned that under the data protection act 1495, or some other outdated legislation, I had acted illegally in obtaining that footage, and had "compromised" it. Now, to be blunt, THEM lying about being in the building, and asking for evidence in the first place "compromised it." I am not sure exactly what happened after that, the CDs were taken from me. The originals, well, to this day they are snug and secure.

We now had a good idea WHO did this. Imagine the police being able to access the CITRAC cameras on the M8. Following the timeline of the vehicle leaving our premises, they could have easily tracked it to the M8, then got the registration. Their argument **INFURIATED** me: "That would never be enough to prosecute." Really, is that where we are? It may not have been enough to prosecute, it would almost certainly have identified the culprit for further investigation, **SURELY**?

I defaulted back to arrogant and insulting comments. "Seriously, you people could not convict Hitler!" was the opener. Followed by me walking about, stepping over a non-existent obstacle, repeating the following phrase as I did so: "A murder was reported, damned if I can see a body," as I continued to step over the "corpse." I don't remember what happened next, I was either arrested or just cautioned. This whole "investigation" was an eye-opener for me and became the subject of a formal police complaint. If the police had come to me and said this was a really low profile and low priority case, I would have accepted that, and appreciated the honesty. Instead, it was handled like something out of a Laurel and Hardy movie, just not as funny.

You'll not be surprised to learn that the perpetrator was never caught. As the weeks and months progressed more and more information came from a variety of sources. No one was interested in hearing the story.

So that was the fire. Dark days. Life goes on, the building was re-built, the equipment was all replaced, and business continued. Thanks to the Disaster Planning, and a lot of people who really had our back.

What Are the Learnings for YOU?

There are massive learnings in this chapter that must be shared. The first one is obvious. In the cool light of day prepare for the worst. Prepare for all your "T-Cup" moments (Thinking Clearly Under Pressure) and also the "Doomsday Scenario." This saved the business.

The other point is insurance. Our broker advised us to take a specific PRINT business policy. That was the **second-best** piece of advice we ever got. This policy covered loads of things that other policies excluded. Be careful about the "warranties" on some of these. Again, the broker pointed these out, and they included things like secure flam (flammable) stores, no dirty rags in bins overnight, no wastepaper bins, etc. As they had been highlighted, the guys were superb at keeping to them.

Why was that the second-best bit of advice? The **BEST** bit of advice was paying the extra £150 to cover a Loss Adjuster who would be appointed for us. In the event of a claim, this firm worked on OUR behalf. Let me tell you, stressful situations don't come any worse than this, and having this firm working behind the scenes on our behalf was a life saver. Insurers work a certain way, speak a certain language, this was like having a P.A. and a translator all in one.

Final piece of advice, honesty. Let me share a story that we later found out was a huge turning point in the insurance claim process. The insurance company sent their loss adjuster, a serious and very unhappy looking guy. Our loss adjuster escorted the visit and we went around the "battle site." This took hours, as he detailed all the damage. When we arrived upstairs the digital press was running at full speed. The company that supplied the machine were keen to get another sale and had issued an "invalidation of warranty" certificate. They claimed the corrosive smoke could damage the machine and cause faults years down the line. As a result, the press was being claimed against the insurance. I don't remember commenting; however, I was later reminded that I said how ridiculous that was, and that there was nothing wrong with that machine, IMHO.

As we progressed into the upstairs offices there was a MONSTER Plasma TV. Back in the day these were mighty expensive items. "I don't see that on the claim?" the adjuster asked. "It's not, that's from our house, there was some warranty work being done, and it was delivered back here the week before the fire, tough shit on us, eh? I'm not sure if the house insurance covers it, I'll check." That was my reply. "It's not a business item," I confirmed. Nobody said anything, it was a throwaway comment, yet right there, right then, that insurer knew I wasn't taking the piss in any way, shape or form.

The whole process was seamless, there were no issues with payments or claims. The final claim was being made after the building was finished. The new carpets, new walls, indeed new everything, made the business **ALIVE** again. We were sitting in the new boardroom, and we presented what we thought was the final figure. It wasn't a massive amount, just a lot of the final bits and pieces. "**My figures don't agree with yours**," the insurance assessor stated. "**Here we go**…"

As he passed HIS final figures to my assessor a wry smile appeared on his face. As he slid the statement over to me it was £4,000 MORE than mine. "OK, we'll go with your figures, then!"

So, that was "Fire in The Hold." A difficult chapter with big learnings for all business owners.

What Doesn't Kill You Makes You Stronger

You may be wondering what prompted this? When our business was at its peak, we were very aggressive and very good at marketing and selling. It's safe to say that we were not well liked by a number of competitors who simply could not keep up. A huge part of our business was menus, we did MILLIONS of them every month. It was becoming a very competitive market, and one competitor in particular was hurting as a result of our increased aggressive nature to gain market share.

In the days after the fire, a number of people phoned me, and the same name came up again and again. This was all passed to the police, and this person was indeed interviewed under caution. Nothing came of it, and business continued, indeed in the months after the fire we turned up the heat on the menu market, and totally dominated it for the next 2-3 years. **Don't get mad, get even**.

That was a risk for sure, you can either surrender or fight. I had worked too hard to even consider the surrender option; besides, they wouldn't dare try that again? The security at the plant now resembled Fort Knox anyway. We had "bullet proof" glass installed that made smashing the windows virtually impossible (planning restrictions prohibited window shutters). We had motion detectors fitted at a few secret locations and an 18-camera, high-resolution recording CCTV system. We had also taken another growth spurt, and were now operating 24 hours a day, 6 days a week.

The fire was just another "chapter," it nearly killed me. However, in business what doesn't kill you makes you stronger.

Finally, and you could not make this up: a few years later I was at a printers' golf day at Gleneagles and partnered with the person that we believed either set the fire or ordered it. **Isn't that interesting**? The wounds had healed, the business was booming, however as we approached the furthest and quietest point of the course, I asked the question… "**WHY did you set fire to my business**?" I asked that coolly and calmly. "Well," he said, "let me tell you something interesting…" **And that, is our little secret**.

I went on to win that game on the final putt on the 18th green on the Queens that day, it was a good day.

Chapter Ten - How to Wreck Your Dreams

Don't worry, things aren't about to get all "woo woo." Bear with me on this one, it's really important. In chapter 3 I discussed Planning and the "Vision Planner." A segment of that Planner was devoted to "Goals" and for a VERY good reason.

Now, let's be clear before we dive in. Goals are not dreams, and dreams are not goals. Goals are set, and when combined with ACTION, may lead towards the dream. However, we're not issuing guarantee certificates here. The achievement here depends on 1) The dream, 2) the goals set, and 3) the action you take. Let's just be clear, before the letters start.

Going by the amount of business owners I have met and worked with, a few of you are undoubtedly rolling your eyes right now. Dreams aren't for you, are they? No, of course not. You're more than happy with the way things are right now. There's no need to change, is there? Goodness me, we can't possibly "dream," we're British, and if you did sneak in a wee dream there, a bit of big picture vision, **there's no way that's being shared out loud, is it**?

Here's the thing, when we were kids, we dreamed big, and reached for the stars. We had ambitions of being astronauts, fighter pilots, explorers, whatever. When we were kids, we dreamed, and we dreamed BIG. What the hell happened?

Now, when you started your business you had a dream, of course you did, otherwise WHY did you do it? What was the dream you had? We're not talking about the 5-year Vision for the business here, we're talking about the dream you had when you started your business. What was it? You know what it was. You might not have told anyone, you do know **exactly** what it is though. Has it maybe become a bit faded?

I have a theory on dreams that I'll share with you, this is it: "**The perception of reality is the killer of dreams**." It's my theory, there's no science behind it. You see, when we're kids, we have no concept of "reality," whatever the hell reality is. As we grow up and experience the roller coaster that is life, and we invariably meet the "Glass-Half-Empty" losers, it taints us, we allow it to dampen **our dreams**, we let ourselves doubt that anything is possible. Does that make sense?

"Oh, hell no, you can't do that." "Be realistic and go and get a REAL job." "Your brother's a solicitor, and you want to do WHAT?" Get the idea? The WAY we are allowed, or allow ourselves to dream changes. The "**reach for the stars and to hell with reality**" attitude we had as kids is replaced by "reach for the TV buttons and to hell with the book." Now listen, that's okay. Sadly, the world needs 99% of people to do that, there's no room for everyone to be an entrepreneur. It's an exclusive club with limited membership.

It's not okay for you though, **YOU are a business owner**, you are the top dog, you are the top 1% that will make it **BIG**. Only if you **dream big**. This is often referred to as "The Millionaires Mindset." Yes, we're back to cash again. It really doesn't matter what your dreams are, cash and profit are the mechanisms that will get you there. So, keep your capitalist hat on, at least for the time being.

Does "FEAR" play a part in your dreams, or lack thereof? The fear of failure perhaps, the fear of being wrong, or proved wrong. F.E.A.R of course stands for FALSE Expectations Appearing Real. In other words, the majority of fear is in our head.

Now, if you're out in the Canadian wilderness, and a huge bear appears, looking for the equivalent of steak and chips, then FEAR stands for something else, Fuck Everything And RUN. Don't get the two confused.

Did you know that when you're born, you have only TWO FEARS "built in?" Yep, mamma nature has put a few fears in there just to make sure you're okay and get past first base. The fear of loud noises and the fear of falling, and that's it. The other fears that we pick up along the journey of life, well, we plant them ourselves for some reason that I'm sure a book somewhere will cover.

The glass is always **100% full**

50% water + 50% air = 100% FULL

All the fears and phobias that many have, they are not there from day one. Hippopotomonstrosesquippedaliophobia is the longest word in the dictionary and, wait for it, this is a real piss take - it's the fear of long words! Seriously guys, this is when you know your fear and phobia chain is being pulled. The world has gone, officially, mad. No one can confirm how many "fears and phobias" there are, it's estimated at 50,000. Oh, just for business owners, many of you suffer from Nomophobia, the fear of not getting a phone signal. Seriously? The best one however is phobophobia, the fear of fears. Wow, and to think we were born with just TWO.

It's All Down to Money, It Always Is

Here's an exercise for you. Write down **THREE** figures (incomes). The first is what you **NEED** just to survive and pay the bills and live a basic life. Now write down what your **IDEAL** salary is, the one that pays all the bills, upgrades the car, pays for 4 holidays a year, etc. Now write down what the **DREAM** salary is.

Does that make sense? THREE figures. What you need, what you want and what you dream of one day achieving?

Here's the thing, I struggled with that. I never asked where you actually are currently, I'm guessing for most it's between NEED and IDEAL, closer to need than ideal perhaps? So why did I struggle? Simply because the DREAM is the 100% focus and I don't allow anything to cloud that picture. Ideal for me isn't a consideration.

There's a couple of illustrations that help explain this, too. The first one is the "Self-Limiting Belief," calm down, it's not woo woo. In our heads we have a lot of noise, interference, previous experiences, advice from the mate in the pub etc, etc, etc. The REAL dream gets trapped behind a layer of "interference" and we settle for a lesser, more achievable dream. This is another reason why you want the morons in your life to exit starboard right.

The other illustration I like to share is, "Reach for the Stars," only because you're rolling your eyes again and sighing, "I've heard that all before," and yes you have. However, don't reach for the stars, reach for the galaxy far, far away. Then, if you do fall short, well, you're light years past the Moon and WAY past the stars. Too many people find the going tough and "re-adjust" the dream - don't downgrade the dream, upgrade the activity.

I am going to hazard a guess that you have a dream that you've never shared with anyone. Why? Is it because we're British and that's just the way we do things? Is it because you're a bit embarrassed about what people may think or say? That never happened when we were kids, what changed? **Are we back to FEAR again**?

There is nothing surer in life than a MORON being present at some point. You know, the one that always has a problem for every solution. Every silver lining soon gets a cloud. Life is tough, and the glass is always half empty? You need to get rid of people like this. I had a "friend" many years ago, honestly, if he could shit gold bricks, he would complain about the income tax implications. He was also an Air Traffic Controller when I was in the RAF. How he never had an aluminium shower amazes me (that's what we call a mid-air collision in ATC.) We stayed friends, however, when I started my business, he really just annoyed me. Morons like that need to be weeded out of your life. Does that sound harsh? Well try this, write down your biggest DREAM, what you REALLY want, and go and share it with your moron mate. I would buy tickets for that. Guaranteed they are going to shoot you down, and tell you to be "realistic." Realistic never killed anyone, maybe just a few million dreams!

Remember, you become the **AVERAGE of the five people you hang around with most**. Who is your average five? Also, and you should try this, you EARN the average of the five people you hang around with most. Isn't that interesting? You see, in life you get what you tolerate.

A Formula for Success, Really?

The good news is, there is actually a FORMULA for success. Here it is. D x G x L x P x A = Success. I am not sure who the original author of that formula is, I am certainly not trying to claim it as my own. What are the key components?

DREAM: every success starts with the dream of what success LOOKS LIKE. Easy one to start.

GOALS: obvious, once you have the dream you start to set a series of goals to achieve it.

LEARNING: now it gets real. You have the dream, you've set the goals, what do you need to know and learn in order to achieve it? This is where we come back to learn and earn. The only time earn comes before learn is in the dictionary. You need to learn the stuff.

PLAN: you knew it was going to be in there somewhere.

ACTION: obvious. You can do all the learning and planning on the planet, and if you don't commit to action then it's just a waste of time. Things won't magically happen just because you have learned and planned. A poorly executed plan will return higher rewards than an exceptional plan confined to the top drawer.

Put that all together and you're on your way to SUCCESS. If you look at any successful business owner or entrepreneur, EVERY component part has been there on their journey.

Are you a glass-half-empty, or a glass-half-full person? Be honest. I'm neither: why settle for half anything? My glass is FULL, 50% liquid PLUS 50% air = 100% full. Now, on a Saturday I have been guilty of having a glass "very empty," not for long though.

You see, it's how you view things. It's a bit like asking an Entrepreneur what $1 + 0$ is. $1 + 0$ can only equal one, surely? That's what we're taught by convention. $1+0 = 10$, you only assumed it was a collocation of the two numbers. Entrepreneurs see things differently, and challenge conventional thinking.

When I had the Ink Shop the dreams were woolly, fuzzy and not written down. There was no formula, or if there was it would be D + H = Fingers Crossed. Dreams + Hope = Fingers Crossed. Hope isn't a good strategy for anything in business; Hopeium is also very addictive.

How To Wreck Your Dreams

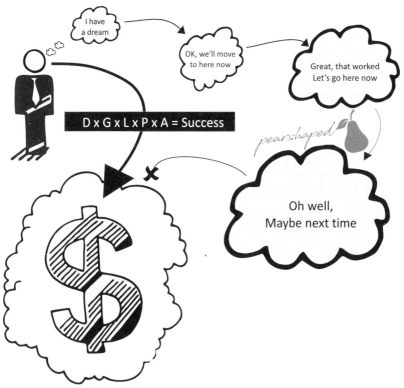

Don't let dreams become clouded or even restricted by previous "fears" or self limiting beliefs.

Follow the formula - dream BIG.

D x G x L x P x A = Success

dreams x goals x learning x planning x action = success

How To Wreck Your Dreams

You need to navigate through the interference - **no one is going to do it for you**. Don't downgrade the dream, **upgrade the ACTION!**

Once you set your dream you need to be flexible with it, this is important. As the journey towards that dream becomes difficult or challenging, downgrade the dream, otherwise you're heading for disappointment. Now remember, this chapter is "How to WRECK Your Dreams," so that's sound advice if that's your goal. The reality for everyone else is, **NEVER**, and I mean EVER downgrade your dream - **INCREASE THE ACTION**.

When I had my business there was a lot of items ticked off the bucket list and "dreams fulfilled." Owning an £186,000 Aston Martin is a DREAM, and a pretty damn big one at that. The thing is, it was never on the long-term dream plan, because there wasn't one. As the graphic shows, it went from "dream A" to "dream B" to "dream C" without any structure or plan. It just so happens that one of these happened to be an Aston Martin. Now here's the weird thing, as much as I loved that car, getting it felt more of an "entitlement" rather than achieving a lifelong dream.

I remember when I was "just a lad," I was with my dad in Johnstone and there was a garage there that had an Aston Martin in the window. It would have been the V8 Vantage, now that was a muscle car that even today looks impressive. I remember gasping at the price tag and asking my dad "Who owns cars like these?"

That reminds me of another Aston story, actually the Ducati fits in here too. It would have been the summer of 2005. I get a call asking me if I would be interested in going to RAF Leuchars for a family day, they were interested in having supercars race the Tornado. After thinking about that for 1.2 seconds, I was IN. The following weekend was duly blocked off in the diary (that I never used).

The rear tyres were looking a tad depleted. They didn't last long, they seemed to be made with a mixture of rubber compound and Blu Tak. I duly ordered two new ones from the Aston Dealership in Edinburgh and arranged to have them fitted en route to RAF Leuchars.

That was an interesting day to say the least. A few "laps" around the taxiways, a few doughnuts with some of the pilot guys, and we were ready to race the TORNADO. The first two were heading out and the Aston was ON. The rules were simple, line up with the jet, and as soon as the jet started to roll, the race would start. The Tornado was on the runway (I feel embarrassed having to point that out) and the Aston was on the parallel taxiway.

Now, if you know your Tornados, you know they have a secret weapon, **AFTERBURNER**. The crew went full power on the brakes, lit the fires, then released the brakes. The Aston was an amazing car with a 6-litre V12 delivering 520 bhp to the back wheels. There is no way on this planet that even the Tornado would outrun this.

The "finish" line was agreed as the point where the jet "rotated," and the front wheel lifted off the runway. That was being recorded by one of the pilots, a wee bit biased there, maybe.

Anyway, it was irrelevant as the Tornado was at least 3 car lengths in front by the time it took off.

Not so the Ducati, in the day this was the bike to have, and my neighbour and I had the only 2 in the country. The Ducati 999R Xerox Replica. Since it was "Xerox" we never referred to it as a replica, instead a "copy." Anyway, the photographic evidence was presented for all to see. When the second Tornado went, the bike WON. It passed the jet before it had a chance to lift off. The pilot (from memory) was Nappie or Napster, so impressed was he by the Ducati, he bought one.

The day continued with much hilarity and a few more drifts and doughnuts, then it was time for home.

The Aston was sold when the business started to hit tough times. Common sense and reality set in. I spoke with the dealership and they offered to buy the car. Clearly it had devalued more than a third world currency and the offer was just ridiculous, probably due to the fact that they would want to make £40,000 on it, too.

I am often asked "would you buy another Aston?" "Absolutely, only with Tier Three Cash Flow, though.

Opinions and A Reality Check

I want to return to "Dreams" now, simply because I did manage to wreck them successfully, although by default, also achieve them.

As you have been reading this book, you will have gathered an opinion. We have more than likely never met, yet you will have formed an opinion of me. Reading the stories of flying by the seat of my pants, the helicopter, the car, there's a high probability that **your opinion is not flattering**?

There's a high probability that some of you are thinking, maybe not saying, just thinking, "This guy's a dick, he deserved to lose that business." Hey, that's okay, because I AGREE with you. I would not have written the book otherwise, or I would have called it, "The Best Way Possible to Fly by The Seat of Your Pants."

The person I was then, is not the person I am today. I am still super-motivated, driven, ambitious, hate lots of detail, and impatient, however that's why understanding DISC is so important. That's just ME. Today, my "High D" DISC style stands for "Dominant," back then, it was "DICK." With the clarity of hindsight, I can see that now. When I had my business, my "Chimp" was running it 90% of the time. You really must read The Chimp Paradox by Dr Steve Peters, it's one of those books that does change your life, **if you WANT it to**.

This whole book has been written in "High D" style: short, abrupt, lacking intricate detail. If I was a "C" or "High C," which is "Compliant" on the DISC system, then I would crave detail, and this would not be the "How to Wreck Your Business" book, it would be 2,000 pages of the "**Encyclopedia of How to Wreck Your Business**."

This all goes back to "**unconsciously incompetent**," you don't know what you don't know. Running my business, I never had a coach or mentor. I had no one holding me to account, or challenging decisions, and God help those who tried. **Do you see the problem**? I was a HUGE reason why that business never progressed towards £5m and £10m - it could have, EASILY. I am not going to say "fail" here, as that arrogance and drive built the business, however what was once an asset soon became a liability that hindered growth. A business that isn't growing is dying!

A few years ago, I met a previous software supplier at a Print Exhibition. I was coaching at this point and was there with a client. We got chatting, and I was telling him about coaching and how it worked, we just chatted generally for an hour or so. We ultimately never went with that supplier although did keep in touch. At the end of the conversation he said something that surprised me, it didn't shock me, but was an eye opener. He said, "Stuart, great to meet you again, and this coaching journey sounds amazing. Let me tell you, YOU are a completely different person now. I am glad we never worked together as I felt you were one conversation away from losing it all the time." **He was of course absolutely right**. I can see that today, **blissfully ignorant then**.

Let me share a few things with you. This book is all about learning and sharing, and that starts with congruency. I do what I say and say what I do. Today, I don't do anything in business without a plan, business plan, marketing plan, systems plan, financial plan, and everything is in a diary and default diary. My "NOT DO" lists are amazing, "this week I am just NOT touching ………………………." The Dreams are much clearer, much simpler, and less financial based. Everything previously was fast cars, fast bike, boats, helicopters, aeroplanes (I did own an aircraft too), just "things."

For this example, I am going to show you how the "Reach for the Stars" illustration works. To recap, there's three levels. Reach for the **MOON**. Reach for the **STARS**. And (my addition) **Reach for a GALAXY Far, Far Away**. The logic is simple. If you reach for the Moon and fall short, you're nowhere. You're in the void of empty space. If you reach for the stars and fall short, well you've passed the Moon. You will have read and seen that analogy 1,000 times?

How To Wreck Your Dreams

Don't reach for the moon, or the stars. **Reach for a galaxy far, far away**.

Dream BIG.

What if you reach for a Galaxy Far, Far Away? Where are you if you fall short? You're still past the stars. More importantly, where are you **WHEN** you achieve that dream? This is all mindset, whether you think you CAN, or whether you think you CAN'T, you're right.

Let's put some text on this now. These are my dreams, okay? If you ridicule them, then you are considered a "moron" and please return this book for a full refund. MORON of course stands for "**M**y **O**pinions **R**eally **O**utweigh (your) **N**onsense (dreams)."

Reach for the Moon: My dream is to be well respected in the business community and drive my business forward to earning levels in excess of what was previously achieved through print (all about ME).

Reach for the Stars: My dream is to be the "go-to guy" in the business community and build a business that is "oversubscribed." For my book to become a "reference" for business owners throughout the UK. To build and create a lifestyle that combines the balance of business and pleasure (Mostly about me, a bit about you).

Reach for a Galaxy, Far, Far Away: My DREAM is to tackle the business failures in the UK and in particular Scotland, which are simply unacceptable. I want to eradicate what is currently 1000s of families torn apart through the pain of business failure, to avoid the shattering of dreams for so many people who had nothing more than a desire to better themselves. That is just not fair or just. My VISION is to have a community, a culture, where business failure is the EXCEPTION, and not the NORM. My dream is to be a LinkedIN "Influencer," where the posts I share have true meaning and value to all business owners, where people follow, and listen intently. My Dream is for the book to be a "lightbulb" for business owners throughout the WORLD, who are trapped or following a similar path, for that book to HELP those who need or want it. To one day to sit on BBC's The One Show and share the story… **I have a DREAM** (all about you).

Not ONCE was money a factor in the "REAL" dream, the **dream is a**

vision, and just try and stop me, isn't that **VERY** interesting?

If you look at the above three levels, you'll see something interesting. They started off "woolly" and not really detailed, and clearly financial based. **More about ME than you**. Hey dude, they are my dreams. Peel back the layers, and the true vision today **REALLY** appears. No mention of an Aston Martin, although if there's one going, I'll take it. I may be off on some crusade, that doesn't need to mean walking with sandals and a backpack - crusades can be equally successful through driving the Aston to the Waldorf Astoria.

I remember reading a quote a few months back about "advice," and the author wrote, "Take advice from someone who has **DONE it**, and not simply read it." Take advice from a failed business owner before you read books on how to be a billionaire, they carried on "**you would never take investment advice from a poor person**," that made me laugh, and I have to agree with every word.

My point, as always, **DREAM BIG**. Be clear on what **YOU** really want, NOT what others may think or say. Does THAT make sense? D x G x L x P x A = **Whatever YOU want it to be**.

Chapter Eleven - How Appropriate (Franchising)

It wasn't deliberate to have this as Chapter 11, there's a subtle irony there. This chapter is going to share what was the biggest mistake in the history of the Ink Shop. This is not to say that franchising your business is wrong, far from it, it's a great way to grow your business, if it is "franchisable," and there is where the problem lay, **and the story begins**.

Before we take a journey down "Franchise Lane," it's important to share some details about our main competitors at this time. The year is 2007, and we're coming to an end of the "Glory Years," and whilst the cracks in the business were there, they weren't yet evident. By 2007 Printing.com had grown a significant network of franchised print outlets throughout the UK, and were getting stronger in Scotland. They operated the same "hub and spoke" model that we did, namely one production facility serving a number of High Street Print Stores.

Now, the thing with Printing.com was they were much slicker and smoother than we were. That's good, having a competitor that keeps you sharp and focussed is no bad thing. Their branding and corporate identity was way more powerful than ours, in fairness they were a PLC and at that time had a fairly significant £20m+ turnover. **We did however, punch WAY above our weight**. That said, they had a better brand and a growing market share, it was the "enemy at the gate."

What developed with Printing.com is best described as a "love/hate" relationship, the two main directors of Printing.com had very different personalities, and we would regularly would lock horns with them, as well as get the odd solicitor's letter. It was usually because we had pushed our luck and maybe infringed the odd bit of copyright here and there. It wasn't copying, it was a homage!!!

In fairness, dialogue between us prevented this going to full-out war, and indeed we would often share "industry-specific" topics that were beneficial to both parties, with maybe the odd red herring thrown in, they were

competitors after all. It's fair to say that over the years a solid friendship and mutual respect was developed, that indeed continues to this day.

Cyber Squatting

There was one particular incident, this is one of those moments when you know you have crossed the line and it could result in a serious arse kicking. I'm not sure what year this was, however, it was before browsers got good at predicting the web page you were looking for. I would make a point of looking at the Printing.com website to see what offers were on, new products, services, and generally keeping an eye for more stuff to copy!!

I can now admit that our product expansion range was down to them, that brought advantages and of course, disadvantages. Our product range was popular and narrow, but as the years progressed the range increased substantially, and the economies of scale that made the business profitable were being eroded with some of the new products. The key of course was keeping the material choices limited, it didn't matter if it was a leaflet, voucher, brochure or booklet, if the paper was the same, then these could all be mixed. Our compromise was to increase the range massively yet keep these to 8 or 10 core paper stocks.

Anyway, on this particular day, in this particular year, I was out of the office and went to look at their website. www.printnig.com returned a **"page not found"** error. Not sure what that meant, I dug a bit deeper, was the site down? Had they not renewed the domain (unlikely)? Then it dawned on me, a typo, **printnig not printing**. Damn!! "Hold on a minute, how many other people did that?" Within a few minutes **printnig.com** was duly bought and pointed to the Ink Shop website.

Content that I was a marketing and strategy genius, I went about my business for the next few months and could see that a fair degree of traffic was indeed coming from that site, **what a result**.

I had the most annoying habit of analysing mail, yes, in those days a lot of posted mail was received. Hand-written white envelopes which were thin were usually cheques, they were still popular. Some millennials might need to Google "cheques." In effect, a cheque was a bit of paper promising to pay you money which was more like playing Russian Roulette as to whether the bank would clear said cheque. Indeed, modern payment methods have eradicated the best excuse for **NOT** paying. When was the last time you were told "**Cheque's in the post**"?

Fat envelopes with a solid "square" were usually orders with disks. Yes, we still used them too. If you're unsure, Google that as well. It was a bonus if they contained cheques, which most of them did, as the model was "**full payment with order**."

Then of course there was the UFO mail, "**unidentified folded objects**." This particular one was well typed, franked, in a vellum laid (nice paper) envelope. It had a "legal look" about it. Yes, indeed it was. It had come to their attention… blah, blah, blah, **printnig.com** had been rumbled.

Now, in fairness, the demands were light. Cessation of all activity, and hand over the domain. Really, this was a **GREAT** marketing strategy. I called our solicitors, a large Glasgow firm whose own letterhead was half the A4, as the list of senior partners, partners, and associates was so vast it took up the other half. I explained the story, what we'd done, the demands made, and then asked do we need to surrender the domain? The reply was **CLASSIC**. "Stuart, are you beside a PC right now?" "YES." "Good, very good, email the CEO immediately and accept the terms of their letter, then follow that with a letter sent recorded delivery to their solicitors confirming the same, and transfer the domain as soon as you put the phone down."

After our solicitor had sighed, and set his stopwatch for billing obviously, he went on to explain the line that we had crossed. "Cyber Squatting," I think he defined it as. Long story short, we could have had our arse severely kicked by that action, yet the guys at Printing.com, who were keen to give us a hard time for using a COLOUR similar to theirs just a few weeks prior, were prepared to let this one go. I don't doubt that they knew just how much that would have hurt us. Nice people after all.

Out of this friendship the annual "Ink Shop - PDC" Golf Day was born. I have no idea how we ended up playing with "camouflaged" golf balls, or whose idea it was to have "Happy Gilmore" tee shots off the 2nd on the PGA Centenary at Gleneagles. Hit that ball right and it **WORKS**. Happy is the boy. The reality of course was a mis-hit either went 4 yards in the right direction, or 400 the wrong way. Good days indeed, and we never took them too seriously, obviously.

Have you ever played golf with your biggest and fiercest competitor? It's really bizarre, it's a mixture of fun, one-upmanship, digging for information and most of all, an amazing desire to win - made all the more complicated when Pro V1s are being shot at right angles 400 yards into the Perthshire wilderness. It was, from the 1st to the 18th, a RIOT.

The Franchise Concept

Printing.com was a FRANCHISE and a very good one at that. Their brand was strong and consistent, it was building quickly in the marketplace and new stores were opening at (for us) an alarming rate. Their stores were quirky yet professional and we were coming up against them more and more. This was an issue that needed addressed. The advantage we had was they were a PLC, and as such released various reports and statements to the "City" and this of course would include their growth plans.

We knew that a storm was coming, and it did, just not from where we thought it would. This is 2007 going into 2008. Fannie Mae and Freddie Mac were now starting to indicate that not all is rosy in the financial markets. I do recall saying, "with names like that they deserve to fail." At the time we thought the storm was going to come from Printing.com, so we watched with envious eyes, and slowly, and surely, we drew up our plans against them. The war of the printing worlds was about to start.

A funny thing happens when you have a strong competitor, especially one with deep marketing pockets. They raise awareness in the marketplace of their products and services, and yours!!! As Printing.com grew, we had a significant increase in footfall, it's the advantage of having price superiority.

Now, that doesn't always work in your favour, very often customers who are purely price driven can be problematic. Not always of course, we do all like a bargain.

The Ink Shop was very aggressively priced in the marketplace. We had the right balance of costs, overheads and retail price. Whilst we were nowhere near as impressive-LOOKING as Printing.com, we were pretty damn good at what we did. The "basic" look of our stores, whilst weak from a BRAND perspective, was superb at keeping the COGS (Cost Of Goods Sold) under control. Where it went pear-shaped for us was the TRADE work. This disrupted the perfect balance of COGS vs INCOME.

This was an important turning point, and worthy of a pause to reflect and really hammer this home. TWO fundamental mistakes are being made at this point, yet all indicators point to these being great strategies to grow the business. All indicators being "gut," and a few calculations on the back of an envelope. Increasing Trade Work and Franchising **seemed** the "right thing to do."

Let's look at Trade work first, and this was before the arse was well and truly ripped right out of this market. The idea was this, to supply smaller printers, designers, and copy shops with our range of print services. This was all full payment with order, so great for cash flow and risk. This meant that we only had to find **ONE** customer, yet receive multiple orders from them, so great at keeping marketing costs down. Ten trade clients would bring more work than potentially one HUNDRED end-user clients. That's the advantages. **Have you worked out the disadvantages**?

Okay, the disadvantages. The easy one, **PRICE**. Trade work was heavily discounted. You'll see the "Dangers of Discounting" and quickly establish that discounting is a MUG'S game. A 10% discount with a 25% margin means you need to sell **67% MORE just to MAKE the same**. Now, here's the thing, the discounts were WAY MORE than 10%. In reality, factoring in all costs, hassle, we were printing for nothing and doing little more than bringing cash into the business.

Trade printing was becoming a race to the bottom. **"You don't want to win that race"** was the common statement. Well actually, NO, that's not correct, that's NOT the worst option. The worst option, the def-con one moment, is coming in SECOND. At least if you win the race to the bottom you have the CUSTOMERS. We had cut our throat and come in **SECOND**, that meant we didn't have the VOLUME needed to balance the economies of scale to actually make this work.

At the time though, this wasn't seen as a huge problem. The full effect of this wouldn't really be felt until a year or so later. We're now in a price-driven, Trade market, we're now not the dominant player in that market, and Trade work is now 60% of turnover, because it was "easy." WAS!! The issue with the Trade market was due to the over-capacity in the industry, a few serious players were entering the market. There's no loyalty in Trade work, so the ONLY way for a newcomer to get clients quickly was to print fast and cheap. The prices were being driven down, and down, and down.

Here's an example to show the insanity of this. Our bestselling product in the "Glory Days" was 5,000 A5 Leaflets, glossy paper for £99. Our customers were AMAZED at that price, and we printed these all day long. The year after the Ink Shop closed the "Trade Wars" went up a few gears and you could buy 5,000 DOUBLE-SIDED leaflets, gloss paper for **£35, delivered FREE**. The arse had well and truly been ripped right out of that market.

As the market became more and more volatile, we stuck to a core range of products and accepted that we were not the cheapest, and never would be. We focussed instead on quality and service, and whilst 80% didn't care, it was price or nothing, that **20% was enough for us**. Everything in business is 80:20. Vilfredo Pareto had worked that one out.

We're going to come back to this again, this is all linked to "Franchising." The Global Economic Meltdown was underway, yet no one could predict the severity. Northern Rock was 2008, we started Franchising in 2007.

The World Is About to Melt

Let's recap on where the business is at THIS POINT. The glory years are coming to an end (that's a hindsight observation), trade work is massively reducing margin, the lucrative menu market was now being copied by the prestigious printers who realised it was actually a cash cow. Our main competitor was growing by the month and dominating the "SME end-user marketplace." The COMBINATION of this, **AND** a decline in print spend, **AND** the Global Meltdown that had now been triggered was **the beginning of the end**.

Imagine we had a detailed PLAN of what we wanted to achieve? Instead, we (sorry, me) felt like a rabbit in the headlights. I had gone from years of doing no wrong, to seeing the business start to unravel. Refer back to the "Right Road and Wrong Track," I was in **DENIAL** that there was anything wrong. We'd be fine, it always was.

This is Titanic stuff, it wasn't ONE error, it was many. We were going too fast, we thought we were "unsinkable," so it was Full Speed Ahead and fuck the icebergs. What was that bang? Even THEN we (Okay ME) still thought we were unsinkable. Even when I was up to my arse in ice-cold water, I could only think of suing the shipyard! Refer once again to the WRONG ROAD. **Blame**.

Meanwhile, Back at the Bat Cave

The Trade Work issue was "running parallel" with the franchise project. We could see the way the trade market was heading, so that only fuelled the desire to carry on with franchising. Not realising at the time, we were about to enter a whole new world of EXTREME pain.

I was smart enough to know that franchising was BIG, and that specialist consultants were needed, I was smart enough to know that. I knew that I could not take on any more, and this project needed handled correctly by professionals who were smarter than me.

 I'll repeat this later in the chapter.

Are You On The
Right Road,
Or The **Wrong Track**?

The Right R.O.A.D.

Knowing You're On The *Right Road* Means...
Responsible For Your Actions
Ownership Is Always Taken
Accountable To Yourself & Others
Decisive In Your Nature

The Wrong T.R.A.C.K.

Knowing You're On The *Wrong Track* Means...
Total Lack Of Respect
Refuse To Acknowledge Issues (Denial)
Attack & Blame Others
Change Is Always Resisted
Keep Using Excuses For Everything

Where are you?

The first thing I set about doing was a SWOT analysis, identifying Strengths, Weaknesses, Opportunities and THREATS. Now, you know what my planning patience threshold was, so this SWOT was more of a **SWAT SWOT**, planning with some flash bangs thrown in, creating lots of noise, a bit of confusion, and getting the hell out ASAP with minimal casualties and reporting back with a "sit rep."

The report created was actually very well detailed (for me), and led onto the creation of the "Franchise Plan." Now, this is a book on its own, so the idea was simple. People would BUY the franchise, operate from a store front in a secondary trading location to keep costs low. They would buy all print from us which would be provided at lower than trade rates, and we'd all sell at the same RETAIL price. This would mean that a company-owned store wouldn't have any advantage over a franchised store. That was the BASIC theory.

The "Franchise Plan" covered all this, the range offered, the store layouts, the marketing concepts and actually was a fairly decent document. Now, there are vicious rumours that a lot of this was "cut and pasted" from the Printing.com literature, and there may have been an element of "homage," I accept that. You do what you need to do to get by. In business, original ideas and concepts are too slow and expensive. Borrow what you can and steal the rest, I always say.

I was introduced to a "Franchise Consultancy" and within a few weeks discussions started, and this "consultancy" pitched for the business. They presented their proposal, which was weighted on **RESULTS** to keep the initial costs low. Well, that made sense, kind of the franchise equivalent of "no win no fee."

You need to understand that things were moving **FAST** here, even for ME things were moving fast, too fast. There was too much emotion and not enough logic being applied to this. The little head... No, we can't say that. Things were moving TOO fast, driven by ego, and lack of planning, shocker there eh?

I loved that though, I LOVED progress and HATED detail. This is where DISC becomes an invaluable resource. Do you think that a HIGH C would have been good for this role? Someone who is systems- and process-driven, craves detail and accuracy? Of course. What we had was a High D client, a High D Consultant, and on off-the-scale HIGH D OWNER of the Franchise Consultancy, which itself was a franchise.

Things got off to a good start, until one fine day at Glasgow's SECC. I was invited along to a "Franchise Breakfast." Now seen as a "mover" in franchise circles, my ego, my CHIMP, was loving it. Now, the Chimp had disappeared off for a banana milkshake and a fight, and I got talking to a VERY respected "Franchise Specialist" from one of the TOP banks in the franchise market. This was "The Guy" that I needed to speak to. We got chatting, and he was super excited about the Ink Shop and the plans, he seemed genuinely interested in the franchise model, and was keen to get a date in the diary and become involved. We would need the route to finance for franchisees. Then two things happened, and these happened almost at the same time. First, he asked a question, second, the CHIMP came back. The QUESTION was "what consultants are you using?" "We're using the Franchise (deleted for legal reasons)." The response was immediate, and threw the CHIMP into a fit of RAGE, talk about going bananas? He said, after a massive exhale of air, "No way, no way are we getting involved with any business, in any way, that uses them. You will be "blacklisted" already." Okay, take it away Chimp, way to go, furball. What the hell did he mean "blacklisted," how dare he? That conversation ended rather abruptly.

That **RIGHT THERE** was a "**Tap on the Shoulder**," one of these moments in life where you get a warning that something good was about to happen, OR, that something resembling World War III, the Great Fire of London, and the PLAGUE COMBINED was on the way. Well let me tell you - it was the LATTER.

I presented this immediately to the "consultant" and "owner." Now, I didn't think I was gullible, I really didn't. I kinda knew I could be short, volatile, arrogant, ignorant, impatient, demeaning, unreasonable, and often all at the same time, I didn't think GULLIBLE was there. Maybe it was the emotion?

Anyway, I accepted their answer.

Their answer was, "**This happens ALL the time**." They continued, "We are so good, and so disruptive, that they hate us for it. We're disrupting and challenging the franchise market and breaking through the smoke and mirrors that have paralysed this sector for decades. Relax, we have our own bank support."

I liked that, breaking through bullshit was my favourite record, I accepted it, and immediately got presented with "Another Gullible Twat Award," behind my back of course. The bank support was from the "Federal Bank of Kawasistan" who would probably lend 1% of the funding requirement with a 100% PG signed by both parents and grandparents, it was a MYTH, another myth.

The franchising continued, and an air of caution was now obvious. Then the day came, the eagerly awaited Franchise Manual, our BIBLE was ready and presented to us. It was obvious that all this negativity around these consultants was **absolutely VALID**. The Franchise Manual, and all associated manuals, contracts, proposals, marketing plans, branding plans, store guides etc was absolute CRAP. It could have been, and probably was, written by a three-year-old.

This was the disaster of ALL disasters. They had not listened to anything, the concept was wrong, the plan was wrong, the financial forecasts were pie in the sky. This was over 6 months' work completely wasted. The Franchise Specialist was bang on. Clearly, I was not the only unhappy client as the firm was now beginning to creak and was on the brink of collapse. Another "investor" was brought in, and after a meeting with him it was clear that nothing had changed. There were two options, shelve the project or "go solo." I'll now repeat an earlier phrase…

"I was smart enough to know that franchising was BIG and that specialist consultants were needed; I was smart enough to know that. I knew that I could not take on any more, and this project needed handled correctly by professionals who were smarter than me."

The above seemed to have been forgotten about. I was furious at the quality of the work this firm had produced. "How difficult can it be to write a few thousand pages of manuals…?"

If you have ever traded shares, you'll be familiar with a "Stop Loss." In the cool light of day, you agree a price that you'll offload shares to "stop the loss." This is where REAL planning comes in. Not only would the progress have been planned, a "Stop Loss" would have been there too. The project carried on, solo.

Throughout the period when these consultants were engaged, I continually asked about membership of the British Franchise Association. Their response was predictable, of course the BFA was wrong, and their new "disruptive" method was the way forward. Now that they were officially "binned" I set about doing this properly and contacted the BFA to apply for "Provisional Membership."

You only have to look at the big players in the franchise market to see that they are all BFA members, it's almost irrelevant what they do or do not provide, it is seen as the benchmark for potential franchises in the same way as ABTA and ATOL is for travel companies.

As we headed closer to 2008 my focus was now 100% on the franchise development. Still convinced this was the route forward. The operations manuals, marketing guidelines, sales processes and financial plans were all ready to submit to the BFA for membership application. The franchise project was nearing launch capability.

BFA membership was attained without any issues at all. The franchise model now looked like a finished product and was finally ready for market testing and development. The focus now shifted to recruitment, and part of the systems and processes written for the franchise was "Selection Criteria." This included a psychometric test. Franchises are interesting, you need to get the right person. Someone with a high "entrepreneurial drive" is unlikely to be a good "franchisee," they will want to change and break things. Someone with print industry experience is also unlikely to be a good fit, they too will "know better," and equally will want to break things. It's important to get an individual who is driven, motivated and will follow the system. We started off with those intentions.

The first franchise was a "trial." No matter how good you think your systems are, the only way to know is to test. The first franchise opened in Hamilton and was taken on by a previous employee who had left to start his own web design business. He felt that print was a perfect tie in with his business and we agreed. The store duly opened in 2008, and so began the "Franchise Journey." It wasn't long before this store was flying and taking on its first employee, a graphic designer. This was ALWAYS the way the franchise model was intended. The franchisee would work ON the business and not get involved in the day to day operations, leave US to do that.

Our Hamilton franchisee followed the system to the LETTER and based on this we were all confident that the model was right, the model worked, and the business was sustainable. For about a year this proved to be the case, then things started to go very badly wrong.

This is where you must have a robust contract and stick to it. It does NOT make you a bad franchisor, the opposite actually, however what happened with the franchise moving forward was pure and simply down to a weak contract, and an even weaker implementation of it.

We already knew the FRANCHISE worked, our Hamilton franchisee was proof of this, it worked, it was making money before projections. It wasn't perfect, and we felt super confident that we were really onto a winner here.

You know there's a "BUT" here don't you? The franchise model was going in the right direction But… some errors of judgement were about to be made. To progress the franchise "model" we decided to sell two of our current own stores, Edinburgh being one. Edinburgh was our second busiest store and could achieve £50k on a good month. We knew it had bags more potential and saw franchising that store as a gateway to achieve it. On paper, Edinburgh could be a £100k a month store: if Glasgow achieved it, why not Edinburgh? So ends the THEORY.

Sell a current trading store as a franchise, buy a turnkey solution with a customer base that guaranteed profitability from day one. A new, motivated owner who could drive the business forward, what could possibly go wrong? In a word, "**everything**."

There were no issues with finding a hardworking, dedicated owner, that was a given and Edinburgh was duly handed over to a new franchisee. Life was good and we were all excited about moving forward. It was VERY exciting times. I want to refer back here to "Right Road/Wrong Track." What followed wasn't anyone's "fault" and how I hate the "blame game," however shortly after taking over the Edinburgh store some serious cracks started to appear.

Unrelated to the above, our Hamilton franchisee decided to emigrate. His partner was Canadian, and they had decided that Canada offered more opportunities and set about the process of moving back to Canada. The Hamilton store was put up for sale. All this was happening at the same time the Edinburgh store was showing some concerns.

Recession, What Recession?

The recession was now real. Trading was tough and the decline in the industry was really biting. There was some serious overcapacity in the industry which leads to only one outcome, MASSIVE discounting and price reductions. Online print was maturing at a crazy rate too, and some new players were establishing themselves in that market. The trade print market was becoming more and more volatile, and this was going to really affect us.

Our franchise model was based on an "imperfect" system, that was not scalable in the long term. The franchisee would buy product from the central production facility (CPF). The goods were bought at a trade price (Base Price.) Easy so far. The franchisee would then sell at the same price as the other stores, they could discount if they wanted, however they rarely did.

This worked well. The franchisee focussed on business development and sales, passed the work to the CPF, had no production issues whatsoever, we even delivered the work. We made money by charging the franchisee the base price, and they made money on the mark up and associated services such as design and branding. It worked, in the early stages. The print market was changing at a ridiculous rate and the franchise system was going to be outdated before it matured.

A further two franchises were reserved, including our first English store in Manchester. It was here that mistakes started to get made. When you create a system or process in the cool light of day, STICK TO IT. With the recession biting, and by and large an unproven franchise model, enquiries and sales were thin on the ground. A second territory was released in Stirling and again, this got off to a good start.

As the recession bit harder, the flaws in the franchise model were about to get blown wide open. That would have massive implications for the franchisees, and US. This was a huge factor for the business failing some three years later, however, make no mistake about it, these next three years were going to be challenging to say the least.

The first issue was our cost base. The factory was superbly well equipped, and this came at a cost. The business was also heavily geared. Printing presses are £1m a pop, finishing equipment varies from expensive to outrageous, and given that we had so many stores our policy was "buy new, look after it, and it'll look after you." Now, any business that is highly geared has two worries, falling profits and/or rising interest rates.

Our BASE PRICES to franchisees were set, that took account of all these costs, including the distribution network, which now included a truck for store and client deliveries. Paper is incredibly heavy, and we had outgrown even the biggest of vans. We had actually been very careful when setting these rates to cover all this infrastructure.

What was happening now in Edinburgh was **FALLING SALES**, not rising. We found ourselves in the unbelievable position of having to discount the "sales" by 25-40% and seeing a **STATIC TURNOVER**. The Edinburgh store was now no longer contributing to our business, we had very quickly **LOST** our second biggest source of revenue. It gets worse.

The franchisee was now concerned that this was no longer working, and who would argue with that? They decided they wanted "more control" and the ability to do digital work "in-house." Now, the franchise contract did permit the provision of services that weren't supplied by the CPF, however what quickly followed was a significant amount of work being undertaken by the franchisee that should have come to the production facility. The net result of this was of course a further decline in sales.

These were difficult times, and it's important to get across that this was not done with any malice or dishonesty in any way. That was why it was tolerated. Yes, we could have been stricter and forced that all work came to us, however being professional and accommodating was seen as the preferred option.

The frustrating issue for us was that some stores had now become production units and time was being focussed on "**doing**" rather than "**developing**." The franchise model was now in chaos.

Not all franchisees played by the fairness rules either. As the print trade slid further and further into disarray, a number of "trade printers" appeared, each more eager to make less profit than the other. These guys were actively targeting our network. The consequence of that was franchisees were now buying sub-standard work outwith the network and passing this off as our goods. This only came to light when a previous client contacted me to complain about the quality and the FRANCHISE. When we checked the quality, it became apparent that we never printed the brochures, although we did end up having to RE-PRINT them to keep the customer happy. As far as he was concerned, he paid "The Ink Shop" - and he was right.

The franchise concept was halted, and we set about trying to regain control of the stores, that was never going to be easy. Edinburgh was now contributing a fraction of what it used to in terms of turnover. Hamilton was not sold, it closed, and we regained control of the Stirling branch.

The production facility was geared up for at least £3m of EXTRA franchise "sales" and the reality was a fraction of that. The overcapacity in the factory was staggering, and layoffs were now essential.

How could an INDUSTRY change so quickly? Was it solely the recession?

Could the franchise model have worked had the recession not come along? Very good question. If we look towards our main competitors, Printing.com, they have not been without their challenges either, however they continue to evolve and adapt, and I'm sure if we had survived we would have followed a similar path.

The plan always was for the franchise to be a mixture of print, design, web, display and business services. Never being reliant on any one area of income solely. The most dangerous number in business is ONE. Being reliant on 1 key product, 1 key client, 1 income stream. The franchise model never got the opportunity to grow and evolve into that "business" franchise; everyone knew that a "print" franchise had a limited shelf life.

The print High Street was dominated by the likes of Prontaprint, Kall Kwik, PDC, Alphagraphics, Kalamazoo Ink and the likes. These stores were all franchised, and by and large are either gone completely from the High Street or massively reduced. Print just isn't cool anymore. I don't happen to agree with that - I think print offers a tactile and "emotional" product that nothing else comes NEAR.

The rise of Trade Print Providers also presented another problem, ANYONE could now set up as a print broker, work from home, and SELL products for less than our franchisees could pay for it. That was never going to work. The market itself is now imploding due to crazy pricing and over capacity.

This has been another difficult chapter to write. Was franchising a reason for the Ink Shop to fail? Absolutely. Could it have been the goose that laid the golden egg? Absolutely. There are factors you can control in business and factors you can't. The recession being one.

One thing is for sure though, recessions have been, and always will be, the way that commerce brings out the dead. The weak shall perish. Whilst you cannot control a recession (and if you CAN, please drop me a note), what you can, and indeed MUST do, is always PLAN your business so that it's financially strong and built on a solid foundation. Read back the timelines for this journey. The business was wounded, heading into a recession, not a great recipe to launch a new product line, let alone a full franchise model.

It was the right idea, just at the wrong time.

Franchising is a great way to grow and develop your business. There's some interesting statistics surrounding franchising, too. The business failures amongst franchises is almost the polar opposite of non-franchised, and it is an industry that continues to grow. Over half franchise businesses turned over more than £250,000 in the last twelve months. This was coupled with the staggering figure of 97% of franchisees reporting profit, with the failure rate down from 4.6% to 2.2% since 2013. The failure rate is DOWN, yet at the end of 2018 the business failure rate in the UK hits a FOUR-YEAR high. If we factor out the franchises in that statistic, then that makes for even more dire reading for non-franchised businesses.

WHY do franchises have a better survival rate? Many will argue it's the brand and that may of course play a part in it. It's not the principal reason, however. The reason why franchises enjoy a higher success rate is down to TWO things. First and foremost, Systems and Planning. Any franchise worth buying will have all the systems and processes ready for you to use from day one. A franchise is a "business in a box" - follow the system, follow the manual. If your plan is not already done for you, the support of any franchise will soon have your business and financial plans ready in zip time.

The other reason of course is YOU. As a franchise owner, with the exception of "man in a van" (I assume that's not PC now, let's try "non-gender-specific carbon unit in a van"), then you will be working ON your franchise and not IN it. Even the "non-gender-specific carbon unit in a van" will have a proven sales and marketing system, as well as a head office backup that ensures many of the marketing and back-office support is provided.

Not every business is franchisable, so keep that in mind. It's a great way to scale up and shape up your business. Just make sure you choose the RIGHT consultants and keep in mind that it will probably take longer and cost more than you budget.

If franchising is on your radar, choose consultants wisely. Go through the British Franchise Association (BFA), and make sure you get references, bucket loads of them.

Chapter Twelve - How to Wreck Your Numbers

Throughout the book there have been various references to a variety of key numbers within your business, and how I had most of them in my head, **maybe you do too**? It made sense to bring this together in one chapter, and briefly go through these again, the reasons why they are important, and **MORE** crucially, showing you how small changes can make a **HUGE difference**.

In Chapter Three we covered Planning and touched on the "Magic Matrix," which can be downloaded from the website. (Knowing Your Numbers/Your Vital Statistics). I want to focus further on this. I saw a similar illustration a few years ago and it stopped me in my tracks.

It's All About the Money

Before we dive right in, this is not touching on the importance of Cash Flow, Budgets, Debtors and Creditors, Bank Balances, P&Ls, and other vital accounting information. **Can we agree that these are a GIVEN**? Can we agree that monthly financial accounts with the above are now seen as an essential part of your business moving forward?

I don't think a chapter is needed to explore those essential accounting basics of your business, not because they aren't important, **they are massively important**. Indeed, if you take **NOTHING** from this book, and **ONLY** focus on your finances, then that's a result. Speak with your accountant and ensure that, every month, you have the financial pulse of your business. Have a look at the "Getting Started with KPIs" guide on the website (howtowreckyourbusiness.co.uk). There's a Quick Start Guide there for creating a "KPI Dashboard," including the KEY financial numbers.

It's all about the money. Remember, the Ink Shop failed in the first quarter of returning to profit. Profitable businesses fail every day, **they simply run out of CASH**. Every business will be different, and have different financial reporting needs. Before you use the excuse of having cash in the bank, refer back to the "Glory Days," I had **£500,000 CASH** reserves in the bank, yet that business still failed some years later. Glad we cleared that up. What are your financial action points? There simply can't be "none."

Business Is Just a Numbers Game

This book will refer continually to the illustration in "Your Vital Statistics," so be sure to have that PDF open, or printed out (download from howtowreckyourbusiness.co.uk).

The reason I wanted to dedicate an entire chapter to this is simple: we need to pad the book! Seriously, I never did **ANY** of this. I had no idea what any of these key numbers were, other than through gut instinct. How many times have I said it now? "**You can only improve what you accurately measure**," that fantastic quote from Brad Sugars.

Why do you set **Marketing Budgets**? I don't understand a Marketing Budget. If I was selling £10 notes for £5, how much "budget" would you set aside for that? "Hey Stuart, thanks for the great offer, I don't have any budget left." Really? The simple fact is you would keep going, and keep re-investing that profit, yes? If you answered no, this chapter isn't for you.

The reason why you set Marketing Budgets is really simple and comes down to **TWO** things, yes, just TWO things. **You simply don't KNOW what's working**, and what's not, OR you **don't accurately track the true cost** of your marketing. Also, ditch the "cost" word. Marketing is only a **COST** to the business when you don't get a return. Marketing of course should be an **INVESTMENT**, invest £20 in Marketing, get £200 profit in the bank. Does that make sense?

One other thing. Unless you know ALL your marketing numbers, then you **WILL** need to set a budget, you need to set a limit because you have **NO IDEA** what's working for you. At what other stage in life are we happy POURING money into something without knowing exactly what the return is? Yet, when it comes to marketing, businesses do **EXACTLY** that all the time.

Another phrase I want to hammer out of business owners is this, "Yes, that worked okay, we covered the costs of the campaign." At best that's breakeven. However, let's not kid ourselves, if that's the case, you're losing money, it's a COST. A campaign that "covered the costs" is not a successful campaign, nowhere near it. Yet, every day, that's what I hear. The only exception to this is when you **KNOW** for a fact that these customers return, and your strategy is to make money on sale two onwards. Refer to the **"Eleven Steps of a Customer Journey"**.

Decide right now what your marketing investment should return. Every £1,000 spent should bring in a clear number of leads, enquiries, quotes, sales, customers and (£) profit. How can you determine the success of any strategy or campaign without knowing that?

Glad we cleared that up. Do you now have the "How to Wreck Your Numbers" chart open? What we're going to do now is dive into a "generic business" and explore their numbers from marketing reach to sale and profit. Not all steps may apply for your business.

Small Changes Deliver BIG Results

Let's start right at the beginning. **Everything you do in Marketing has a "REACH."** In today's data-mad and analytical world there's no excuse for not knowing very accurately what that **REACH** is. You can track views on LinkedIN posts and articles, you can see exactly how Facebook ads and posts have been performing, you have full visibility of social media activity, and you can use analytics to track every visitor to your website. You will know how many prospects your team has visited, you know how many flyers you posted, and you can estimate the reach of the magazine advert. See, by doing this you are going to gather an **approximate REACH** for your marketing. That will be a BIG NUMBER: is it a **big COST**, or a **BIG investment**? Don't worry about getting this figure EXACTLY right, an accurate estimate is good. You now have a NUMBER, and from that number you can work out the cost per engagement.

The 11 Steps Of **Your** Customer's **Journey**

Download these resources from the website at
howtowreckyourbusiness.co.uk

The 11 Steps Of **Your** Customer's **Journey**

The way we buy has changed massively in recent years, yet the vast majority of businesses still focus on Customer SERVICE and not the Customer **EXPERIENCE**. Think of this as a Journey. Get the Experience wrong, and they'll never see your Customer Service, and you'll probably never know.

Let's look at the journey. This isn't applicable for every business, and some steps will be skipped. you'll get the idea though.

The Thinker: every journey starts here. The customer is now thinking about your product, service or perhaps your business. This invariably leads to **Browsing**, almost certainly online, having a look at you, and without doubt - your competitors. How good do you look online? Is it exciting?

The customer is now interested, so they become a **Researcher** and start looking a bit more at your business and product or service. Your ratings and reviews will almost certainly be getting viewed now, as will your website, and social media pages. **Researchers** are very clever these days. At this stage, you don't even know they exist, they however, **know a LOT about YOU**.

This could then lead to an **Enquiry**, and this is where it goes pear-shaped for many. They don't agree the next steps and simply answer a question with no clear "next step." Oh dear!

The sale eventually comes, the first order, this is **The Tryer**. They are not keen on moving away from their current tried and tested supplier yet. If they liked what they got, and return for a second time, they are now a **Shopper**. There's bit of work to do yet, though.

They like you and your business and return for a third time. You now have the MAKINGS of a **Loyal Customer**. At this point you have worked hard to get and retain them, and this is where the **Danger Dot** is. The Danger Dot is "Perceived Indifference." Where the customer "thinks" you don't value their business, you do, it's just not obvious to them. **You have just been too busy getting other new business**.

This is why you must get your customer to become a **Card Carrying Member.** Offer benefits that say "thank you." Priority bookings, the best table, enhanced service levels - RARELY a discount. Provide value that exceeds any discount.

Once you have done that you now have a **True Ambassador**, a customer who, when asked, will refer and recommend you to their friends and colleagues. Keep going though, there's work to do.

Once you get the Customer Journey nailed, you have a **Raving Fan** who tells the whole world, without prompting, just how awesome you are. **And you are, bloody awesome!!**

In our example, a £5,000 budget saw a 12,000 reach, which equals 42p per engagement. Every person that saw, engaged or reacted to your marketing "cost" you 42p.

That brings us to **Conversion #1: Marketing Reach to Initial Enquiry**. If your marketing is pressing all the right emotional triggers, you have generated interest, or that prospect is READY to buy, then the next stage is an ENQUIRY. Perhaps by phone, email, web, it doesn't matter, just make sure you make it EASY for them to make that enquiry. This will likely be a "do you do…" type conversation. In our example, we have shown a conversion rate of 10%. From our 12,000 reach, 1,200 enquiries are made. That now equals a "cost" of £4.17 per enquiry.

Enquiries are GOOD, **Qualified LEADS** are better. If you're selling conservatories, 100 enquiries from people living in flats is not good (I assume). Your next step is to QUALIFY these Leads. That brings us to **Conversion #2, Initial Enquiries to Qualified Lead**. Your qualification process will be unique to you. However, in very simple terms, it will mean this prospect is your target market, and ready, willing and able to BUY whatever you are SELLING, either now or in the future.

In our example, we have 1,200 enquiries, and a conversion rate of 25% to Qualified Lead. That gives us 300 Qualified Leads, at a "cost" of £16.66 per qualified lead.

It's getting exciting, sorry I just LOVE this stuff now. I just wish I knew all this back in the Ink Shop days. **Conversion rate #3 is Qualified Lead to Quote Issued**. This may be a quote, or proposal, or maybe another meeting. Whatever it is, it's now going to be a demand on your time, so you really want to make sure your Qualification Process is working. In our example our 300 Qualified Leads saw a conversion of 50%, and 150 Quotes were issued. If your Qualification Process is **RIGHT**, and you're asking the right questions, providing the right benefits and delivering exactly what the customer WANTS, then you would expect a high conversion here.

Pro Tip: Watch out, this conversion rate may be **FALLING**. If your campaigns aren't targeting the right market, then **your conversion rate after QUALIFICATION may drop**. This is a good indicator that all is not well with your marketing campaigns. This won't apply to you though, you have tested and measured every marketing strategy, haven't you?

We now know that our "cost" per quote is £33.33. Something else is about to happen though. Valuable time and resource are about to be invested in generating that quote.

BREAK TIME: can you see the "cost" rising? Can you see why it's essential to track this? Here's why this is so important. Up to this point it's been MARKETING. If the conversion rates from reach, to initial enquiry, to qualification are POOR, then your message is wrong. You're either not targeting the right market, or not targeting the right market WITH the right message. Does that make sense?

Is this good stuff to know or what? Please, if this gets you excited, please write to me. I genuinely want to know who starts using this.

Conversion Rate #4 is Quote Issued to Customer Sale. Now, when I start to talk about conversion rates, this is usually the ONLY one people think about, rarely KNOW, just think about. You can now see there's a hell of a lot more work needs done beforehand. I also find it amazing the number of business owners who want to "start a marketing campaign" and don't know this number. That is a new kind of stupid, let me tell you. How can you start a new campaign without knowing this? Improving this number may mean that you could DOUBLE sales without spending a penny extra. Here's another consideration. Marketing raises **AWARENESS** of your product or service. If you can't close a door, never mind a sale, then YOUR marketing is generating **LEADS** and **SALES** for your **COMPETITOR**. Let that sink in for a moment.

Pissed off? Good, pissed off is good. Beats being bankrupt.

In our example here, the conversion from Quote Issued to Customer GAINED is 40%. 150 Quotes issued, 40% converted, provides 60

Customer Sales which equals a "cost" of acquisition of £83.33. Is that a good conversion rate? I am asking YOU. Is that a GOOD conversion rate? **Do you know what YOUR conversion rate is**?

Conversion rates vary from business to business, however, I would say NO. In this type of business where quotes are issued after a proven qualification process, then no, I would expect a conversion rate north of 60%. Go to the Marketing Plan in the "Planning Tools" section on the website and see how you can create a **SIX-touch follow-up process**. Hold on tight, **your conversion will ROCKET**.

Whilst Conversion 1 to 3 is marketing, not so Conversion 4. If you are NOT converting sales after quotes issued, then it's YOU. Sorry, just need to be blunt here. Is your price competitive? Did you highlight the VALUE to your client? Did you provide benefits or focus on features? Were you clear how you would make their life so much better? Did you provide the WOW factor? Did you follow the quote up PROPERLY? Did you present the quote in a professional way, AND get it out on time?

You see, the days of sending feature-ridden, poorly-created TOSH to your prospects and waiting for the phone to ring, well those days are gone, long gone. The only reason it worked in the past is because EVERYONE worked that way. The smart guys WIN the business **EVERY** time. Sorry, just needed to be a bit blunt there.

Has this made sense so far? Don't focus on these numbers, these are made up. Find out and FOCUS on what YOUR numbers are.

We're now going to move on to the "Customer." How many sales does your AVERAGE customer give you? In a month, or year, how many times does that customer return? In our monthly example, the average is 2, which is great as it reduces that "cost" of acquiring the sale nicely.

The next consideration is the AVERAGE spend VALUE. In our example it's £495.

Let's put all this together now. 60 customers, visiting us TWICE and spending £495 gives a turnover of £59,400. These figures, by the way, can be monthly, quarterly or yearly.

From our £59,400 of monthly sales, our margin is 30% and we make a profit of £17,820. Just to be really pedantic, we then work out what "investment" was needed to generate that turnover. In this case it was 8p. Every £1 of turnover required 8p of marketing investment. Why bother with that? Simple, **do you want to grow your business**? Then you need to know how much you need to invest in marketing to generate "x" turnover.

When you have these numbers accurately recorded, you know what ACTIVITY is needed to generate leads and sales, and how MUCH you need to invest. Not doing, or knowing these figures, really is the way TO WRECK YOUR NUMBERS (and everything else).

Finally, we have a profit, and again, we know what we need to "invest" to generate that profit.

Great, so now you have all these figures. They are what they are. If you discover that conversions are lower than you thought, relax, this is GOOD. It means you have some **amazing quick wins just around the corner**.

And Now, the Small Changes

What I want to show you now is how a **really small improvement can make a HUGE difference**. The "Small Effect." I am sick, and I mean SICK of books and social media posts on how to 20x, 50x or 100x your business. Jeez, the chances of that are so small, so remote, to be ridiculous. Yes, some of you will do it. This book is for the majority, not the minority. Does that make sense?

If you can 50x or 100x your business, crack on, please. Just make sure you have the systems, structure and cash reserves to do that first.

We're going to look at what a simple, and **EASILY** achievable 5%

improvement makes. Except, we're NOT going to increase the marketing spend and NOT going to increase the reach. We're going to do **MORE** with the **SAME**. Best grab another coffee first.

Marketing Reach to Initial Enquiry, currently 10%. How do we improve that by 0.5% and get that conversion to 10.5%? Did you think we were going to add 5%, and take that to 15%? No, it's 5% of, not 5% on. Now, in fairness, some of these improvements will deliver WAY MORE than 5%, however, let's just show the "The Small Effect."

Do you think you could get an extra 0.5% onto your conversion rate from marketing reach to initial enquiry by just being a bit **more focussed**? Really targeting your ideal market and tweaking your initial message to excite that audience, and address what they **REALLY** want?

Let's say that's a yes, then your conversions to initial enquiries go from 1,200 to 1,260 and your investment per enquiry is now £3.97.

Initial Enquiry to Qualified Leads, currently 25%. How do we improve that by 1.25% and get that to 26.25%? Same as above really, target the pain the customer has. When you become the "Nurofen" for your customer's pain, that's where the magic starts. Think about this, the client is making an INITIAL enquiry. Do they know your full product range?

The example shows 1,260 initial enquiries being converted to give 331 Qualified Leads, which reduced that "investment" to £15.11 per qualified lead.

Now here's another thing about the qualification process - your prospect is qualifying YOU just as much as you are them. So, make sure your qualification process addresses their needs, wants and desires, too.

Now, as you move to **Qualified Leads to Quotes Issued**, it's VERY important to point something out. This conversion rate very much depends on what PRECEDES it. If you fill your sales funnel with crap leads, then IMPROVE your qualification process, that conversion rate will actually

DROP. Of course it will, you're weeding out the poor leads. We'll assume, for this example, that your targeted message to your targeted market has been awesome. How do you then improve the conversion rate from Qualified Lead to a Quote or Estimate Issued? We're only looking for 2.5% here, going from 50% to 52.5%. **The biggest improvement will come from SCRIPTS**. Scripts ensure consistency.

You now know that every person at this stage is target market, so ASK the right questions. Generate a bit of excitement. Make your prospective customer think "these guys are amazing." Who's NOT going to ask for a quote or estimate at this point? Always, always, always agree a "next step" and an "action" with your prospect. This is NOT pushy sales, though. At this stage in the process your conversion rate should be WAY more than 52.5%. Does this make sense?

We're doing great here, and got the Quotes issued up to 174 and in doing so reduced the "investment" from £33.33 to £28.74.

The Quote has been issued, great, now sit back and wait for the phone to ring. That's How to Wreck Your Numbers. You're not going to do that. You're going to improve your **Quotes Issued to Sale** from 40%, by just 2%, to 42%. Let me be honest here, this next step is really where the magic happens, and when followed consistently will improve that conversion rate MASSIVELY.

You're going to create a "6-Touch" follow up process, this is covered in the "Marketing Plan." A follow up process so smooth, and so slick, that you'll be AMAZED, and perhaps annoyed that you never did this years ago. One word of warning, this ONLY works when it is tested and measured, (every business is different) and done **CONSISTENTLY**. Remember Brad's quote, "**You can only improve what you accurately measure**."

The reason this works is really simple. We know that the vast majority of customers (around 86%) will be ready to buy after a minimum of 6 "touches." Not 6 stupid, pushy sales calls - 6 well-constructed touches that address their needs and wants. Yet, bizarrely, the vast majority of SALES people give up after the SECOND touch.

Now, if you leave the customer to decide, and have not differentiated your business, what's that decision going to be based on? More than likely PRICE. Eenie, meenie, miney… **PRICE**.

I want to touch on one element of the "6-Touch process" and that's the "WOW" Pack. The "**WOW**" pack is usually a gift. It's NOT a pen with your logo or a mouse mat, get that out your head right now.

Touch point **ONE** will be the initial meeting, there has more than likely been dialogue before this, however for this example we're using the INITIAL meeting as "touch point one". The purpose of touch point one is to issue a quote, estimate or proposal. Remember, touch point one doesn't have to be face to face.

The quote, estimate or proposal is emailed for speed, this is usually Touch point **TWO**. When doing this, you want to be FIRST. It shows professionalism. It astounds me the number of businesses that can't get a quote out on time. What message does that send to the customer? If you can't take the MONEY, what the hell is the aftersales like? That's what THEY think. You know I am right?

You then send the "WOW Pack." This is Touch point **THREE**. It still has the quote, printed this time. Nice letter, not a jumble of corporate bore though, PLEASE. "We thank you for the opportunity to provide an estimate…" Oh, please! Are we stuck in the 70s? WRITE as if you were talking to your customer in the pub. No, scrap that. Write as if you were talking to your customer socially.

The **WOW** pack contains an appropriate gift, not TACK. In MY pack, I always make sure I provide the proposal, and a BOOK that I know will be a game changer for my prospective client. I ALWAYS handwrite a note, something like "Hi Pete, I have highlighted this page, I know you'll LOVE this."

Get the picture about the WOW Pack? Oh, by the way, you POST the "WOW pack" first class the same day that you email the quote or proposal.

Touch Point **FOUR** is the first call. Now, some of you may be thinking this process won't work. Allow me to disprove that right now. When you call the client, the purpose of that call is to make sure they got the quote. You can ask some light questions, of course you can, just don't go into hyper sales mode. The purpose is to make sure the quote was received. Here goes, you'll LOVE this. "Yes, we RECEIVED your quote this morning in the post." NOT ONE person has EVER referred to receiving the email, they ALL comment on receiving the "WOW" Pack. Why? **Because it WORKS**.

Before the letters start, the "WOW Pack" will clearly depend on your sale value. I can't possibly know what your business is. I can tell you one thing though, EVERY business can add MORE WOW.

There's one other VITAL consideration during this call (**Touch point 4**), you are ASKING for permission to call back (**Touch point 6**) and you will email again before calling (**Touch point 5**). You will always agree a next step, or an action point for you or the customer. Do not fall into the **RIDICULOUS** "British" phrase, "Oh, that's great, I'll leave it with you, just give me a call if you need anything."

Your sales process should be mapped out so the TIMINGS of each step suit your business. This process may be completed over a few weeks, or many months.

If this has got you super excited, download the Planning Pack from the website (Planning Tools).

Back to the NUMBERS now. The conversion rate from **Quotes Issued to Sale** goes from 40% to 42%, just 2% of an increase. I think we can all agree it will be way more than that? That now gives you 73 customers, and you'll see that cost of acquisition drop to £68.49.

A Simple Six Touch Follow Up Process

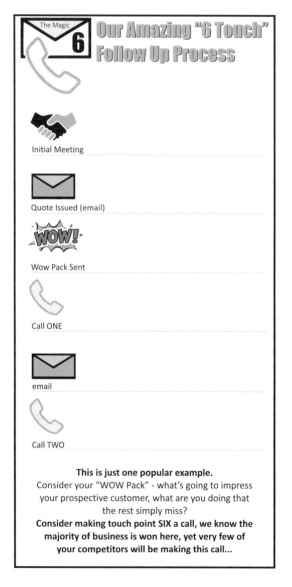

The above has been taken from our "Marketing Plan" - download the full plan at **www.howtowreckyourbusiness.co.uk**

The next TWO areas we want to look at are **Average Sale Value**, and the **Number of Average Sales**. We want to improve both of these by 5% too. We want to get the number of sales up by 0.1% (not an error: this is POINT ONE of a PERCENT), and increase that sale value to £520.

How this is done will vary from business to business. Making sure your customers know your full product range is a simple start. We call this your Product Ladder. Here's one for you. The Ink Shop started doing a lot of display and promotional items and we quickly gathered a lot of new customers. Time and time again we would find print customers that didn't know we did display, and display customers that didn't know we did print. Never assume your customer knows. Do you think THAT ALONE would give you 0.1% more AND increase the average sale value?

Cross-selling, up-selling, bundled deals, these are all EASY ways to increase and improve the Sale VALUE and Sale FREQUENCY. A Beauty Salon client was very good at booking customers in for their next appointment. They would know the average time between appointments was five weeks, so they would book you for an appointment in four weeks' time. A handy strategy to increase the number of transactions. Or they would book in the five-week slot, then send a message that there's been a cancellation.

Whatever your strategies are, there's THOUSANDS of simple ways to improve those two numbers.

Now, let's add all this up. This is where the magic happens and why we call this the "Magic Matrix."   Look at the turnover and profit, up 5%, yes? NO, Turnover is up around 35%. The improvements MULTIPLY down. Amazing isn't it? The profit is even better, around 41% improvement, and all by adding just 5% in those KEY areas.

Use the blank template (on the website) and FIND your numbers, then look at what a 5% improvement can deliver. If you really want to blow your mind, go for 10% improvements.

And that's why I wanted to devote a separate chapter to this. **How to Wreck Your Numbers**. Let me finish by saying this: I have NEVER met a business owner yet who had this level of detail known. That's why with clients now I hammer this home.

You're maybe thinking, "What an arse, he's just shown in a BOOK how to do this." Yes, I have, here's the thing, though. Less than 2% will read and action this, few will follow it through, and fewer still will follow it consistently.

OUR secret is safe.

Is it now becoming clear why the business failure rate is so high? That's rich coming from me, the marketing spend at the Ink Shop could be as high as £10,000 a MONTH, and none of these figures were known. That "budget" could have been dropped to £1,000 and achieved TEN times more had I known this stuff. Let me correct that, I did know this stuff, you know it too. I haven't invented time travel here. It's not about knowing, it's all about DOING, that's what makes the difference.

If you don't read anything else in this book, and you **ACTION** this, it will have been a worthwhile "**investment**" of your time.

Chapter Thirteen - The End Game, a Bunch of Bankers

Well, here we are, the final chapter, and again another part of the story that was never intended to be in the book. On reflection, it needed to be. The reason this was never intended to be written was again the wounds. Let me tell you right now that there's a terrible, dark portion to this chapter, and you'll know when you get there. For that reason there can be no names, there can't even be any smart-arse hint at names. Those who know, know, and we need to leave it there.

I mentioned earlier in the book that we can often be slow to react and "work in pain" for long periods of time because it becomes "normal," and what's "normal" has a resistance to change. We can become comfortable being uncomfortable as the thought of change seems daunting. This was me, this is what happened to me and the business. You see, the end came slowly at first, it creeps up on you when you're in "denial." When we talk about the "Glory Years" it's easy with hindsight to look back and see when the dark years started. 2007 to 2010 were challenging, 2011 to 2013 were hell on earth. The downturn in the industry, the recession gathering pace, a disastrous franchising model were all about to attack a business that simply was not ready for what was to become **"The Final Battle."**

Always Have a Plan B

A strange thing happened a few years ago. In coaching we're always looking forward with clients, planning, learning, growing ourselves as well as the business, testing, measuring… positive, positive, positive. You only ever look back to LEARN. Does that make sense? A coaching client was progressing like a steam train, the business was always slightly ahead of even their most ambitious targets. Turnover was only outperformed by PROFIT, and the team that was being built around this was beyond exceptional. This business owner was delighted and was now seeing the real benefits of a structured business that could run without them. Family time was a priority, the dream holiday was booked, and the dream car was ordered. This business owner and I shared a lot in common, we were the same DISC, enjoyed the same taste in music (mad AC/DC fans), loved the same cars, and both had lost businesses in a horrific way. As you can imagine, this business was being built on a foundation of enthusiasm, knowledge, commitment, massive action, yet CAUTION, and it worked.

Shortly after they published the first set of accounts with me as their coach I was called in to a meeting. The accounts told them nothing they didn't already know. They knew to the penny what was in the bank, they knew to the % what the profit was. That wasn't the reason for the meeting. They called me in to say "Thank you." That was nice, there was no need of course, it was them that did all the work. I was thanking them, and to this day still do. The reason for the meeting was to discuss something that I never came across before. Now, plenty of businesses have a "Plan B," not one like this though.

In the cool light of day, with no financial pressures and no emotion to cloud the journey they wanted to create a plan to save the business. I thought about this for a moment and asked a question, **"Would a plan like this have saved your previous business**?" The answer back was abrupt and instant - **"YES**." "Same here," I said.

Then, unknown to anyone outwith the owners and senior directors, the plan was created based on a number of "what if" scenarios. To this day, that plan is updated as often as the main plan is. It clearly shows what immediate actions will be taken when a series of "trigger" situations occurred.

[UPDATE: at the time of editing (March 16th 2020), the UK is in the grip of the worsening Coronavirus. This prudent plan came into effect last week (trigger actions occurred). This business is now significantly ahead of their competitors.]

This goes back to a previous example using a "Stop Loss" system when trading shares. What had been put in place was simply that, a "Stop Loss" system. Should "X" ever occur, we'll immediately do "Y." As I found out to my peril, when "X" does happen, you are emotionally compromised as is your decision-making process. There's always a great debate about having a Plan B or not. Some argue having a Plan B takes your real focus and drive off Plan A. Others argue that a Plan B avoids pushing bad decisions. Personally, I believe in a SOLID Plan A. A well-thought-out approach where nothing is left to chance, that includes a Plan B. That's just me though.

Their plan was now becoming obsolete, this business had passed the danger point, and their wealth had been protected. They are also approaching their "Exit Date," and by the time you read this, that will almost certainly have happened. However, it's still updated, our "comfort blanket," as they described it. They also added that during due diligence the new owners loved it and vowed to do **TWO** things. Keep it in place, and NEVER use it.

You see, we both agreed that when our businesses were distressed that decisions were made too late as they were clouded by **EMOTION**. It's worth noting the fable about the frog. If you put a frog into boiling water it'll instantly jump out, if you put a frog into tepid water and slowly increase that to boiling point the frog does not perceive the danger and just sits there and boils to death.

A distressed business owner can react in the same way, we both knew this is exactly what happened previously, and why they insisted on the "Plan B." Readiness to act should the water ever start to get hot.

Go back and look at the "Right Road/Wrong Track" image again and you'll understand that something else took place with BOTH these businesses. Can you see what it is? Blame would follow. The killer was **DENIAL** and **EXCUSE**.

We both agreed that we suffered from what we called S.D.A. syndrome, Stupid Dumb Ass. Denial that anything was seriously wrong, and an excuse for every negative situation that appeared.

In my business, as profits dipped and cash reserves dropped, the **water was warming up**. The Denial and Excuse was the fact that the franchising had been such a disaster, the recession was real, and that the underlying business was good and would "bounce back," classic behaviour that is completely on the **WRONG TRACK**.

Despite my impatience and drive, I was very slow to react to "people changes." When you look at DISC, an "S" profile person would walk on hot coals before letting people go. Despite having almost ZERO "S" in my profile, I was slow and reluctant to make people redundant. Was that due to caring for people, **or a deeper-rooted denial of the admission of failure**?

Those were challenging years indeed, 2007 to 2010. I am not going to dwell too much on these years other than to say this is where it could have been turned and saved. Drastic and decisive action in this period would have seen a scaled-back business survive. All the signs were missed, and you need only look again at the "Wrong Track" and you'll see why.

2011 to 2013 were, as you can imagine, hell on earth. Every day was pressure, stress, robbing Peter to pay Paul. By this time action was of course being taken. Nonperforming stores were being closed, however the nonperforming franchise was the real killer for us. Leases, where possible, were being re-structured and the entire business model was being reviewed. It was **ALL REACTIVE** though.

At this time, it was carnage in the print industry. It seemed that business failures were being reported every day. What was being reported was the "Phoenix" and "Pre-Packs": print businesses closing on Friday, ditching all debt and starting on the Monday with the same machines, with the same staff, in the same premises and the same, blissfully unaware, customers. What was worse, they were often supported by suppliers who were only too keen to keep the business and mitigate their losses. I was very vocal on this.

It eventually got so bad UK-wide that print businesses united and agreed that any supplier that continued to supply a Phoenix would not be supported. This was on the back of a VERY high-profile Scottish business failing. They were horrible times, it was a war zone indeed.

2012 was the turning point. I can't remember exactly what the trigger point was, three quarters of consecutive losses? Anyway, 2012 saw us appointed with a bank manager from the "Specialist Banking Team." Towards the end of 2012 numerous changes were made and the business was slowly, and surely starting to breathe again. The business was still losing money, we could however see that the changes were working. No thanks to the "Specialist," who was completely useless and unhelpful and if anything, hindered progress.

Regular meetings between me, Bobbie, our Banking Manager and the "Specialist Banking Manager" were commonplace. We were getting ready to close for Christmas (2012) and were right on the overdraft limit. Previously our manager had let us drift over that limit, and sometimes WELL over, however this guy was having none of that.

We finished up for Christmas 2012 with a degree of cautious optimism, the changes were working and for the first time in a long time - light appeared at the end of the tunnel.

The holiday period is usually a cash-flow challenge. Slow trading before Christmas, closed for two weeks, then a slow start in January was the usual. We had a very busy December and a great start to January. This was really encouraging, making it past the hurdles and heading towards a busy period (March) was a real boost, we thought!!!

January and February were challenging, but no real drama. The problems came in March. This month was nowhere near as busy as it should have been. The marketing budget had been wiped out, the marketing had stopped, and we were really paying the price for that now. The marketing should never stop. Marketing is simply OXYGEN, cut that off and the brain quickly dies. Looking back, the bank's only concern was to reduce the overdraft. Pay absolutely NOTHING and cash as much as possible. The "Specialist Banking Team" isn't a business turnaround department, if they were, they would have known that killing the marketing kills the business. They are a hatchet department as would be proven later. They were in to shut us down and mitigate their losses, IMHO.

By the end of March 2013 things were looking dire. March was what we would have expected January to look like.

At the end of March, we all sat down, and I presented what HAD to be paid. Payroll was priority, it was agreed not to pay HMRC, and a few leases. The "specialist" looked at a payment to another bank and asked what it was for. We started using invoice discounting, which is a stupid name - FACTORING. I was never a fan of it and although there was £30k in the account, we had never drawn it down. He was furious about this and insisted it be transferred. "NO CHANCE, that's the rainy-day fund for when we can't meet the payroll," I was insistent on that. "Look outside, it's RAINING" he barked. It was actually a glorious day and it seemed to piss him off no end that I mentioned that.

He reluctantly agreed, then agreed to pay the wages, the standing order for the factoring and our main supplier bill.

As March rolled into April, the payroll was met, however EVERYTHING else was bounced. I had promised our supplier that we would pay them. Word was clearly out, and another supplier took a £30,000 payment EARLY which meant NO CASH for our main supplier. The bank also bounced the payment to the factoring company and that account had now been "locked."

We had gone from looking positive pre-Christmas to knowing we were now in SERIOUS trouble. As we ended Q1 2013 we knew this was it. As if March wasn't tough enough, we also lost our best friend in the world, Dougal the dog. He was our 13-year old German Shepherd "pup." These were dark days, **I can't even BEGIN to share that with you**.

Q1 of 2013 was the first quarter that saw us return into the black. That was interesting as turnover was well down, the simple fact was we were no longer doing ANY low-margin work. An emergency meeting was called by me, and this time, I was not messing about. I was ready to pin this guy against the wall.

This meeting comprised me, Bobbie, our accountant, our manager and the

"Specialist Banking Manager." I had been warned to keep it calm, which I took on board.

The meeting was Monday 15th April, it started with me asking WHY the agreed payments hadn't been made. I accepted the fact that one supplier had been sneaky, I got that. What I didn't understand was why the small amount to the factoring company had been "bounced"? Our Bank Manager (good guy) didn't know this, and to our amazement, the two of them had a "heated exchange." Our Bank Manager was a good guy, a true gent.

I cut straight to the point, "Look, we have a £1.4m property portfolio with low borrowings, we need to release that equity." The bank had been asked about that previously and would NOT do it, point-blank refused. They had security on the property and of course a floating charge on the business. They were "safe" in the event of failure. They also had a PG (personal guarantee, they couldn't lose!!!

Specialist Dude again refused that option. Our accountant then took over and said that based on that information the business was insolvent, and continuing to trade and accrue debt would be in contravention of the Companies Act blah, blah, blah.

Specialist Dude then made a suggestion. If we increased the PG to £250,000 they would release some equity to allow trading. The picture was clear, the corner had been turned. This was needed to get the business back on track.
I was only interested in releasing the equity of the properties, or going to another lender, or SELLING them as a final option. The bank was having NONE of it. I wanted £500,000: £250,000 to clear the overdraft and £250,000 to provide working capital to drive the business forward. Not a chance. The most realistic option was to get £250k to clear the overdraft and keep us breathing. I didn't like it but it was the ONLY option on the table.

Specialist Dude only repeated the increased PG, it's all he mentioned.

At this point my accountant asked for a ten-minute break and the three of us (Bobbie, the Accountant and I) headed to my office. Bobbie was distraught,

NO WAY to the PG. One hurts us, two kills us. Of course, I wasn't looking at it from that angle, it was going to work. Our accountant butted in, "Guys, the PG is irrelevant at this point, I don't like what I am seeing, so I suggest this course of action…………….." We were being set up.

We went back into the meeting and I said "OK, you're right. To show our commitment, we will agree to the £250,000 PG, on one condition: the bank must agree, in writing, today, to keep the overdraft in place, at the CURRENT limit for 12 months."

He refused. Our accountant was right. As soon as that PG was signed this bastard was pulling the overdraft. I could tell by the colour of our Bank Manager's face that's **EXACTLY** what the game plan was. He wouldn't even make eye contact.

I sat back in my seat **STUNNED**, and gutted. I was done. They had won. I took the keys out of my pocket and slid them down the table. Call in the receivers.

9am the following day, receivers were in, and the business was dead. It was the receivers that pointed out that the business's Birthday was that day, **20 YEARS.**

You'll have read some of this in previous chapters, the team refusing to leave until the work was done, despite being made redundant and told to go home. The receivers also commented on the amount of work that was still coming in. The phones rang constantly, customers came to the door, the website was on fire. "What are we doing here" they asked?

"That's a VERY good question" I replied.

I have only highlighted the key points, as you can imagine there was 100 times more going on. Today, I see things differently. Yes, the bank had behaved in a deplorable way. Do you remember the antics of the banks at the height of the recession? It was outrageous what they were doing, and getting away with. No one cared, no one cares. The irony was, it was THEIR financial recklessness that caused the problems in the first place. An irony you could choke on.

The fact remains I had put the business in harm's way. I had allowed the future and decision-making process of "my baby" to be taken away from me. I could go off TRACK here and blame others - the fact is I must, and have, taken RESPONSIBILITY that this happened on my watch, **MY WATCH**.

The Vultures

The "vultures" had gathered. I wasn't privy to those conversations although I did end up joining one of our main competitors as their Production Director. What a team that was. Together we created a £10m business with a £2m net profit, yes, in PRINT. That business went on to win numerous high profile awards and was acquired by a global player in 2015. I knew right away that "corporate life" was not for me and sacrificed a significant six figure "bonus" to walk away. For the first time in my life I was driven by the **HEART** and not the **WALLET**. For reasons I can't and won't divulge, that was the **RIGHT** decision.

I saw an advert for "Action Coach" in a business magazine and liked the idea of helping businesses. After all, there was a lot of learning and expertise here.

I made a few enquiries, getting more and more interested each time. Now clear that this was the route I wanted to take, I went on one of their "Discovery Days." That was where things started to change. As I looked at the system it was so obvious where all the mistakes were made. I now regretted telling the Action Coach I had met during the "Glory Days" to go away!!! They would have been in that business ten minutes and identified the dangers. Would I have listened? Well, that's a whole other question. I'll take the 5th on that.

So began another journey, another chapter, that continues to this day.

There's been tough patches along the way. The learning has been extraordinary though, every day is a learning day, both with coaching practices and clients. My appetite for learning is only equalled by my appetite for your success. I have completed numerous coaching qualifications and continue to grow and learn.

I did say this chapter had a dark edge. I was actually going to leave this out. When the business failed, my Bank Manager (I'll call him X) and I agreed that we'd shake hands and walk into the sunset. He knew I appreciated everything he did for us. He bent rules, he fought our corner - he was just a lovely, lovely guy. A true gent, and a rarity in commercial banking. I can't go into any more detail than that. There was nothing dodgy, trust me, this guy was poker straight, he was just a GENT.

Not long after I started my new role my accountant called, "Have you spoken to X?" he enquired. I told him that we shook hands and agreed to walk into the sunset. "Oh," he said. "Why?" I asked. He continued, "X was a senior partner at the bank and was summoned to a meeting. At that meeting, reported as heated, X left, cleared his desk, went home - and committed suicide."

To this day, I don't know any more than that. Did X do something to help us that later caused him to be reprimanded? We just don't know, nor will we ever know. I think about X every time I see the bank he worked for.

Where are we in society when the pressures of work lead to this?

Let me finish with this. When you have a business that is distressed, you would be shocked by the "friends" that are no longer there. I could count on ONE hand the people that have remained friends today, indeed I could count on one hand with three fingers missing who those people are.

This book has been written to share a story, to share a learning. A true story, my story, a Horror Story. It's not a motivational book, it's not a "How to Increase Sales x 100" type book. God knows, there's plenty of them. If you can take points to help you and your business, then great. The one thing you need is ACTION, things won't magically happen.

Get a coach, you'll be amazed what they see that you miss. The biggest success my clients have shared is accountability. Years of running their business with no one DARING to ask them, "Why have you not done that?" Then DARING to challenge the bullshit excuse that often followed. Hang around with people smarter than you. I found the Chamber of Commerce was great. I would make a point of speaking to loads of people there, starting the conversation with "I'm selling NOTHING, I'm genuinely interested in your business and your views on ……………………." I found out more about the impact of BREXIT through four conversations than any government source would ever reveal.

Get a "Business Buddy" too, someone that you can REALLY talk to, over a beer. Someone that "gets it." My Business Buddy now, in Lossiemouth, is John Straw, Google him. We put the world to rights every Sunday over a beer, with Troy too, my faithful German Shepherd "pup," he's 10 now.

That's something else worth a mention. Dogs don't judge, they are immensely loyal and won't leave your side. They are there for you during the good times and bad. We can learn a lot from our four-legged friends.

Enjoy the journey, and please, Do NOT Wreck Your Business.

Stuart

Let's Wrap This Up - So What's in it For You?

The book has told a story, a condensed story, however a true story. That's not the purpose of the book, though. The purpose of the book is to realise a vision, to make business failure the exception and not the rule. To eradicate business failure that rips thousands of families apart every year, when all that was being sought was the opportunity for a better life. Simply telling a story does not help achieve that.

The book thus far has been written in a particular style, a style that reflected the person I was then, not today. My journey through the "story" and onwards into senior roles, and finally into business coaching has opened my eyes, and changed my view of life, and not just in business. Today, I am now more interested in the "simple pleasures" in life, and from my home in Lossiemouth, Scotland, I am much happier sitting outside a local restaurant with a cool beer watching the sunset. What you didn't see there, I typed "sunrise" in error, I know I'm Scottish, it's definitely **SUNSET**.

This chapter, therefore, with your permission, will take a much more serious approach. Throughout the book there have been many learnings shared, this chapter brings them ALL together. I did say that "Eight Fundamental Errors" caused my business to fail, this chapter is all about those eight errors, and what you can do to avoid them.

Business isn't about right or wrong, good or bad, errors or perfection, it's about **LEARNING**. If we can all be better tomorrow than we were yesterday, what an incredible business community we would have today. What an incredible future we would all have.

Before I dive into the "Eight" it's worth noting that one element has been left out - Chapter 11, Franchising. Whilst this indeed was a significant part of the failure of the business, that was not down to the franchising idea or concept. The crazy thing is, franchising the business could have saved it, and propelled it to achieve the success intended. There were too many other factors at play that meant that project was doomed before it started. If you are considering franchising your business, give me a call, or message me through LinkedIn. There are a few books I want you to read, and if you're UK based, a few people I want to introduce you to.

Today, I get to work with many business owners; what a privilege that is. I guide them to achieve what they want in business, what's important for them. Today though, I say no more often than yes, and that frustrates me. Why no? How's that congruent with my opening statement? CNEs, **Critical Non-Essentials**. Clients who are not prepared to work on the "eight" are not serious about taking their business forward. These are what I call Critical Non-Essentials. There are not essential for you as a business owner, they are not law or compliance regulations. They are however, in my view, **CRITICAL** for your future success. Following these points will not guarantee success, however, as I have proved, not following them…. Well, we've covered that.

Let's get down to serious business now. No humour, no jokes - serious business. The book title is "How to Wreck Your Business" - the purpose is to make sure that you learn from the mistakes I made. This chapter and the associated downloads now move more towards "Here's How to... Plan, Grow, Develop etc. This entire book and resource has been written with the smaller "would-be entrepreneur" in mind, and as such the intention is to provide guidance that is delivered in a short and sharp manner. What is missing? **What can't I provide**? The **ACTIONS** you now take, **that's up to you.**

1 of 8 - Planning

Everything starts with a plan. Chapter Two covered this, however, let's have a quick recap here. The website has "The Planning Tools" which allows you to download and create your own Marketing Plan, 5-Year Vision Planner and 90-Day Planner, as well as giving you the instructions on how to get started. This is serious stuff, the lack of CLARITY around planning was a significant issue for my business. The reason I say CLARITY is that you may still think that a plan in your head is OK - trust me, it's NOT. Plans need to be workable and achievable, which is why the "Vision Planner" is so good. It's a start, it does require additional plans too. However, once you see your Vision come to life, I'm confident that you'll soon have it all nailed.

So how does the Vision Planner work? Very simply, it focusses on eight key areas of your business: Turnover, Profit, Marketing, Team, Personal Goals, Assets and Investments, Office and Plant, and PROFIT. The plan encourages you to look out, create the VISION of where the business will be in five years, then bring it in to three-year MILESTONES, one-year MUST DO's, and where the business is today.

Each segment challenges the other, so by the end of this, you'll have that all-important **CLARITY**.

Plans don't stop here, how can they? Other PLANS you absolutely must have in your business are 90-Day (Quarterly Planning) and a Marketing Plan. Each of these is also ONE page.

Your Action Points from #1 are

Create your 5-Year Vision Planner
Build your 90-Day Plan
Complete your Marketing Plan

The one thing I would add is, know your numbers before starting your Marketing Campaigns. There is no point in spending valuable resources on marketing if your sales messages aren't right, your conversion rates aren't known and your follow up process (if applicable) isn't bang on. All you are doing is creating MORE leads that you can't, or won't close. Start there first, you'll thank me for it later.

(All the above are available at **howtowreckyourbusiness.co.uk**, Planning Tools, "Hit the Planning Button.")

2 of 8 - The Dangers of Discounting

This is really important, it's not that you can't discount, just be fully aware of the Dangers of Discounting. For me, I was haemorrhaging PROFIT every month through reckless discounting. Printing was, and still is, a very competitive market with over capacity. In such instances you have TWO choices: discount, and start a race to the bottom, or NICHE and command a sensible margin for the work you specialise in. I chose the former.

All of our competitors were discounting and as the recession bit harder this became more common. A race to the bottom is never a good idea, it's a race you don't want to win. The trouble is, we didn't win, we came second, and that's worse. Not only had my brilliant strategy failed, we had now discounted to the point of LOSSES, AND still hadn't won the customers to make it almost worthwhile.

I made **THREE** errors of judgement, and I want to share these with you right now. Number **ONE**: I never appreciated the TRUE dangers of discounting, and how much more product we had to sell to make a campaign work. Do you? Have a look at the Discounting Matrix on the website, Discounting Advice, make sure you read this before starting any campaign.

A 10% Discount which is NOTHING, on a 25% margin means you need to sell 67% more just to stand still. The thing is, a 10% Discount EXCITES no one, it's nothing. We would often lead with a 20% DISCOUNT. Do you know how much extra you need to sell then just to stand still? If you don't, then you are making the same mistakes I did. **The answer is 400%.**

Now, let's be honest. It needs to be a superb campaign to bring in 400% MORE. Think of the extra resources you'll need, the extra stock required. Staffing costs, overtime, the additional cash flow pressures, all to make the same.

You may discount certain products at certain times, and that is absolutely fine, just be AWARE of the full effect of discounting. There may even be times you sell at a LOSS just to clear old and dead stock, that's fine too. Maybe buy smarter next time, just saying!

The **SECOND** error of judgement was this: people who buy on price are lost on price. When you build a business based on being the "cheapest," what kind of customers does that attract? Yes, you guessed it. We had a client that had used us on three occasions, we had to discount every time to win the business. Every time we under-promised and over-delivered, as you should. Every time we had to fight to get paid, as you shouldn't. Then, "D Day," the client (a design studio) finally came to us with a HUGE job. The discounting strategy had paid off. Our over-delivering had paid off. The first three orders must have been a "trial." We quoted for the job as keenly as possible, and waited for the order. The order never came (we were terrible at follow-ups, that's for later). When we did follow it up, we were told that we lost the business to a competitor - they were £400 cheaper than us. This competitor had let them down with quality and delivery issues before, yet they won the job by being £400 cheaper - on a £10,000 catalogue job. It was then I realised, too late, the ridiculous price-driven market we were in. Customers who you win on price will almost certainly be LOST on price. There is always some idiot prepared to do it cheaper. **Too often, we were the idiot!**

The **THIRD** error of judgement was discounting products when customers were prepared to pay full price. This is REALLY important to explain. Our DRIVER was to win NEW BUSINESS, gain NEW CUSTOMERS. To do that, incentives and discounts were offered. These offers were invariably published online, and as such our existing customers would see them, and order at the discounted price. Who can blame them? What we then had was a discounting strategy to win new business that meant we needed a 400% increase just to stand still, AND we were losing the higher margin to hundreds of customers that were prepared to pay full price.

A lesson learned too late: it's both easier and cheaper to sell existing products to existing customers. "Brand New Customers Only" is a poor strategy best left to the banks who seem to still think it's a good idea.

Your Action Points from #2

Have a look at the "Dangers of Discounting" and work out what a 20% DISCOUNT means for your business. Before starting any sales campaign that involves discounting be clear on the outcome for that strategy. What makes it a successful campaign?

3 of 8 - Knowing the Numbers

We'll start off with the obvious numbers first. Monthly Accounts (P&L, Balance Sheet), Cash Flow and Budget. Our accounts were all produced in-house, we used Sage at the time. Every month these were sent to the accountant and monthly Management Accounts were duly produced and forwarded. All going well so far?

There was no Cash Flow produced, nor any Budgets - so we're starting to come off the rails a bit now.

I rarely took the time to fully interrogate these numbers. Focussed more on turnover and production KPIs, I would rarely look beyond the top line and bottom line. This doesn't work in a growing business.

Lending institutions love businesses that are in financial control, know their numbers, and can see any storms long before they happen. What they don't like is businesses that are not in financial control, have no clarity on the finances of the business, and come looking for overdrafts or loans the DAY they need them.

For YEARS I convinced myself that since the business was profitable, cash RICH, with no overdraft, a cash flow and budget was not needed. Had I used them, I would have been able to track the storm as it approached, as it ripped the roof off, and tore apart everything I had worked 20 years to build.

The business operated without an overdraft for 18 of its 20 years.

Work with your accountant and agree what key numbers YOU need to know. Make this a DEFAULT diary task EVERY MONTH. You should know to the nearest £100 what your turnover is, what your profit is, and how much is in the bank on any given DAY.

There are many other numbers that are vital in your business. On the website have a look at "Knowing Your Numbers," "Your Vital Statistics." This is a MUST-do exercise for every business.

What is your conversion rate? Do you know it exactly? Did you know, that in most businesses there's FOUR conversion rates you need to know?

The example on the website breaks every element of your business down. Marketing Reach to Initial Enquiry to Qualified Lead to Quotes Issued to Customers Gained to Sale Numbers to Sale Values to Monthly Turnover to Margin and finally Profit. It will then challenge you to not only know the numbers, to allocate a cost to each section too.

This is where it gets **REALLY** exciting. The example then illustrates how a small 5% improvement can make a significant difference.

Have a look, **KNOW YOUR NUMBERS** and start looking for those 5% improvements.

I never knew any of this, I was never shown this stuff. When I saw this being presented for the first time it BLEW me away. Since then, I have modified it and added to it. It's a VERY powerful tool.

Your Action Points for #3

Agree what your daily, weekly and monthly FINANCIAL KPIs will be. There's a guide on the website at "Finances and KPIs" that shows you how to get started with a basic KPI Dashboard. Don't try to measure every number, every variable. If you try to measure everything, you'll measure NOTHING. Pick the most important numbers, start there and build from that.

Download the worksheet from "Knowing Your Numbers," your Vital Statistics. Complete your own numbers on the matrix. This is going to give you an overview of your entire marketing, enquiry and sales numbers. It's unlikely that you will have EVER had this clarity before. This is GOLD for any business.

It instantly shows your **TRUE** cost of client acquisition. It shows you clearly what your conversion RATES are, making improvement easy. **You can only improve what you accurately measure**. This is ACCURATE measurement at its finest.

Once you have all your current numbers, look at what a small, 5% improvement does. Why not try 10% too? If this doesn't motivate you to measure and **IMPROVE**, I'm not sure anything will.

4 of 8 - Your Team

I could, and probably WILL, write a book on this topic alone. It does seem that today though, that "Team" is a tad over-used on Social Media. Without a doubt, the people you surround yourself with make or break you, and your business. You become the average of the five people you hang around with most. Almost certainly, that means colleagues.

We had a GREAT bunch of guys (guys being gender neutral, okay?) at the Ink Shop. Our gang were hard working, focussed and well paid. We knew very early on that good people were a vital resource. The staff turnover at The Ink Shop was incredibly low, 80% of the gang were the ORIGINAL people hired when the job was first created. There was a reason for that. Yes, the place was manic most of the time, they did however all "buy in" to what we were trying to do. Read the previous chapter to see what happened when the receivers arrived. I doubt they had seen that before, or since.

You may be asking why is this in as a fundamental reason for the business failing? Despite having GOOD people, I never empowered them enough. The reason (and the result) was, never being able to let go. The business was reliant on my presence for even the most basic of decisions, and it did not have to be that way. **You get what you tolerate**.

Chapter 7 covers a lot of this. The same excuses were used time and time again when foreign holidays were cancelled. I chose this, I allowed and permitted this to happen. Not because I had incompetent people working for me, the exact opposite. I simply never gave THEM the opportunity to shine.

Training plays a HUGE part with developing your Team, that includes you too. **"What if we train them and they leave? What if we DON'T and they stay?"** That quote summarises training PERFECTLY in my view.

"No one could do the job as well as me." The reality is, they would have done it better. The team is only as strong as the LEADER, and I found out way too late a great quote: "Don't ask for my permission. Ask for my forgiveness." In other words, just do it, and if it goes pear-shaped, we'll sort it. I never did that, I never GOT THAT.

I would be too critical, sometimes openly critical, and simply built up a culture where my **EXCEPTIONAL** team wouldn't make decisions. I was very fortunate to have those amazing people, I just failed to use it to MY full advantage.

I read the most amazing book, "Turn the Ship Around" by David Marquet. David was a US Navy Submarine Commander and introduced what he refers to as "intent-based leadership." Not only did this change the entire way the NAVY operated, it transforms BUSINESSES in a most amazing way. This is your Action Point for this section - **you MUST read this book**.

Your Other Action Points for #4

Roles and Responsibilities should be created for each member of your business team. How can your team perform at their best when they don't know exactly what their role is, what their responsibilities are, and what is EXPECTED from them? **You get what you tolerate**.

Organisational Charts are a must for a growing business. Create an Organisational Chart for the business in your five-year plan. Many of the roles won't exist yet, or some people may be doing multiple roles. That's absolutely fine. SHARE this with your team. Let them see the vision you have for the business, and THEM.

Vision Mission and Culture is always overlooked. When was the last time you shared your vision with your team? Do they know, understand, and believe your "mission?" What CULTURE are you building within your business? Are you building your business with the RIGHT people? If I picked members of your team at random and asked them, "What is [your business] all about, what does it stand for?" How would they answer? **Could they answer**?

DISC Profiles are a great way to understand yourself and your team MUCH better. DISC reveals the way we behave, and why.

Team Meetings held weekly or monthly should be short and sharp. Structured to provide information and keep those information channels flowing. How often do you share updates with ALL your team?

Training Plans will make sure you have your team continually learning and developing. What do YOU want to train them in. What do they want to do? Have you ever asked them?

5 of 8 - The Systems for Success

I have not met a business owner yet who couldn't achieve further improvements quickly, by simply introducing **better Systems**. The Ink Shop had systems, just not enough. They were either too complex or manual. Now, some systems may have to be complex, however, the majority probably don't. Let me share a "**System**" with you.

There is a procedure that is designed to be understood by people who are aged 8 or 80. By people whose first language may not be English. This system will be used by people who will be under EXTREME pressure and anxiety. Sounds like a challenge doesn't it? Yet this system is delivered on a single A4 sheet. It is of course an Aircraft Emergency Card. You know, the one you ignore EVERY time you're on the plane. That's okay though, it's designed to be understood by those who ignored the safety briefing.

Systems and Processes don't have to be complex. They can be simple "Checklists," they may have a variety of scripts. The key with systems and processes in YOUR business is to make sure they are understood and used CONSISTENTLY.

The world has moved on at a huge pace in recent years. There's a software program or app for virtually every business in every industry. This makes systemising your business so much easier. How well do you utilise software? **Do you have ten Excel Spreadsheets when ONE system would do?**

What I hear and see a lot today with business owners is "there's just so many systems I need." That may indeed be the case, that's a reason to **DO IT**, not an **excuse not to**. Have a look on the website for "Some Systems Help, A System for a System." A handy guide to get started.

Let me share with you the systems that I did NOT have that would have made a HUGE difference in my business. The reason I want to share this with you is because I see so many businesses today that either don't have these in place, or don't have them being followed consistently. **Consistency is the key**.

1) **No consistent system to track leads**
2) **No consistent system to record lead SOURCE**
3) **No consistent follow-up process**
4) **No consistent manufacturing process for on-time production**
5) **No consistent quality control process**
6) **No structure for a Customer Service system**

You'll see my continual use of "consistent." The issues we had were simple: sometimes it was done, sometimes it wasn't. Sometimes I would do it this way, John would do it that way. Does that make sense? The "system" was actually there, or was it?

Your Action Points for #5

Your action point for this section is simple. REVIEW your current systems and processes and score your business out of TEN for each of the following:

1) The **right systems** in place
2) The **right training** in place for those systems
3) The way the systems are **consistently** followed.
4) The **review process** to make sure the system is still working perfectly.

Now, scoring out of 10 is all relative, you'll get what I mean. If you feel your business is in a bit of "Systems Overwhelm" just remember, that's the **REASON** to do it, not the **EXCUSE** not to.

If you want to do it, you'll find a way. If you don't, you'll find an excuse.

The "**System for a System**" on the website may help you get started. Start off simple, do NOT try to re-invent the wheel here. When creating ANY system or process in your business be VERY CLEAR on:

1)   **What will the system deliver, what's the benefit to the business?**
2)   **What are the CONSEQUENCES if this isn't done?**
3)   **WHO is taking ownership of this project?**
4)   **WHEN does this start?**
5)   **WHAT is our completion date?**

6 of 8 - Time, Not Enough Hours in the Day

There are loads of resources on "**Be a Better You**" on the website. Time is a huge challenge for many business owners. A lot of this has been covered already, and the amazing book by Brian Tracy, "Eat That Frog!" is a must-read for anyone who feels time-challenged.

I was actually GOOD at managing my time. I would use a "To Do List" and was very good at sticking to it. What I was **DREADFUL** at, was putting the **WRONG STUFF ON IT**. That's what I want to hammer home here. This was a huge issue for me.

I recently found an old "Ink Shop Brochure," and read a statement that stopped me dead in my tracks. In one message, it hit me how wrong my mindset was. This was it, "**You're more likely to find me in the print room than the boardroom**." We're really back to "unconscious incompetence" here. At the time I THOUGHT that showed passion and commitment, and it probably did. However, what it proved was that I was working IN the business and not ON the business, WAY TOO MUCH.

This is where it all starts to join, or unwind, I'm not sure which. Working too many hours, always stressed and under pressure, unable to take decent time off. Systems, Structure, Training.

Rather than explore Time Management, I want to focus here on "YOU" Management, and here's how to do it. I wish I knew this before.

Work out what your SALARY should be. Not what it is, what it **SHOULD** be. Now write that figure here:

£ …………………………………………………………………. **WOW**!
See the space I have provided for that? Now divide by 52 to give you a weekly number, then by 40 to give you an hourly rate. Remember this is what it SHOULD be. If you work less than 40 hours, adjust that. If you work more than 40 hours, **leave it as 40**.

You now have an hourly rate, **YOUR** hourly rate. The next bit is simple. When you are doing tasks in your business you simply ask yourself this question. Would I PAY someone that hourly rate to do this task? If the answer is NO, **then what the hell are YOU doing it for**?

The biggest single improvement you will make in your business is focussing on the BIG PICTURE tasks, the BIG hourly rate jobs, and working **ON** your business and **NOT** in it.

There endeth the lesson.

Your Action Points for #6

On the website in "Time Saving Tips" review the following:

The Time Target - where do you spend most of your time?

The Hourly Rate Challenge - what are your hours worth?

Time Money Challenge - are you sacrificing time for money, or money for time?

Start using To Do Lists and Default Diaries

This is essential - read "Eat That Frog!" by Brian Tracy.

7 out of 8 - Learn Before You Earn

"Read a book a week for the rest of your life." I heard that quote from Brad Sugars who had previously heard it from Jim Rohn. The late, great Jim Rohn had an even better quote, and it went something like this, "Work harder on yourself than you do on your business. **Work hard on your business and you'll earn a living, work hard on yourself and you'll earn a fortune.**" BOOM, that's it!

Why is it that when we were at school we learned continuously? That continued and indeed intensified with college or university. Yet, when we start a BUSINESS, which is WAY more complicated than ANY school subject, the majority of us STOP LEARNING? Why is that?

I could count on one hand the number of books I read in The Ink Shop's 20 years. Let me be clear, I mean business improvement books - the Beano doesn't count. In fact, I could count on one HAND with three fingers how many it was. Is this you?

How can you possibly grow as a person and a business LEADER if you aren't constantly and continually LEARNING? Reading, attending seminars, training, re-training, gaining qualifications?

I was shown a "formula" that I want to share with you. I am not sure who the original author of this is, so I am going to attribute it to the person that showed me it first: Brad Sugars.

Be x Do = Have. In business, and life, we quickly realise that to HAVE more you DO more. If you DO more, you can HAVE more. Does that make sense? Let's put a few numbers on this.

Be (1) x Do (1) = Have, which can only be 1.

Be (1) x Do (10) = Have, which is now 10. This is easy, to have more, I just DO MORE. That's where most business owners, including ME, come off the rails. It's NOT scalable.

Now try this: **Be (5) x Do (5) = Have (25)**. Oh, hang on: BE better, DO less, HAVE more. Going back to Jim Rohn, work harder on **YOURSELF** and you'll make a **FORTUNE.**

Your Action Points for #7

The action point here is simple, work on your BE. What is that? What can you do right now to make yourself better? A good example was a client who had some confidence issues around public speaking. To "be" better they wanted to work on that. They came out of their comfort zone and attended Toastmasters meetings. Today, speaking on a stage in front of thousands is nothing. **BE better, do less, have more**.

8 of 8 - It Could Only Be Me - You Figured That Out

A great way to complete the chapter and indeed the book. The single biggest reason for The Ink Shop failing, for all those amazing people being made redundant, for those suppliers that lost thousands, and all those dreams shattered was ME. **Me and me alone**.

To fully understand why you do things the way you do, you need to understand DISC Profiles, behaviour patterns. How we behave, why certain things annoy and frustrate us. There's no way this can be covered in the book. I have included a DISC worksheet on the website in the "Be a Better You Section".

When you understand DISC, you'll appreciate as a "High Dominant Style," I have some challenges. As a "Dominant" style I get shit done, I am very fast paced, and hate lots of detail. Don't dare send me a 3-page Word document when 3 bullet points on an email would do. This is GOOD for a business owner though, yes?

However, Dominant styles are impatient, insensitive to others and are poor listeners. Under pressure a "High D" will also be dictatorial and critical. Now that we're reaching the end of the book, is this now making a lot of sense?

If only I had known about DISC back then. Then again, would I have listened?

This had a huge bearing on the direction of the business, and I have worked hard to address these issues. Although, please, just send me bullet points. There's another book that I want to share with you, "The Chimp Paradox" by Dr. Steve Peters. I was lucky enough to hear him at a recent Business Excellence Forum event. If you have ever wondered why you do what you do, this is a MUST READ.

On the website I have also uploaded a graphic that covers "The Right Road or the Wrong Track." Today, I make a point of operating on the RIGHT ROAD, always. In years gone by, sadly this was not the case. Again, I just didn't KNOW this stuff. In the Ink Shop days, I was constantly on the WRONG TRACK. I was too quick to blame others, it's clearly you, not me. I would have an excuse for everything, it's the weather, it's the economy, it's the industry and then be in complete denial that there's anything wrong with that picture.

When I have been writing this book, I have shared many of the chapters with a number of friends, business colleagues, and a few previous Ink Shop customers, suppliers and employees. They all say the same thing, sharp exhalation of air, followed by "you've changed, a LOT." Sadly though, too late.

I can see now that I was the business's biggest asset. Driven, motivated, enthusiastic, and creative, very creative. Yet, sadly, I was also the business's biggest liability, and that is How You Wreck Your Business...

The ~~End~~ *Beginning*

Intentionally Blank